Entrepreneur *M*ADE EASY *Series*

*M*ASTERING BUSINESS GROWTH AND CHANGE MADE EASY

JEFFREY A. HANSEN

12/20/05

To Rick with many thanks for your support!

Jeff

EP Entrepreneur Press

Editorial Director: Jere Calmes
Cover Design: Beth Hanson-Winter
Composition: CWL Publishing Enterprises, Inc., Madison, WI, www.cwlpub.com

This publication is designed to provide accurate and authoritative information in
regard to the subject matter covered. It is sold with the understanding that the
publisher is not engaged in rendering legal, accounting, or other professional services. If legal advice or other expert assistance is required, the services of a compe-
tent professional person should be sought.

> —From a Declaration of Principles jointly adopted by
> a Committee of the American Bar Association and
> a Committee of Publishers and Associations

ISBN 1-932531-64-5

Library of Congress Cataloging in Publication Data

Hansen, Jeffrey A.
  Mastering business growth and change made easy / by Jeffrey A. Hansen.
    p. cm. — (Made easy)
  ISBN 1-932531-64-5 (alk. paper)
    1. Management—Handbooks, manuals, etc. 2. Business planning—
  Handbooks, manuals, etc. I. Title. II. Series: Entrepreneur made easy series.

HF5686.C7L6542 2004
658.15'11—dc22
                                                      200403233

Printed in Canada

10 09 08 07 06 05   10 9 8 7 6 5 4 3 2 1

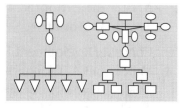

Contents

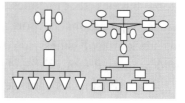

Foreword

THE LEADER OF AN INNOVATION-DRIVEN, GROWTH-ORIENTED BUSI-
ness manages many opposing forces and aspirations. You seek
to develop an organization that can pursue goals and implement
strategies with deep passion and commitment. Yet you must
also change these goals and strategies as your business circumstances require. Failure to keep these forces in balance leads to weakness for
both you and the business.

Mastering Business Growth and Change Made Easy will help you recognize what's needed at critical turning points as your business grows—and it
will help you become a more effective leader. It begins by helping you understand what kind of leader you are and in what situations you're most likely to
be effective doing what you like to do. Knowing this is critical: your job as
leader changes over time—you can't always dictate the nature of your most
important priorities. As your business grows, you must be able to identify how
your organization is changing and what it will take for you to be effective in
each new situation. A successful leader must champion different priorities at
different times.

When I read this book, I was struck by the insights it provides into my
own experience as an entrepreneur leading a company that is now large and
diverse. Russell Investment Group is a collection of different businesses,
started at different times. It was founded by my grandfather in the 1930s as a
mutual fund company with a local clientele. I joined the firm in 1958; since
then, the company has evolved from a retail mutual fund company to a diverse

global business that includes a pension fund consulting business that serves an elite group of global corporations with more than $2 trillion in assets, a thriving stock index business, a trust bank, and a developer of multi-manager funds sold as mutual funds through various distribution partners.

These businesses took several decades to develop and there were many lessons learned along the way. But it is clear in hindsight that there were several clear transitions that required Russell to change the way it operates, much as described in *Mastering Business Growth and Change Made Easy*. While our company of over 1,800 people is considered by many to be quite complex, the conceptual framework for business growth embodied in this book's "Choice and Change" model clarifies where we have been and where we have needed to go.

One of the first innovative breakthroughs that led to Russell's growth and industry dominance occurred in 1969. I was trying to figure out how to successfully interest pension fund executives in investing in our mutual funds. I got a chance to present my funds concept to the chairman of one of the country's leading conglomerates and sold $50 million worth of funds—a sizable piece of business in those days. But I learned something that was much more valuable than that new account. Big pension funds didn't want to invest in mutual funds. They wanted somebody to analyze institutional money managers and give them objective rankings and insights so they could make sensible business decisions about which group of managers they should retain to manage their pension assets.

The main point is that it was an intuitive flash. I could see the broader implications of this single piece of information. As a small, agile organization, we remade ourselves to take advantage of the opportunity. I began calling on large pension funds, offering to perform the service of selecting money managers.

The response was so immediate and so positive that I quickly decided to dissolve the mutual fund sales force I had developed, which was doing quite well with 350 salespeople, and to concentrate on pension consulting. Good intuition helped me to discover the right business to develop at the right time. A few years later, the adoption of the Employee Retirement Income Security Act (ERISA) essentially mandated the kind of service we offered and validated the insights we had years earlier. Russell's pension consulting business continues to flourish around the world even with all the changes since 1969.

In 1980, we realized that the advice we were providing on a custom basis for large pension sponsors could be made available to a larger number of clients through packaging our advice differently. This new application for an existing capability led to Russell's multi-manager funds. The growth of the business has been guided by a series of highly capable leaders who have carried it through many of the phases detailed in this book. We have needed all types of leaders at all times.

I have long believed that I am an intuitive decision maker and the self-test in *Mastering Business Growth and Change Made Easy* confirms it. While my intuitive nature led to many successes, it also had its drawbacks—many of them similar to what this book describes. The leaders I hired had to learn to compensate for my biases, along with their own, to pursue Russell's goals and strategies with passion.

Viewed through the lens of *Mastering Business Growth and Change Made Easy*, Russell's continued success has come from our ability to spot attractive opportunities and then structure ourselves to take advantage of them. I believe it's not enough to simply have a good idea. You also have to be able to build on it, sell it, and deliver the promised results. At the same time, you can't rest on your laurels; you can't stop innovating. It's important for leaders to be honest about their own strengths and weaknesses, so they can surround themselves with people who bring the needed, complementary skills to the table. I have always hired people smarter than I am to implement new ideas.

As a success-oriented organization, Russell has always been interested in the professional development of our people, our most important asset. We have used a wide range of training approaches over the years. *Mastering Business Growth and Change Made Easy* does not replace this training; it sets the context for it. It provides a guiding framework for the right time to address issues.

The overarching message of Jeff Hansen's book—that wisdom, conscious choice, and disciplined action are the most important traits in leaders—is an absolute truth. *Mastering Business Growth and Change Made Easy* will empower and strengthen leaders to lead with greater success over a wider range of situations. I am grateful for the insights it provides.

—George F. Russell Jr.
Chairman Emeritus
Frank Russell Company

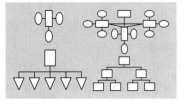

Introduction

I N THE WORLD OF HIGH-GROWTH BUSINESSES, NOTHING LEADS TO FAILURE like success. There's simply something about achieving a high degree of success that plants the seeds of failure within a business. Most of us can think of a business that is very successful, perhaps even coming to dominate its particular market niche, and then stumbles, even when the fundamental product concept or idea lives on and is made successful by another firm. During the successful periods, the leader and the organization act as a single entity. The organization and the way it operates are extensions of the leader—they act as a single entity. In turn, the ways the leader leads and the organization operates are perfectly synchronized to their business environment. But after a certain period of time or after some unnoticed internal or external change, all the parts are no longer working in unison. The way the organization operates is poorly suited to its circumstances and the leader and management team are out of step with both the organization and its business.

While this shift can happen in companies of any size and maturity, the shift is particularly dramatic just after the entrepreneur validates the basic business concept and the business starts to grow. The most important business goals for the leader shift away from innovating and validating the business strength of the innovation toward building a business.

The trouble that entrepreneurs have making this shift is tragic because so many entrepreneurs invest a great deal of time, resources, and personal commitment into the validation phase. They are unprepared for and overwhelmed by the confusion of falling out of synchronization and the magnitude and depth of the changes that must be made.

For the last 25 years, my passion has been to analyze and define the internal threats to long-term success. As a college undergrad, one of my hobbies was to follow the activities of small businesses and to predict which ones would succeed and which ones would fail. I had observed many entrepreneurs among family friends and noticed that success and failure did not seem to relate to qualities I'd assumed would be critical.

At the time, I could see that marketing contributes greatly to success—as do adequate funding and a great product. But what surprised me was that, all things being equal, the entrepreneurs who were intelligent and tenacious and worked hard did not appear to have a greater success rate. In fact, it almost seemed like those who were particularly intelligent and tenacious had a *lower* success rate, especially if they had already experienced some success in their endeavor. With a success under their belt, they would continue to grow for while, but then would fail quickly and decisively. It was as though they hit a wall in the dark and could not find a way over or around it. The harder they tried, the more exhausted and fragmented they would become until they expired.

I was intrigued. In fact, clearing up this disconnect was what prompted me to go to graduate school and study organizational behavior. I wanted to find some answers.

Hitting the Wall: Is There a Common Denominator?

Many questions come to mind about these entrepreneurial companies that hit the wall. Why didn't they find their way over the wall or around it? If their products are successful in the marketplace, why didn't they stay on top of it and keep growing? Was it because of some external and uncontrollable force—something unrelated to the company or product? Or was it because of some internal force or dynamic that, if identified and understood, could be managed better? Would a better understanding of the wall have been enough to enable these businesses to continue on their growth path? After several years at graduate school and research on venture capital funded companies, I found some answers to these questions beginning to emerge.

A Leader's Personal Style Sets the Tone for the Entire Organization

One of my most memorable classes in graduate school focused on the importance of an entrepreneurial leader's personal decision-making style on the success of the business. There were two key points:

1. We manage others in the same way as we make decisions for ourselves.
2. A small firm's business and organizational strategies and culture often mirror the leader's own management style.

These were earthshaking insights. Had the failures I'd observed been caused by the leader's personality? Are we ultimately limited by the very personal qualities that cause us to be successful in the first place?

These were the questions that haunted me. Determined to find answers, I set out to study a large number of entrepreneurial businesses, their leaders' management styles, and their strategies for business growth. It was the early 1980s: hot demand for high-tech hardware and software jump-started hundreds of businesses up and down the West Coast. I decided to focus my research work on companies that had been evaluated for funding by venture capital investors. This was a good pool of subjects for several reasons.

First, someone other than I had carefully evaluated these companies, so my biases would not influence the evaluation. If a company got venture capital funding, an expert had determined that it had a product with a competitive edge and had a better chance at long-term economic success than those it did not fund.

Second, the leaders of these companies and their growth strategies were targeting high economic growth. Thus, businesses started purely for lifestyle reasons (e.g., the satisfaction of being your own boss) would therefore not dominate the pool. These were companies that wanted to grow economically.

Finally, venture capital (VC) investors are fairly quick to replace ineffective leaders. This meant that as I looked at small, medium-sized, and large organizations, I would be able to see the type of leader that the venture capital investors thought would be providing the company with what it needed to achieve its long-term objectives.

I was able to evaluate the businesses that tried but did not receive venture capital funding to determine what differences might be observed objectively. I was also able to evaluate the leaders of funded companies who lost their jobs and the people who were hired to replace them. This pool gave me a good chance to see which management styles and approaches to leadership are most effective at different stages of growth and for different types of companies.

I compared various groups of leaders—those who personally developed the innovation on which their company was based, those who were brought in after the innovation had been validated, leaders of companies that sought venture capital funding, those who got funding and those who were rejected, and so forth. The message was clear: venture capital investors favored companies managed by different types of leaders at different phases of growth.

Of course, statistical research did not tell the whole story. For two years I traveled up and down the West Coast interviewing CEOs of high-tech companies to determine how their management styles related to their business priorities, organizational structures, growth culture—and ultimately their level of success.

This work confirmed the statistics and validated the strategy of VC investors: different styles of management are indeed more effective at different phases of organizational growth. Moreover, problems develop when a business moves from one phase of development to the next, from one type of business environment to the next, and its leader and organization fail to keep pace with the changes. A business is weakened when it applies in its new circumstances a strategy best suited to its prior circumstances. To the thoughtful leaders of the business, it makes perfect sense to solve problems the way they've solved them successfully in the past. They would ask, "Why not repeat what produced your earlier success?" This began to explain what I had seen years before. Nothing leads to failure like success.

It's tempting to conclude from this research that business organizations should, if they're serious about economic growth, have a succession of leaders, each with the "best" management style for a particular phase of growth. I resisted that blanket conclusion. There are thousands of businesses that depend on the presence and accumulated wisdom of singular individuals, both leaders and members of leadership teams. The knowledge and skills of specific people are crucial to ongoing business success. As my work evolved, I sought to gain a broader understanding of businesses that were headed by indispensable leaders. I wanted to know what challenges they faced as they tried to shift gears from one phase of growth to the next.

Investment Management Teams:
The "Fruit Fly" in the Laboratory of Management Effectiveness

I found an ideal pool of businesses with indispensable leaders: investment portfolio managers and their teams. These are professionals who invest billions of dollars of retirement assets in mutual funds and other types of investment products. Some of these portfolio management teams are small boutique firms. Others are groups within larger investment firms, such as mutual fund companies and the investment divisions of banks and other financial companies. Each of these larger firms consists of dozens of smaller entrepreneurial investment teams, all of which go through their own developmental process.

Since the early 1980s, my colleagues and I have evaluated hundreds of the most prominent investment teams and firms in the United States, Asia, and Europe. We have worked with a wide range of firms, from very small entrepreneurial boutiques to large global investment firms. Some of these investment firms were evaluated as part of a larger investment manager research and selection process for the Russell Investment Group. Others were evaluated while I have been with Blue Heron Consulting, a small management consulting firm specializing in helping insight- and innovation-driven businesses develop and deploy their insight more effectively. Most of our work has been with investment management firms that retain Blue Heron to help them implement their investment strategies and programs more effectively. Our clients have a combined asset base of almost $1 trillion. Improvements in how well they support their investment activities make a big different for their clients and their businesses.

Regardless of whether these investment teams represent a single firm or reside in a larger firm alongside many other investment teams, they typically start as entrepreneurial efforts by someone with deep conviction that he or she can beat the stock market—or at least competing investment firms. If this vision is right and produces investment success, the business will experience growth just like any other successful entrepreneurial enterprise.

But for my purposes, certain features of investment teams make them particularly good subjects for studying effective approaches to organize people, their insights and efforts, and systematic processes to solving problems, which are important elements in business leadership.

First, investment firms are essentially pure decision-making organizations. Their main purpose is to collect data from a wide variety of sources, process it into useful information, and make and implement decisions. To separate themselves from the pack and make money for their clients, they need to collect better data, develop better insights and innovations in the interpretation of the data, and implement the resulting decisions faster than their competitors. The organizational influences on investment success are tremendous and many manager evaluation experts, such as the Russell Investment Group, focus their effort on evaluating people, philosophy, and process when assessing the strengths of an investment firm.

Second, all investment firms invest in the same capital markets and have access to roughly the same information, regardless of where they are located geographically. One investment team may be a large, established firm located in London and the other may be a boutique based in Seattle. If they are investing in the same part of the capital market (large company stocks in the United States, for example), they are competing head to head and the results of their decision-making efforts—their investment portfolios—can be compared side by side. There are few local market effects except those that relate to the pool of talent that they hire from. With many of the external variables being the same, we can isolate the effects of how they organize and operate as it relates to their performance. It is possible to compare a large number of organizations around the globe and see more deeply into what drives the success of their internal management efforts. We can compare the relative success of two organizations that produce directly competing products but differ in their types of decision-making processes, organizational structure, caliber of investment staff, and use of systematic computers and tools. We can test in a very controlled set of organizations various questions, like "Is bigger better or is it better to be small and agile?"

Third, measuring the results of their efforts is a relatively objective process. Their success is indicated by numeric measures of investment performance and this performance can be evaluated against objective benchmarks, stock market indices, and the performance of other firms. It's easy to tell which team has been effective in which type of situation, regardless of their marketing hype or how rich and famous their people have become. It's all in the numbers.

Fourth, the innovation and implementation cycles of most investment teams are relatively short. In most cases, they must conceive insightful investment ideas each quarter and implement them in portfolios immediately. One can see the results of their decisions within a few months. If there's a change in the management structure of the team that doesn't go well, the effects of the changes are often revealed in the numbers a short time later.

Finally, when you buy an investment product like a mutual fund you must focus on selecting the investment management team, not the product it produces. The short life of what the team produces—a particular portfolio of securities—becomes obsolete in a few months; it must be refreshed. So one must focus on how well the investment team can create the next portfolio of securities, and then the one after that, and so on. Investment teams must be operating in the right mode for the current and future circumstances, not the past. In many other types of businesses, one can focus only on the product that is currently being produced or has been produced in the past. If the current management team is not right, the members can be replaced with others more suitable to current and future needs. These special features of investment teams make them the fruit fly in the laboratory of management effectiveness.

My experience with investment management organizations confirms the following findings, which are consonant with the research of high-tech ventures cited earlier:

▶ Long-term success is more likely when the ways in which decisions are made and organizations are structured evolve over time to keep pace with the changes in the organization's size, purpose, and technological systems and the capabilities of the people it employs.

▶ Investment firms that are experiencing performance problems often use organizational structures, decision processes, and control mechanisms that are better suited to the firms' past circumstances (staff count, expertise levels, use of systematic tools, and so forth) than to its current circumstances. Their structures and processes seem to follow paths of least resistance—if a change is difficult, it is usually avoided.

▶ Even when they recognize problems in how they operate, leaders and their organizations are reluctant to change what has been successful in the past. It has been embedded in their cultures, their concepts of who they are and what they stand for.

▶ When leaders and their organizations do step up to the task of changing the way they operate, they are able to develop modes of operation different from the past and to improve their performance.

- ▶ Emulation of a naturally effective leader can be almost as effective as actually having a leader in place who is naturally effective. But it can be as successful or more successful long term because the enterprise can avoid the cost of changing leaders. Faking it can work.

- ▶ If changes are made quickly and early as the organization moves through the transition from one phase of growth to the next, emulation is a good strategy in most cases.

As a consultant for 15 of those years, I've helped companies develop effective organizational strategies to help them continue to thrive. My work with various businesses over the years has reinforced these points time and time again. This purpose of this book is to provide you with the information and perspective needed to lead your business (small or large) through the various phases of growth effectively—so you can take full advantage of the business opportunities provided by your insight and hard work.

The Bottom Line

Clearly, businesses fail for many reasons. We develop businesses strategies, marketing strategies, product strategies, and financial strategies to help us contend with changes within different business realms. These strategies, even if informal, help us anticipate changes that will affect our efforts. And they can help us respond in an appropriate way more quickly when our circumstances change.

Yet, as leaders, we tend not to have strategies for managing some relatively controllable forces that impact business success. This is the way our enterprise itself operates—its *mode of operation*. The mode of operation is how people and tasks are organized to achieve objectives and encompasses the structure of the organization, the formal and informal priorities being pursued, cultural values, and how the entire organization is controlled.

With initial success, a business grows, stabilizes, and becomes more complex. With these changes, its mode of operation should change—just as managing a four-person team during start-up is different from managing a 40-person organization with a product in the market. How the mode of operation changes over time can be thought of as an *organizational strategy*. Thus, just as you should have a marketing strategy that covers a product from development through introduction to contending with competitors, you should also have an organizational strategy—an idea of how your mode of operation will change as your enterprise grows and develops.

If we get the organizational strategy right, we can increase our chances of being successful *over the long term*. A tremendous benefit of having an effective organizational strategy is that you can control the key variables that influence success. Your enterprise's mode of operation is fundamental. Not only does it influence your current success, but it also impacts how you develop and execute the other important strategies. With an effective organizational strategy, you can focus less attention on the internal threats to success. That frees up your energies to concentrate on the main event: your external opportunities and your external threats to success.

Most of our experience at Blue Heron has been with high-tech and investment companies. But developmental cycles seen in these insight-driven businesses seem to mirror similar patterns in other industries. I have heard from many of my readers that my descriptions sound exactly like their own businesses—that I must have been in the room when their conversations were taking place. I have heard this from people in health care, churches, governmental agencies, design organizations, and, of course, from the high-tech communities and investment management.

Although there are many benefits of working with investment management firms, one drawback is that their stories do not make good reading. It is more interesting to hear about their investment strategies than their organizational strategies. Considering this reality, I will use some examples of investment management shops but will try to keep them to a minimum. Instead, I will draw on stories from other industries to illustrate important points.

Also, I'd like to highlight the potholes in the pathway. I enjoy reading about stories about how things go right for someone. It makes a pleasant read. I like to hear how Starbucks grew. I like to hear about Bill Gates living in a nice house in Seattle. It makes me want to try to do what they do. But we need to look at the trouble spots as well. The success stories are often well documented, and descriptions of what has happened to a dozen or two dozen people in the world to make them extremely successful may not be as useful to my readers as knowing what typically trips ups hundreds and thousands of businesses. A good leader learns from his or her mistakes—a great leader learns from the mistakes of others. Therefore, I have listed a few success stories but I will focus on telling you where the potholes are so you can navigate around them. (The examples of the enterprises have been disguised so I don't get sued.)

When you see where the potholes are along the way, when you see where the walls are that you have to climb around, when you see more clearly what lies down different paths, you can make better decisions immediately about how to better lead your enterprise. When I see a real-life enterprise avoid a pothole and move more smoothly, efficiently, and successfully down a path that is right for it, this is much better than hearing a good story—this is witnessing the beginning of a great story.

How This Book Is Organized

Chapters 1 and 2 provide an overview of the entire territory that a growing enterprise may traverse, the different phases of growth, and the management styles that are naturally most effective in each phase. A self-test in Chapter 2 will help you evaluate your own management style for making decisions in a certain way.

Chapter 3 covers the first growth phase—*Concept Development*. There is a significant wall between these two phases. It goes into detail about the requirements for success in this phase and how the naturally effective management style models the right operational mode for that phase.

Chapter 4 describes some of the classic indictors that it is time for the enterprise to shift into a transitional, Foundation Building mode. These indicators will help you gauge where you might be in this early part of the developmental cycle and help you see the wall before you run into it.

Chapter 5 discusses the transitional, Foudnation Building phase. It details what is necessary for succes in this phase.

Chapters 6, 7, and 8 describe three more growth phases—*Rapid Market Expansion*, *Crowded Marketplace*, and *Niche Development*. These are intended to help you see what operational mode might be right for your business so you build the right foundation.

Chapter 9 summarizes the growth phases and presents an integrated model to help you assess where your business is in a more integrated manner. It also discusses how enterprises get off track.

Chapter 10 lists ten survival tips that summarize the key points of the book. I will cover various phases, modes, styles, and other frameworks. This chapter will highlight the key universal points.

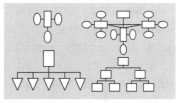

Chapter 1

The Perils of Success

MANY OF THE LEGENDS IN THE BUSINESS WORLD BUILT THEIR enterprises on their visions and passions. Henry Ford, J.P. Morgan, John D. Rockefeller, Bill Gates, Michael Dell, and others pushed new frontiers, changed the business landscape—and experienced phenomenal successes. Their visions and their companies affect our lives every day. But the most astonishing feat accomplished by these visionaries was that they built on their initial start-up success to lead their companies on to industry dominance. They realized the dream of growth and long-term success that so often eludes entrepreneurs.

The far more common experience is that the creative visionary and his or her company achieve initial success and then both falter as the business grows. At first the enterprise grows nicely and seemingly quite naturally. But then, all of a sudden, it hits a wall. While the leader may believe they are climbing over or going around the wall, it has stopped them dead. The thrill and camaraderie of early success give way to anxiety and panic. The cohesive team fragments, the leader fears losing control, business opportunities are missed, and internal management issues consume ever-larger shares of management attention. Poor decisions are made; the business weakens and then, ultimately, fails under competitive pressures.

What is the cause? Has the leader suddenly become a bad leader? Has the leader failed to give up control? Perhaps. Has the staff become a collection of malcontents? Perhaps. More likely, the fundamental problem is that the situation changed and a new approach to management was needed within the enterprise. But this simple explanation does not really imply much of an answer.

A statement attributed to many great thinkers goes something like this: "For every complex problem there is a clear, simple, and wrong answer." The sentiment behind this statement fits the management challenges faced by innovative entrepreneurs and the leaders of other innovation-driven business. There are many variables that influence how effective any management approach is in a particular situation.

The more complex answer begins something like this: "An enterprise and its leader each react differently to success." After a period of success and growth, an enterprise moves on to encounter different situations and different needs. Sometimes the most pressing issue is to develop a new product. Sometimes it is to enhance and sell more of an existing one. Sometimes the pressing issue is to develop internal processes to manage efficiently the day-to-day complexities of the business.

The leader, however, emboldened by success, typically continues with renewed vigor, using the same management practices and priorities that have been successful in the past. The leader reconfirms the same way of doing things. Instead of setting objectives that address the enterprise's most pressing needs and managing in a way that is well-suited to the current requirements, the leader often simply repeats what was successful in the past. Thus, the management situation changes with the growth of the enterprise, but management practices do not. It is the business version of "Generals are always fighting the last war."

But the answer continues from there. As the leader of an innovation-driven business that seeks to grow successfully, you must understand three things to keep your management practices aligned with your enterprise's most pressing and important needs.

First, you must understand that the most important issues to which you should devote management attention do indeed change over time, and that they do so in phases. The key of successful leadership is, of course, identifying the most important issues that you must address and then addressing them.

While this sounds so obvious, it is not easy to tell which of the hundreds of issues that are confronting you each day are the ones on which you should focus your leadership attention. Some issues may appear more important than others simply because of their past importance. Luckily, the most

A statement attributed to many great thinkers goes something like this: "For every complex problem there is a clear, simple, and wrong answer."

2

important needs and issues tend to cluster in time and create fairly well-defined phases of growth and development. During each phase, certain types of issues and needs tend to be most important to long-term growth and therefore should dominate leadership attention.

Second, you must understand when your enterprise is likely to shift from one phase of growth to the next. There is a standard sequence of phases that fits many innovation-driven enterprises. While not applicable to every enterprise, the standard sequence is a good reference point for every firm. With this sequence as a backdrop, you can see where you've been and where you are likely to go. If you understand the sequence of phases and what forces mark the end of one phase and the beginning of the next, you can anticipate and prepare for the changes that must take place within your enterprise.

Third, you must understand how you should respond to the new growth phase. You need to develop different management practices, promote different management priorities, and develop different organizational structures. In short, you will need to promote a different way of doing things in each phase. The "way of doing things" is what I call an *operational mode*. It is how people and tasks are organized to make decisions and to achieve objectives. It encompasses the structure of the organization, the formal and informal priorities being pursued, cultural values, and how the entire organization is controlled.

Thus, a better understanding of these elements of the longer-term developmental path of an innovation-driven enterprise will help you achieve long-term success. You will identify the shift from one growth phase to the next earlier and more successfully. You will make the transitions from one operational mode to the next more quickly and with fewer missteps.

Let's take a look at the standard sequence of growth phases arranged into a developmental path (Figure 1-1).

The four distinct phases of growth shown in Figure 1-1 cover the development of the initial idea and business setup through the maturing of the organization and its products. These four growth phases are interspersed with transitional foundation-building phases, which are represented by the starbursts.

The different phases indicate how the enterprise changes its focus as it exploits the potential of its main innovation in a way that largely reflects the product development cycle espoused by Geoffrey Moore in *Crossing the Chasm* and *Inside the Tornado*. The correlation will be discussed in greater detail in Chapter 3. Each growth phase expands the enterprise in a particular way that is important to its long-term success: developing its main con-

If you understand the sequence of phases and what forces mark the end of one phase and the beginning of the next, you can anticipate and prepare for the changes that must take place within your enterprise.

3

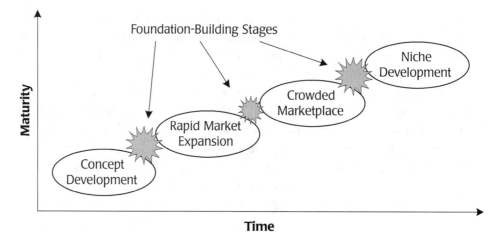

Figure 1-1. Growth phases

cept, moving quickly to dominate a rapidly expanding market, then focusing on cost efficiency in a more stable and mature market. The culmination of these growth phases consists of customizing the basic innovation to fit the needs and demands of smaller market niches.

The transitional phases (occurring between growth phases) focus on making more rational and transparent the work processes developed in a prior growth phase and developing efficient structures to support future growth. The transitions from one growth phase to the next are challenging for a number of reasons:

1. They are accompanied by doubt and uncertainty about what lies ahead.
2. People dislike change in general.
3. Learning and adopting new ways of operating take time and resources.
4. The work required in these transitional phases—making work processes more transparent, rational, strong, and better suited to future needs—is often not as interesting as work done in the growth phases (e.g., developing a new product, entering a new market).

But doing the transitions well is a key part of avoiding the fate of so many businesses that fail to keep pace with their changing circumstances. Yes, these changes will keep you up at night and periodically knock you and your team off balance. But how you as a leader adapt to the changing needs of your enterprise will determine your long-term success.

The size and the jagged edges of the starburst represent the relative difficulty of the transitions. The transitional phases between the first and second growth phases and the third and fourth tend to be the most difficult.

The Origins of These Phases

I developed this scheme of phases in the early 1980s in my evaluation of the management styles of CEOs of high-tech companies that sought venture capital funding. I evaluated the management styles of those who were awarded funding and those who were rejected. I evaluated the CEOs who developed the innovation on which the company is based and the CEOs brought in later by the venture capital investors to promote growth and development. I compared the management styles of CEOs of companies at different sizes and in different types of businesses (e.g., service, manufacturing). My research suggested that venture capital investors believe different types of leaders are more effective in meeting certain objectives. The phases defined in Table 1-1 are based on the differences in management styles of the CEOs judged by the venture capital investors to be most effective in addressing the current and future needs of the company. The table also indicates the growth associated with each type of leader, based on the objectives they are well-suited to meet.

As it turned out, I was not the only one making this type of observation. Many others have determined that different growth phases require different leaders. Many have similar schemes and labels such as inception, adolescence, maturity, etc., reflecting a life cycle perspective. (See Appendix A.)

Over the subsequent 20 years, my colleagues and I at Blue Heron

Who They Were and What They Did	Their Management Style	Phase
Innovative founder	Decisive Visionary	Concept Development
CEOs brought in to make the business processes more rational and robust for future growth	Collaborative Planner	Foundation Building
CEOs with a narrow focus on sales and production	Decisive Commander	Rapid Market Expansion
CEOs focusing on refining their manufacturing processes and procedures	Analytical Planner	Crowded Marketplace
CEOs focusing on the customer service processes	Collaborative Visionary	Niche Development

Table 1-1. Leaders, styles, and growth phases

Consulting have worked with hundreds of organizations contending with growth and development issues and have elaborated these concepts into the model described in this book.

Conscious Decision to Change

The stair-step depiction of the growth phases in Figure 1-1 is a version that we have used in our consulting work and is similar to that used by other authors. It's tempting to assume that moving through these phases will come naturally, much like the phases of human development. Starting out as an infant, Mother Nature takes over and the infant grows into a toddler, the toddler into a child, and so forth. Similarly, some phases of human development are more challenging than others—and the transitions between the phases of human development can be trying and filled with doubt and uncertainty. Indeed, anxiety is practically inevitable, but so is the ultimate course of development. You can't halt development. Reaching "maturity" is largely inevitable.

Businesses and their leaders are not programmed in their DNA to make the needed transitions.

The human development analogy is useful only up to a point. Businesses and their leaders are not programmed in their DNA to make the needed transitions. While you can reasonably assume that an infant will develop into an adult, you can't reasonably assume that an entrepreneur will automatically lead his or her enterprise through these different phases. Nor can you assume that the disorienting transitions between the phases will ultimately be transcended. In fact, these transition periods produce many casualties. Some enterprises fail to make any change in how the business operates as it grows and becomes vulnerable to stronger, more operationally effective competitors.

With this framework in mind, my goal is to help you reduce the size and to smooth out the edges of the starbursts. Your enterprise will shift its mode of operation as smoothly, swiftly, and with minimal trauma when the most pressing needs and issues it faces change. If this is accomplished, then your success or failure depends more on the strength of your innovation and product than on the internal organization and management practices of your enterprise. In order to do this, you need to better understand the transitions. And to understand the transitions you need to have a better idea of each of the phases and what it takes to be successful in each.

The Phases of Growth

Let's take a closer look at each phase and the developmental path that this scheme suggests.

Concept Development Phase

During the Concept Development phase, the most pressing needs and issues of your enterprise are to anticipate the needs and demands of the marketplace and to discover a breakthrough innovation. You seek to discover an innovation that will present such an enticing benefit that customers will start buying your product and stop buying competing products. Discovery is often a trial-and-error process and the competitive advantage goes to the team whose members can work together well and that is quick and creative. Each member of this close-knit team is a generalist and is able to sense directly or indirectly the changes in direction that are inevitable when going through a trial-and-error process.

Think of the circus act in which six or seven people ride one bicycle. All seven performers are in physical contact and feel any minute change in the equilibrium that the team has achieved. Each team member can make small position changes to help the team down the road. The dominant controls in an Innovating organization are the compelling vision, how to achieve it, and the personal interaction among team members, especially the supervision of the leader.

This mode of operation works great for developing and validating a breakthrough innovation. Developing this operational mode comes most naturally to those with the Decisive Visionary management style. Decisive Visionaries favor these practices and priorities. In this way, their natural practices and priorities model and inform the practices and priorities appropriate for this growth phase. But this mode has a soft underbelly—just as does every other mode. The primary weakness of the Innovating mode is its lack of capacity. Innovating enterprises have limited abilities to make and sell a wide range of products; there are also limits to the number of people who can be "on the bike" and still produce a smooth and coordinated effort.

If your business is successful in the Concept Development phase, it will experience growth—which ironically will then undermine the very qualities that led to its success. I will discuss the specifics of this phase and the other phases of growth in detail later in the book. But for right now, the key idea is that each mode of operation has inherent limitations that can harm your enterprise if you are not aware of them and/or don't take action to overcome them. After your original concept has been developed and validated in the market, its success requires you to shift gears.

Discovery is often a trial-and-error process and the competitive advantage goes to the team whose members can work together well and that is quick and creative.

Transitional Phase

The next phase is not a growth phase but a transitional and developmental phase. This is when you shift gears to the next growth-producing operational mode. The most pressing objectives are to make more rational and transparent the work processes that were used to develop and validate the concept and to develop a stronger business infrastructure to support future growth. All of these are important to managing the larger scale of your enterprise and its product line. During this first transitional phase, all the formal controls like organizational structure, formal plans and procedures, and so forth are initiated. Very often, introducing these formal controls represents a huge change for an enterprise and is one of the most challenging for the leader, as we'll discuss in Chapter 4. The Collaborative Planner is naturally best suited to meeting these objectives and to building the systems and controls, weighing the strategic alternatives for future development, and preparing for future changes in operational modes. The mode of operation that is modeled by this management style and that works best for this transitional phase (as well as subsequent transitional phases) is the Foundation Building mode.

The most pressing objectives are to make more rational and transparent the work processes that were used to develop and validate the concept and to develop a stronger business infrastructure to support future growth.

The soft underbelly of this and other transitional phases is that business momentum is consumed. It *costs*—and a classic challenge for a small business is to be able to afford this cost. A small business must have enough business momentum to enable it to turn a portion of its resources and leadership attention away from generating business and toward developing new systems, plans, and procedures that will drive and support future activities. The amount of business momentum consumed can be reduced if the transition is attempted early in the developmental cycle, while the enterprise is still relatively small and the outmoded activities are less deeply entrenched.

Making the transition quickly can also reduce the amount of momentum consumed. Preparing for the subsequent phases of growth and implementing the plans promptly will enable your enterprise to hit its stride with these new management practices and priorities and start receiving the business benefits of the new growth phase.

Unfortunately, many leaders do just the opposite. Instead of moving through this phase early and quickly, they delay starting the transition and then they do it too slowly. As a result, their enterprise can't operate as effectively as it could, and more management resources and attention are devoted to internal problems and stalled plans and initiatives. A prolonged and incomplete transition saps the life from the enterprise.

Rapid Market Expansion Phase

For many enterprises, the next growth phase is Rapid Market Expansion. You enter this phase of growth if your product creates or participates in a market that is rapidly expanding because the market has become more aware of the benefits of your specific product or the product category as a whole. This phase represents an opportunity for your enterprise to grow quickly by producing more of select *existing* products without adding new breakthrough features or developing customized ones. The goal is to gain market exposure faster than any competing enterprise. This is an opportunity to build business momentum quickly. Not every enterprise is going to be lucky enough to experience this phase of growth. Those that don't will move instead to one of the other growth phases.

Not every enterprise is going to be lucky enough to experience this phase of growth. Those that don't will move instead to one of the other growth phases.

The Decisive Commander management style is best suited to a focus on sales and getting the product out quickly and efficiently. The organization they build could be characterized as a platoon of implementers and its activities are controlled by the plans and objectives for market penetration and by the supervision of the leader. This structure is key to taking full advantage of this opportunity. Innovation, deepening expertise in manufacturing, detailed marketing research, or personalized customer service are not the highest priorities. In fact, the basic theme of this mode of operation could be described as "do it." Their structures and priorities describe the Producing operational mode.

The weakness of the Producing mode is, as we can expect, the flip side of its strengths. When market expansion slows and competition is fought on the battlefields of price and feature comparisons, this mode of operation ceases to be most effective.

Crowded Marketplace Phase

When the main competitive battle is about price and features, the phase of growth is called Crowded Marketplace. The goals during this phase are cost reduction, performance consistency, and functional efficiency. The organizational structure of this mode is a hierarchy of functional groups in which the complex operations of the enterprise are broken down into segments and a group or department is created to focus its efforts on each particular function. The naturally effective management style is the Analytical Planner and the most effective mode of operation for this phase is the Planning mode. As one would expect from the Analytical Planner style and Planning mode, the controls are primarily the "hard": plans, processes, and procedures. The weakness of this mode is its rigidity and inability to customize.

Niche Development Phase

Here, the ability to identify niche markets and develop products and services attractive to these customers is important to the growth of the organization.

If customizing your product can increase your margins, your enterprise has an opportunity to move to the Niche Development phase of growth. The objective during the Niche Development phase is to customize products to the needs and demands of different market niches. Here, the ability to identify niche markets and develop products and services attractive to these customers is important to the growth of the organization. The Collaborative Visionary management style and the Adapting mode excel in these kinds of environments. The structure of an Adapting organization is a federation of market-driven teams. Each team within the enterprise focuses on the needs and demands of a particular market segment, and each consists of members who represent all the primary functions required to support that segment.

An Adapting enterprise controls its members and processes predominantly through soft controls. These are elements like the vision and culture of the organization, along with indirect controls like performance feedback. The weakness of this mode of operation is its high cost. There is some redundancy in functions and practices across the market segment teams. This higher cost is acceptable as long as customers place a higher value on the customized features offered.

If they cease to appreciate these enhancements, however, and/or if the features become commoditized, then the cost structure may be too high in the face of competitive pressures. This is the force that you will need to contend with; your options then are to go back to a more structured and cost-effective Planning mode or to hope to develop a new breakthrough innovation (using the Innovating mode) or both.

Phases and Modes of Operations

In describing these phases and the modes of operation, a few points become clear.

First, different forces drive an enterprise's progress through the different phases. Sometimes it's internal forces, such as the increased scale of the enterprise, the need for greater internal control, or the need for restructuring, that push the enterprise into the next growth phase. Sometimes it's an external force, such as an expanding market opportunity or the pressures of a more competitive marketplace, that drives change. Sometimes it's a blend of internal and external influences, such as the perceived opportunity that the development of a breakthrough innovation will propel the enterprise forward. The leaders of the enterprise must take a comprehensive view of their developmental phase and their current mode of operation and what's at stake in order to move smoothly and quickly from one phase to the next.

Second, the sequence of phases is not entirely predetermined. Yes, a transitional phase follows each growth phase, but the sequence of growth phases is variable. There are choices to make. Not every business starts out with or is based on a breakthrough innovation. Some enter this sequence midway. And some businesses never experience some phases—not every business is lucky enough to experience a rapidly expanding market. Also, if you do have the opportunity to focus narrowly on a rapidly expanding market, you can choose not to do so. You can continue to pursue new product innovations (Concept Development phase) or focus on mastering the deeper complexities of manufacturing and the like (Crowded Marketplace phase). There are key strategic decision points along the way that must be well understood. At each decision point you should assess the benefits and costs of alternative paths. The path does make a difference.

Third, Niche Development is not the end of the road. While a new small business may need to devote itself entirely to a particular operational mode in order for its single enterprise to be successful, a larger business is a more diversified set of enterprises. A large diversified business should be able to manage each of its internal enterprises in a manner appropriate for its phase of growth. A business may emphasize different modes at different times and for its different enterprises. The business must be able to fire on all cylinders at the right time and in the most appropriate sequence. In this way development and growth continue without end. We often want, in Jim Collins' words, organizations "built to last." We want them to live on indefinitely and to grow and adapt to new as opportunities present themselves and as their own capabilities and performance levels change.

The sequence of phases is not entirely predetermined. Yes, a transitional phase follows each growth phase, but the sequence of growth phases is variable. There are choices to make.

The Right Gear at the Right Time

In thinking of the growth of an enterprise, there is an analogy for long-term development through different phases of growth. Think of a highly flexible sports car driven by someone who knows the car and the road exceedingly well. The car is designed to operate differently in each gear. With an eye on the road ahead, the driver uses the right gears at the right time and moves masterfully across the business terrain.

In order to do this like Mario Andretti, you must know the car. You have a car with four gears. First gear is in the upper left; fourth is in the upper right. There is no reverse.

11

You must determine where you are. Are you going from a standing start or are you already moving? Are you on a hill? Do you need short-term power or higher speed?

You must exercise some judgment based on what you see ahead and how the car is responding. If you try to shift too soon, you may stall the engine. If you try to shift too late, you could do it damage. And once you decide to shift gears, you need to assess how fast you are going and if you have enough momentum to carry you through the process of changing gears. If you don't have enough momentum, you may not have enough speed to use the new gear and you may be forced to downshift back into a lower gear.

Shifting gears is all about timing. If the timing is right, you need to make the change to keep moving forward at higher speeds. When you shift gears, you put in the clutch and take the engine offline for a short time. If you don't know where the next gear is and delay too long, you'll lose momentum and have to shift back to a lower gear, build some momentum, and try again later. If you don't have the coordination down right, gears will grind, sparks will fly, and you may have to pull over to the side of the road and let someone else take the controls.

To be a good driver you need to understand what is going on in the car and out on the road. You need to decide how you are going to shift gears before you do it—and timing is essential.

This is a better analogy because it says that to be a good driver you need to understand what is going on in the car and out on the road. You need to decide how you are going to shift gears before you do it—and timing is essential. Restated: you need wisdom and knowledge of the situation, you need to make conscious decisions, and you need deliberate and disciplined action. So let's move away from a linear life-cycle concept of development to a map that better reflects important complexities of the real world.

Not a Linear Path

We can revise the stairstep chart presented earlier to better fit this view of enterprise growth. Rather than arranging the phases in a line with a beginning and an end, let's bring the phases into closer interrelationship and do away with the start and finish lines. The result is the Choice and Change model—a map of operational modes that presents the same phases and modes of operation growth, plus the key themes and controls of each mode (Figure 1-2). There is one growth phase at each corner, with the Transitional phase in the middle.

A new enterprise begins in the upper left quadrant in the Concept Development phase. As it grows and develops, it moves to the Transitional

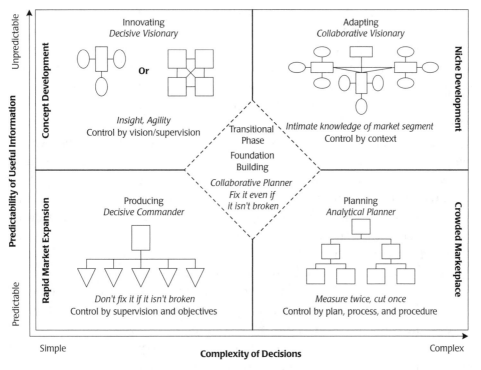

Figure 1-2. The choice and change model

phase in the center. From there, a strategic decision point, a choice is made regarding whether the enterprise is in a rapidly expanding market and, if so, what opportunities that may present. From this point in the middle of the diagram, the leaders can also decide to move to a Crowded Marketplace phase of growth or Niche Development.

Once you've moved to any one of these phases, each move to a subsequent growth phase involves a move back to the Transitional phase shown in the middle of the diagram. Here is where you'll build the foundation, using the Foundation Building operational mode, for the next phase of growth. Clearly, your first experience of this phase is the most dramatic and comprehensive. Later Transitional phases can be more brief and targeted to the areas of your business that require change.

This description of the progression through different phases of growth, with each being executed most effectively by a particular mode of operation uniquely suited to it, may sound complex. But knowing this framework can help you understand where your enterprise is in its development, how it must operate to be effective, what may lie ahead, and how to prepare for it.

Few enterprises move through these phases as crisply and strategically as I have described. There are few real Mario Andrettis. Yes, many enterprises change the way they operate as they grow, but the vast majority do not make these changes as completely as needed: they don't take full advantage of the business potential of their current phase of growth.

There are many reasons why change is incomplete, resisted, or both. People in general dislike change. Surveys have indicated that many people fear public speaking more than death and change more than public speaking. Obviously, there are many reasons why change is resisted that are more specific to business enterprises. Every time an enterprise changes its mode of operation it must change in some way its culture and its power structure (who reports to whom). These changes shake the essence of the organization and its business activities. The resistance to change can be immense.

But there's another reason why change is difficult. The naturally effective management styles in subsequent growth phases may not only be different, but they may be dramatically different. The Choice and Change model (Figure 1-2) shows the management style of the leader that is naturally most effective in managing each mode of operation.

The naturally most effective management style for the Concept Development phase, for example, is *Decisive Visionary*. These leaders are creative and can make quick decisions easily. They are comfortable working with small, informally organized teams pursuing a larger vision. The Decisive Visionary scans the horizon for new opportunities and concepts. He or she collects input from eclectic sources to form a holistic worldview. The validity of the opportunities is sensed intuitively. Objective research is usually done to test the concept or vision, not develop it. Decisive Visionaries are comfortable defying conventional wisdom that says, "It cannot be done," because they see the vision vividly and are not highly influenced by the opinions of others. Their decisive side provides a specific to-do list for getting from where they are to that point on the distant horizon. The Decisive Visionary picks a point on the distant horizon and drives the team toward that destination.

In contrast, naturally effective leaders during Transitional phases are *Collaborative Planners*. They focus on the problems at hand and analyze large amounts of information before developing a solution. They solicit opinions and use them to guide their decisions. They want to make informed decisions that represent the best judgment of the team and external experts. These two decision-making approaches are not only different—they are diametrically opposed.

One can easily imagine that a leader effective in the Concept Development phase of growth would feel like a fish out of water in the Transitional phases, while a leader effective in a Transitional phase would be out of place in the Concept Development phase. This also means that what the leader not only has to do something different from one phase to the next, but also has to do the complete opposite.

The dramatic changes also suggest some benefit in bringing in different leaders to execute each growth phase. Indeed, changing leaders is often done. But having a leader who is a natural fit is not always possible or practical. Their experience, expertise, and familiarity with the business make some individuals indispensable. There's clearly another significant issue at work here as well: some enterprises cannot afford the search process or the salary of a new CEO. Also, the new leader would still need to make the changes in structure, practices, and priorities that make an enterprise effective in the new phase.

A leader effective in the Concept Development phase of growth would feel like a fish out of water in the Transitional phases, while a leader effective in a Transitional phase would be out of place in the Concept Development phase.

Developing Workarounds—A Focus on Operational Modes

If you want to lead your enterprise through the right succession of growth phases, it will be necessary to develop different ways of adequately addressing its most pressing needs. If a leader cannot be effective naturally, then he or she can be effective consciously by focusing on the development of the right operational modes. The objective of the workaround is to develop the right operational mode. This can be done by developing a management team that provides the range of styles needed. It can also be done by having a leader emulate the practices of the naturally effective leaders. In both cases, the leader or leadership team must decide which operational mode to develop and when to do so. Any of these workaround strategies will be more effective by raising the awareness of everyone in the enterprise that changes are needed well before the need for change becomes imperative. Recognize the successes of the prior operational mode and then move on to developing the needed operation mode.

Management Style—More Important Than It Should Be

I believe the personal management style of the leader is more important than it should be. We should not be held captive by our personalities—they should not drive business success or failure. The good news is that you can consciously champion the practices and priorities of a type of leader different from you in order to meet the needs of your enterprise. You can change the way you work, simply by being more aware of the dynamics of growth and different organizational modes of operation.

By recognizing these fundamental dynamics, you can make wiser choices about the priorities you set, the structures you create, and the culture you sculpt within your organization. You can create a greater distinction between your personal preferences and priorities and those practices that will be most effective in your organization's current operations.

By recognizing these fundamental dynamics, you can make wiser choices about the priorities you set, the structures you create, and the culture you sculpt within your organization.

Fortunately, when entrepreneurial leaders understand the impact of their management styles on their organizations, they can make a conscious choice to alter their management practices and priorities. They can begin to place the structure, culture, and priorities into alignment with the requirements of their business opportunities. Ultimately, their flexibility allows them to remain effective over longer periods of time and in a wider range of situations. Leaders who survive one phase of success to be successful in another place a higher value on success than on insisting on hewing to a management orientation and structure that best suits their personal style.

Ironically, the more successful you are in one phase of growth, the more dramatic subsequent changes must be. The more you optimize your organizational mode of operation for innovation, the more successful you are likely to be in that phase. The more successful you are, the more effort you will have to expend to create the next appropriate mode of operation. The saying, "Nothing leads to failure like success," rings true. The answer is not to avoid focus and specialization; if you do not specialize in a mode, you may not be effective or competitive. Be flexible.

Thus, in the remainder of the book, I will discuss most how an individual should respond to the different growth phases. This approach will help those without a leadership team and it will help those building a team to determine what type of leadership is needed.

Let's review the important points of this chapter. Table 1-2 shows the phases of growth and the most pressing needs and issues the business faces.

It shows the management style of leaders most effective in addressing these needs and issues; the right structures, practices, and priorities naturally spring forth from this type of leader. I have listed for each operational mode the structures and dominant controls and the inherent weaknesses of each. Finally, the table indicates the emerging force that pushes the business forward into a new phase. With appropriate leadership, growth takes place and brings other issues and opportunities to the forefront. The enterprise is forced into the next growth phase.

Growth Phase	Pressing Needs and Issues	Naturally Effective Management Style	Most Effective Operational Mode	Organizational Structure	Dominant Controls	Weaknesses	Emerging Force Requiring Change
Concept Development	■ Anticipating customer needs ■ Discovering the form the concept will take ■ Validating the form in the market ■ Survival ■ Breakthrough innovation	Decisive Visionary	Innovating	Focused Team of Generalists	Vision and Supervision	■ One-generation activity ■ Sensitive to personal chemistry and team dynamics ■ Limited business capacity	■ Increasing scale of enterprise and its business
Transitional Foundation Building	■ Making processes more rational and transparent ■ Building systems ■ Weighing strategic alternatives ■ Developing plans	Collaborative Planner	Foundation Building	Functionally Segmented Team	All Controls	■ Consumes business momentum	■ External market opportunity
Rapid Market Expansion	■ Focusing on selling more of what the company is already selling ■ Simplifying ■ Gaining market exposure faster than any other company	Decisive Commander	Producing	Platoon of Implementers	Supervision/ Assignments	■ Promotes little insight or innovation ■ Lacks planning for divergent and complex issues	■ Competition that is close in price and features ■ Greater operational complexities

Table 1-2. Growth phases and business needs and issues (continued on next page)

Growth Phase	Pressing Needs and Issues	Naturally Effective Management Style	Most Effective Operational Mode	Organizational Structure	Dominant Controls	Weaknesses	Emerging Force Requiring Change
Second Transition Phase							
Crowded Marketplace	▪ Cost reduction ▪ Consistency ▪ Functional specialization ▪ Integration according to plans	Analytical Planner	Planning	Hierarchy of Functional Groups	Plans, Processes and Procedures	▪ Tendency to produce optimal pieces but a suboptimal whole ▪ Not responsive to varying customer demands	▪ Margin squeeze ▪ Demand for customized service or productrs
Third Transition Phase							
Niche Development	▪ Developmental innovation ▪ Following external cues ▪ Cross-functional teamwork ▪ Mass customization ▪ Customer-driven strategies	Collaborative Visionary	Adapting	Federation of Market-Driven Teams	Vision, Culture, Standards, Performance Evaluation, Integrated Systems	▪ Costly—requires scale and marketing muscle ▪ Requires sophisticated management and infrastructure	▪ Commoditization of product features

Table 1-2. Growth phases and business needs and issues (continued)

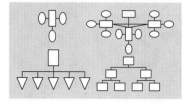

Chapter 2

Management Styles

Y OU'RE PROBABLY FAMILIAR WITH TESTS THAT INDICATE APTITUDES and preferences for certain professions. Perhaps you've taken one or more of them. You may have been advised to become a flight attendant, a surgeon, or an architect. The key to happiness, the logic goes, is to seek the profession for which you are best suited. This strategy is fine for stable professions, but leading a small or rapidly growing business organization defies simple categorization. There is no one single set of aptitudes you will need to draw on as your business grows and matures.

The job of the leader changes as the enterprise grows. When you become the leader of a growth business, you expose yourself to a wide array of situations, challenges, choices, and risks. Some of what you will be required to take on will match your aptitudes, experience, and interests. But some will not. Innovating, Foundation Building, Producing, Planning, and Adapting: the mode names describe the scope of priorities the leader will need to champion. As the creative leader, owner, and business manager, the entrepreneurial leader confronts it all: incidental issues, people problems, and technical problems requiring great creativity or extensive research.

These are all aspects of the real world. As the leader, you must see problems for what they are in cold reality and respond in ways that address the most important issues and effectively move the enterprise forward. You can't be successful over the long term in a growing business by being a set of solutions looking for a particular type of problems. The problems force themselves on you. You cannot be completely selective about which ones you will address and which ones you'll leave unattended.

Adaptation and Change

So many of an enterprise's characteristics emanate from the leader and his or her style of management is a crucial factor determining the success of the venture. A new enterprise rarely has formal business and organizational strategies to guide it as it moves forward. Instead, the leader personally guides the enterprise with countless decisions. Strategies emerge from the totality of those decisions and reflect the leader's decision-making biases. The direction a leader favors personally is often the direction his or her company takes.

The leader's management style often becomes the benchmark for determining if others are behaving as needed.

The leader's management style often becomes the benchmark for determining if others are behaving as needed. If you value spontaneity, for example, you likely view other spontaneous people favorably. If you do thorough research before making a decision, you often view positively others who do the same. Your management style has tremendous impact on the strategic direction of the firm and its daily operation.

As discussed in the prior chapter, leaders with different management styles are most effective in different phases of growth. If you want to be an effective leader in every phase of growth, this means that you'll have to change your management style to be so. However, changing management style is difficult—some say impossible—because it is deeply rooted in our psychology and perhaps our biology. Is this type of personality change advisable? Is it even possible?

We May Not Change—But Our Priorities Can

My colleagues and I have asked recognized experts if people every really change fundamentally. The experts have been in fields that give them direct observation of people who are trying to change in some way, like psychologists and organizationally development professionals. (The fields include developmental psychology, cognitive psychology, organizational psychology and development, neurolinguistic programming, humanistic development, transpersonal development, personal growth, management, and personal coaching.) The consensus is that our basic personality traits remain essentially the same over our lifetimes. People don't really change who they are. An individual can mature and see situations from more perspectives and can learn new skills, but change is at the margin of our character, not its core. Basically, we all must continually work with the raw material with which we came into the world.

My own experience and observation are that people do not change their management styles in any meaningful way over long periods of time. I have tested a number of people, using the same test in this book, at different points over the last 20 years and have found little change in their management styles. My own personal career experience is that my style hasn't changed much and it indeed has had an impact on how effective I am in certain situations. None of my family members have changed the way they go about making decisions.

We have seen the power of people working together to change the priorities they set within an organization, how they organize themselves, and the processes they develop.

But in our work with many organizations we have seen the power of people working together to change the priorities they set within an organization, how they organize themselves, and the processes they develop. We have seen them consciously establish the right structures and develop the right controls, the right culture. In short, we have seen them develop the right mode of operation—even if it different from what they would do simply considering their own preferences. They develop the right operational mode because they believe it will help them be more successful in their current situation. They know it is right for their particular growth phase and the challenges they will face in the future. They seek to develop the right mode of operation because they value success over personal comfort. They are able to do this because they know themselves, including their limitations and the ways in which they see the world.

If you know your natural preferences and what is required to be effective in a particular situation, you can consciously change your priorities and your behavior. Even if you cannot execute all the required priorities personally, the intelligent and effective use of other people in your organization can provide your enterprise with much of what it needs.

Management Styles: Making Decisions

For our purposes, your management style is simply a reflection of your own unique mix of preferences regarding how you make decisions. The purpose of this exercise is to identify the components that make up your management style. Your management style is based in your personal decision style; by identifying your dominant and backup decision styles and how you compare with the general population, you can gauge your management style. This approach is based on the decision styles developed by Dr. Alan Rowe of the University of Southern California. The inventory evaluates preferences, not skill or intelligence. Identifying your personal style now before reading the rest of the book will place your own preferences within a context that will help you get much more out of the material.

Answer each question by assigning to each of the four responses the following points depending on how well that response describes you:

8: most like you

4: moderately like you

2: little like you

1: least like you

You can assign each score only once within each question and you must use all four numbers—8, 4, 2, and 1. For example, for the first question, you might assign the following scores:

	Column	I	Column	II	Column	III	Column	IV
1. My prime objective is to:	Have a position with status	4	Be the best in my field	2	Achieve recognition for my work	8	Feel secure in my job	1
2. I enjoy jobs that:	Are technical and well defined		Have considerable variety		Allow independent action		Involve people	

Table 2-1. Example of assigning scores on a management style component inventory

Please remember these points:

▶ Consider your *ideal* work situation.

▶ Generally, the first answer that comes to mind is the best one to put down.

▶ Relax when filling out the inventory.

▶ There are no right or wrong answers.

▶ Recognize that the inventory simply reflects your preferences, not abilities.

▶ Each person is different and will answer each question differently.

Decision Style Inventory

Complete this inventory using the following scale to score yourself:
8 = most like you, 4 = moderately like you, 2 = little like you, 1 = least like you

	Column I		Column II		Column III		Column IV	
1. My prime objective is to:	Have a position with status		Be the best in my field		Achieve recognition for my work		Feel secure in my job	
2. I enjoy jobs that:	Are technical and well defined		Have considerable variety		Allow independent action		Involve people	
3. I expect people working for me to be:	Productive and fast		Highly capable		Committed and responsive		Receptive to suggestions	
4. In my job, I look for:	Practical results		The best solutions		New approaches or ideas		Good working conditions	
5. I communicate best with others:	Orally and directly		In writing		By having a discussion		In a group	
6. In my planning I emphasize:	Current needs		Meeting objectives		Future goals		Organizational needs	
7. When faced with solving a problem, I:	Rely on proven approaches		Apply careful analysis		Look for creative approaches		Rely on my feelings	
8. When using information, I prefer:	Specific facts		Accurate and complete data		Broad coverage of many options		Limited, easily understood data	
9. When I am uncertain what to do, I:	Rely on hunch and intuition		Search for facts		Explore a possible compromise		Delay making a decision	
10. Whenever possible, I avoid:	Long debates		Incomplete work		Using numbers or formulas		Conflict with others	
11. I am especially good at:	Remembering dates and facts		Solving difficult problems		Seeing many possibilities		Interacting with others	
12. When time is important, I:	Decide and act quickly		Follow plans and priorities		Refuse to be pressured		Seek guidance and support	
13. In social settings, I generally:	Speak with others		Think about what is being said		Observe what is going on		Listen to the conversation	
14. I am good at remembering:	People's names		Places we met		People's faces		People's personalities	
15. The work I do provides me with:	The power to influence others		Challenging assignments		Achieving my personal goals		Acceptance by the group	
16. I work well with those who are:	Energetic and ambitious		Punctual and confident		Curious and open-minded		Polite and trusting	
17. When under stress, I:	Become anxious		Concentrate on the problem		Become frustrated and annoyed		Am concerned and compassionate	
18. Others consider me:	Aggressive and domineering		Disciplined and precise		Imaginative and perfectionist		Supportive and compassionate	
19. My decisions are:	Realistic and impersonal		Systematic and abstract		Broad and flexible		Sensitive to the needs of others	
20. I dislike:	Losing control		Boring work		Following rules		Being rejected	
Column Totals								

Table 2-2. Management style component inventory

Scoring Your Self-Test

To score your responses, add up the numbers in each of the four columns and enter the total in the four boxes at the bottom of the questionnaire. The combined scores should total 300 points.

Interpreting Your Score

The management style determination table (Table 2-3) will develop a two-word description of your management style using these scores. An example is shown below.

Write the scores for each column on row A of the table. The style components are indicated under each column heading. The higher the score, the more you favor that particular approach to decision-making.

On row B, enter "#1" under the style with the highest score. This is your dominant style. Enter "#2" under the style with the second-highest score. This is your backup style. These two are the decision-making styles you favor most. Also on row B, place an "X" under the style corresponding to the lowest score. This is the style you least prefer. The mix of styles described in row B compares your preference among the style components.

Section C of the table will help you determine how your scores compare with those of the average American. Circle the range of numbers in which each of the scores listed in row A falls. Do this for all four columns. This will give you an idea of how extreme your scores are relative to the general population.

Section D will develop a single label for your combination of style components. Circle the label in line D1 that corresponds to the highest relative score category (e.g., very high, high). If there is a tie, circle the style that has the greatest numerical value. This label represents your dominant style component relative to the general population.

For your secondary style component, consider only columns in which your circled range is average or higher (lines C1 through C3). Find the next-highest circled range and circle the label in line D2. If there is a tie, circle the style with the greatest numerical value.

If no columns have scores that are average or higher for this secondary style component, circle the label in D2 that corresponds to your dominant style. This means that the single dominant style is a good indication of your management style biases.

Decision Style	Column I Decisive Commander	Column II Analytical Planner	Column III Creative Visionary	Column IV Collaborative Facilitator
A. Your Decision Style Scores (column totals from Table 2-2)				
B. Relative Dominance				
C. Relative to the Average American				
1. Very high (15% of population)	90 and higher	105 and higher	95 and higher	70 and higher
2. High (15%)	82–89	97–104	87–94	62–69
3. Moderately high (20%)	75–81	90–96	80–86	55-61
Average	75	90	80	55
4. Moderately low (20%)	68–74	83–89	73–79	48–54
5. Low (15%)	60–67	75–82	65–72	40–47
6. Very low (15%)	59 and below	74 and below	64 and below	39 and below
D. Labels				
1. Dominant	Commander	Planner	Visionary	Facilitator
2. Secondary	Decisive	Analytical	Creative	Collaborative

Table 2-3. Management style determination

Next, enter the labels you circled in section D in Table 2-4, which indicates your management style.

	From Line D2	From Line D1
Your Management Style		

Table 2-4. General management style

The resulting management styles are Decisive Commander, Decisive Planner, Decisive Visionary, and so forth. There are 16 combinations of the four style components.

The results of this simple self-test should give you a good idea of your biases, which will be important as you read through the rest of the book. Please keep in mind, however, that there are important dimensions related to your management other than those profiled here. Your lowest score, for example, indicates an approach to decision making that you will avoid. I will mention some of these more nuanced points later. Nonetheless, the results of the scoring tables will give you a workable description of your management style.

	Column I	Column II	Column III	Column IV
Decision Style	Decisive Commander	Analytical Planner	Creative Visionary	Collaborative Facilitator
A. Your Decision Style Scores (column totals from Table 2-2)	82	43	115	58
B. Relative Dominance	#2	X	#1	
B. Relative to the Average American				
1. Very high (15% of population)	90 and higher	105 and higher	95 and higher	70 and higher
2. High (15%)	82–89	97–104	87–94	62–69
3. Moderately high (20%)	75–81	90–96	80–86	55-61
Average	75	90	80	55
4. Moderately low (20%)	68–74	83–89	73–79	48–54
5. Low (15%)	60–67	75–82	65–72	40–47
6. Very low (15%)	59 and below	74 and below	64 and below	39 and below
D. Labels				
1. Dominant	Commander	Planner	Visionary	Facilitator
2. Secondary	Decisive	Analytical	Creative	Collaborative

Table 2-5. Example 1

The individual decision style components will be discussed after the following scoring examples.

	From Line D2	From Line D1
Your Management Style	Decisive	Visionary

This person has a clear dominant style, Creative Visionary, and a clear backup style, Decisive Commander. A single label that combines these two styles is "Decisive Visionary."

These are the scores of a Decisive Visionary and a true serial entrepreneur. This person has a clear dominant style, Creative Visionary, and a clear backup style, Decisive Commander. A single label that combines these two styles is "Decisive Visionary."

Example 2 shows the scores of a person who started a manufacturing business in Seattle in the early 1990s and is the CEO of the business today.

Decision Style	Column I Decisive Commander	Column II Analytical Planner	Column III Creative Visionary	Column IV Collaborative Facilitator
A. Your Decision Style Scores (column totals from Table 2-2)	57	86	114	43
B. Relative Dominance		#1	#2	X
C. Relative to the Average American				
1. Very high (15% of population)	90 and higher	105 and higher	95 and higher	70 and higher
2. High (15%)	82–89	97–104	87–94	62–69
3. Moderately high (20%)	75–81	90–96	80–86	55-61
Average	75	90	80	55
4. Moderately low (20%)	68–74	83–89	73–79	48–54
5. Low (15%)	60–67	75–82	65–72	40–47
6. Very low (15%)	59 and below	74 and below	64 and below	39 and below
D. Labels				
1. Dominant	Commander	Planner	Visionary	Facilitator
2. Secondary	Decisive	Analytical	Creative	Collaborative

Table 2-6. Example 2

This person has a clear dominant style, Creative Visionary, but none of the scores for the other styles are average or higher. The label "Creative Visionary" best describes her management style.

	From Line D2	From Line D1
Your Management Style	Creative	Visionary

This person is also very close to being an Analytical Visionary, because the Analytical Planner component is strong compared with the other styles. She would have least difficulty emulating the Analytical Planner component.

Decision-Style Components of Management Style

These are four decision-style components of management style:

- ▶ Decisive Commander
- ▶ Analytical Planner
- ▶ Creative Visionary
- ▶ Collaborative Facilitator

Although everyone displays aspects of each of these four style components, for most people one is dominant. The next most preferred style, the backup style, is typically used when the dominant style leads to an impasse. Combined, these two describe your management style.

Although everyone displays aspects of each of these four style components, for most people one is dominant.

Decisive Commanders

These decision makers are characterized by an emphasis on the here and now. Decisive Commanders tend to make decisions quickly and consider only specific, objective facts. Their priority is to get the job done. They are directive, action-oriented, and decisive—and look for decision-making speed and results. Decisive Commanders like short reports with summarized conclusions, tend to have many people reporting to them, and maintain tight control of the decision-making process. They tend to control others through supervision. People with this style can be autocratic and readily exercise their power and control to influence others. They sometimes feel insecure and want status to protect their positions. They are often viewed as militaristic.

The strength of this style is an ability to quickly mobilize resources to meet specific task-oriented objectives. They can be heard saying, "Let's just get on with it." The weaknesses of this style are a tendency to follow instincts and to avoid formal long-term planning and being harsh in their working relationships.

Analytical Planners

Analytical Planners tend to seek the best-supported solution to the problem based on a defensible and logical organization of the facts. They make decisions after reviewing the facts, *all* the facts. People with this style see the technical aspects of situations and enjoy solving complex problems. They search for complete, accurate information and scrutinize it to see what possibilities exist. Analytical Planners like long written reports and are most comfortable taking action after the decision and all its implications have been clearly defined. People with this style can often be highly autocratic. They place high priority on using rules and procedures to control others and like well-defined organizational structures.

Analytical Planners tend to be good at solving complex problems, conducting thorough research, and following detailed plans. They can be heard saying, "What do the facts tell us?" The drawbacks of this style are the potential for analysis paralysis, an endless cycle of studies and reports, and a strong interest in controlling the activities of others.

Analytical Planners tend to be good at solving complex problems, conducting thorough research, and following detailed plans.

Creative Visionaries

Creativity and a big-picture perspective characterize Creative Visionaries. They are conceptual and seek something larger than the best solution; they seek universal truths. They scan the horizon for opportunities and threats. They are intuitive in decision making; they make the decision first and then gather information to support or challenge their decision—and then repeat the cycle again and again. They are flexible, curious, and open-minded. They value independence and dislike following rules. These decision makers are perfectionists, especially in issues related to their visions. They want to see many options and are concerned about the future. They are creative in finding answers to problems and can easily visualize future alternatives and consequences. They have a high commitment to their organizations and value praise and recognition. Creative Visionaries prefer loose control and are willing to share power. Communication is open and wide-ranging.

Strengths of this style are creativity and vision. Creative Visionaries can see broad realities that are not apparent to others. They can be heard saying, "Let's take a step back and look at this from a different perspective." But the weaknesses of this style are the tendencies to look for new solutions when current ones are sufficient, to rely too much on intuition and feelings, and to be erratic on issues, especially on issues that do not engage their interest.

Collaborative Facilitators

Collaborative Facilitators are the most people-oriented of all four style components. They are sensitive to others and consider others' views when making decisions. These leaders can be political in their approach to problems and can quickly identify the common bonds among people that create effective coalitions. People with a collaborative behavioral style are supportive and sensitive to suggestions, show warmth, use persuasion to influence others, accept loose controls, and prefer verbal over written reports. They focus on near-term problems and are action-oriented. They want acceptance and care deeply about the organization and the development of its people. These leaders tend to rely on meetings to exchange information and to develop a consensus; in fact, for Collaborative Facilitators, meetings are an important part of the decision-making process. Achieving understanding, agreement, consensus, and a positive working environment are important priorities for them.

The strength of this style is the ability to create common understanding and consensus. They can be heard saying, "Let's get together and discuss the situation." The weaknesses of this style are that decision making can be time-consuming and often requires the presence of people knowledgeable in the relevant matters and that this style can cause people to be overly influenced by the opinions of others.

Achieving understanding, agreement, consensus, and a positive working environment are important priorities for Collaborative Facilitators.

Comfort Zones

It's important to note what is *not* indicated by these personal decision styles and the management styles they create. While they describe an individual's preferences and personal priorities, they do not measure wisdom, intelligence, ambition, motivation, or energy, all of which are vital ingredients for success. What they do indicate is who will be most comfortable in each mode and phase. The ranges, in terms of modes of operation over which each of the four component styles is most effective, are shown on the Choice and Change map in Figure 2-1.

As you can see, the ranges overlap. These ranges indicate the blend of component styles that constitute the management style that's most naturally effective for each phase of growth. To find the situations best suited to your management style, find the coverage range of your dominant style. It is in these areas that you will be most naturally effective. Find the range of your lowest score. This is where you are least in your element and where your success will be driven by the quality of your workarounds.

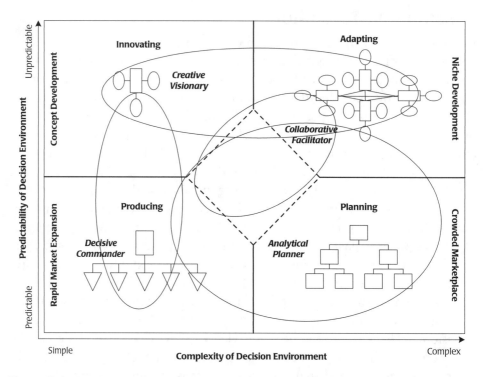

Figure 2-1. Comfort zones of the four management-style components

Five Naturally Effective Management Styles for Growth and Development Phases

The four components discussed above can be grouped in various combinations to describe different management styles. Of the many possible combinations, I'd like to focus on the five that are most effective over the different phases of growth and development, ones that model the practices and priorities effective in each phase. I am going to discuss each of the five management styles in greater detail within the context of the phase in which they are naturally effective, but I will mention them here along with some of the finer points of the mix of the style components that model the operational modes (see Table 2-7).

The *Decisive Visionary* management style is characteristic of someone who is more of a Visionary than the average person, is not much of a Planner, and has Decisive Commander as the primary backup style. An important nuance for Decisive Visionary that models the Innovating operational mode is a lower-than-average score in the Analytical Planner decision style.

Phase	Operational Mode	Modeled by
Concept Development	Innovating	Decisive Visionary
Rapid Market Expansion	Producing	Decisive Commander
Crowded Marketplace	Planning	Analytic Planner
Niche Development	Adapting	Collaborative Visionary
Transitional	Foundation Building	Collaborative Planner

Table 2-7. Summary table

The *Decisive Commander* (one of the four "pure" component styles) is highly directive. Those who best model the Producing operational mode have a Decisive Commander score of 82 or higher.

The *Analytical Planner* (one of the four "pure" component styles) is highly analytic. Those who best model the Planning mode have an Analytical Planner score of 97 or higher and usually have a Creative Visionary score of 73 to 80.

The *Collaborative Visionary* style is characteristic of one who is a conceptually oriented visionary with a strong collaborative and people orientation. Those who best model the Adaptive operational mode have an Analytical Planner score of 83 to 90.

The *Collaborative Planner* style is characteristic of one who is highly analytic and tends to be a more collaborative leader than average. This leader models the goals, practices, and priorities of the Foundation Building phases.

Table 2-8 shows the style score ranges for each of the five management styles. As you will see, these scores represent a more detailed profile for each style.

		Decisive Commander	Analytical Planner	Creative Visionary	Collaborative Facilitator
Operational Mode	**Management Style**				
Innovating	Decisive Visionary	75 and higher	89 and lower	87 and higher	
Producing	Decisive Commander	82 and higher			
Planning	Analytical Planner		97 and higher	73 to 80	
Adapting	Collaborative Visionary		83 to 90	87 and higher	55 and higher
Transitional	Collaborative Planner		90 and higher		55 and higher

Table 2-8. Style score ranges for each of the five management styles

Don't panic if you do not fit one of these profiles—these are profiles of the management styles that best model the five operational modes. (For a more complete analysis of your management style, you can visit our web site: www.bheron.com.) For a more complete analysis of your management style, you can visit our web site: www.bheron.com. You can often easily emulate the practices and priorities of the styles closest to your own.

Not only are certain leaders more naturally suited to certain phases of growth, but these management styles actually help define the enduring characteristics of each mode of operation. If we assume that a management style is most naturally effective in a given mode, we can infer what goals, practices, and priorities will work best. These leaders are our models and we can emulate what they do.

These five styles simply model the most effective goals, practices, and priorities. They are simply estimates of management behavior, not skill, wisdom, or discipline.

If your management style is one of the five styles identified as the model for one of the modes of operation, you will be most comfortable leading an organization operating in that mode. Remember: these five styles simply model the most effective goals, practices, and priorities. They are simply estimates of management behavior, not skill, wisdom, or discipline. You should identify the management styles that are closest to your preferred decision style combination. What this tells you is that these styles will be the easiest for you to emulate. It doesn't purport to tell you that emulating any of these styles is going to be out of reach. This is an important point: while we may not have precisely the right personality to be effective in a particular phase, we can set the right goals, practices, and priorities—we can consciously create the right mode of operation.

Master the Art of the Appropriate Response

As a leader, you are faced with three courses of action when a management style other than your preferred style is needed. You can:

▶ Relocate yourself to a situation that is a better fit for what you like to do or change the situation to fit you.

▶ Personally emulate the needed management style by creating the appropriate structures and setting the appropriate priorities, creating the right operational mode.

▶ Collaborate with other people to develop the right operational mode for the situation.

Your strategy could well be a mix of these alternatives.

Relocate

One can change leaders or change the business. One can get a management style that is in alignment with the requirements of a situation by removing the leader and bringing in someone whose management style is a better fit. This strategy is sometimes the only long-term solution. New leaders may be able to follow their instincts more closely and be more effective than prior leaders. They may also be more energized by the situation and growth phase than were their predecessors.

But this approach has serious drawbacks. First, there is a loss of experience. Leaders accumulate experience and wisdom; the loss of these assets can have a significant negative impact on the business. Second, the new leader may be well suited for just one phase and might need to be replaced later on when the situation changes again. The new phase that drives out one leader and pulls in another may be temporary and the new leader may be no better prepared for the subsequent growth phase than was the previous one for the current phase.

Leaders accumulate experience and wisdom; the loss of these assets can have a significant negative impact on the business.

You can also relocate the business a different business growth phase, one that corresponds to the leader's preferences and presumably skills and aptitudes. This is a decision not to pursue growth according to the phases described above. If an individual excels at innovation, a business can be developed around this mode. There is a cost associated with this strategy, though: some growth phases will not be exploited to their fullest. Selecting this strategy can be appropriate if the costs and risks are considered in the process. Unfortunately, many businesses that decide to stay with a particular operational mode also decide to pursue a growth phase for which the mode selected is a poor fit. The resulting lack of alignment is a source of weakness.

Neither of these relocation options may be consistent with the leader's or the firm's long-term interests if business growth is the objective. The organization may be reacting to short-term needs or might be assuming a greater future stability in its business situation than will actually exist.

Emulate

The second course of action, which is personally more difficult for a leader, is to personally emulate the appropriate management style by deliberately creating the right mode of operation. This is accomplished by shaping the organization's structure, management and cultural priorities, and methods of control. If these variables are shaped to reflect the appropriate mode, the leader's style of management matters less. To be successful in this approach, the leader has to become more sensitive to the requirements of the situation and manage in a more conscious manner.

For example, if you are in your element as a Decisive Commander taking full charge of rapid market growth, you may be ill at ease when new developments require you to take on the role of Collaborative Visionary. Suddenly you are called to be people-oriented and creative. But if you emulate this style, many elements can fall into place. You can deliberately act in ways that will be uncomfortable for you but that will help you to achieve the desired results.

Let me give you an illustration. Macintosh and Intel-based computers running Windows are very different. The Mac has a certain computer architecture that has important strengths. Intel-based computers also have strengths. For many years, Intel-compatible software would not run on Macs. However, software programs are now available for the Mac that enable it to emulate an Intel machine and run compatible software. When a Mac is running the emulation software, it runs more slowly than when it runs Macintosh software, but it works nonetheless.

I believe that the performance of someone emulating the appropriate management style will not be as effective or strong as the performance of someone for whom that style comes naturally.

Just like this analogy of Macs and PCs, I believe that the performance of someone emulating the appropriate management style will not be as effective or strong as the performance of someone for whom that style comes naturally. If you're behaving in a way that is fundamentally different from your psychological makeup, you may be a little slower and you may need to be more deliberate and more conscious of what you do. However, in many cases, your efforts will be sufficient to help you achieve your organization's long-term goals. Remember that the phases do not last forever. The period of discomfort you experience may disappear when your business moves into a later phase.

Creating the right mode of operation for your phase of growth is the thrust of this book. But even if you do so, it's important to recognize that there may still be deficiencies. In my experience, emulation is about 85 to 90 percent as effective. While this is an immense improvement from a leader who is *not* trying to create the right operational mode, it is still short of 100 percent. At certain times, enterprises may need the inherent creativity of a true Visionary, for example, but you can get by with someone of another style if he or she is flexible and given more time.

Collaborate

Another course of action is to work with others. You can create a management team that includes people with different areas of expertise and different management styles. Here's an example. An enterprise might have been founded by a Decisive Visionary, a defiant innovator who is the archetypical leader of the Concept Development phase. Who should take on a relatively greater role as the company emerges in the marketplace? Someone who is a Collaborative Planner, who can do what is required internally and be methodical and attentive to a broad set of opinions when selecting the next growth phase. Then, during the Producing mode, someone who is a Decisive Commander can have greater impact on decisions. And so on. Using a team approach is effective, yet it can be costly and requires extra coordination skills and efforts.

Wise leaders usually use some combination of emulation and collaboration. You should consider all options to make sure that organizational variables are aligned with your organization's purpose and that the right modes of operation are being created. In the end, the ultimate solution lies in wisdom, conscious choice, and deliberate and disciplined action. Either individually or through team efforts, the right options must be selected and implemented.

You should consider all options to make sure that organizational variables are aligned with your organization's purpose and that the right modes of operation are being created.

The Road Ahead

The hard reality is that most of the people who now survive as effective leaders can do it because they haven't in the past. They have learned the hard way, by making mistakes and learning from them. This learning process requires time, an opportunity for another chance, personal tenacity, introspection, and a tolerance of personal discomfort.

Although the learning process takes time, having a clear view of the path ahead and seeing your situation from a broader perspective can reduce the time required. If you can see the subtle indicators that change is afoot and then anticipate and prepare for the changes before they become imperative, you will stand a better change of surviving.

Fortunately, new ventures pass through reasonably distinct and predictable phases of development. A business generally begins in the Concept Development phase, which is most effectively exploited using the Innovating mode, and moves to the right as it grows and develops, although the sequence of phases is not the same for all businesses.

The phase is the situation; the mode is how you respond. The phase is the shape of the hole; the mode is the shape of the peg. An organization is most effective when its response is best suited to the situation, when the shape of the peg is aligned to the shape of the hole.

A Common Mistake

Before leaving the topic of management styles, I'd like to point out a common mistake. Some leaders and organizations seriously misuse information about management styles. They frequently use management-style questionnaires as the chief selection criterion when hiring staff. Some people place too high a value on getting the right management style fit. They do not give enough weight to wisdom, conscious choice, and deliberate and disciplined action.

It is a mistake for management style to be the first screening criterion when evaluating candidates for a position. There is no guarantee that, for example, all Decisive Visionaries will be good at creating innovations for your company. Not all Decisive Commanders will be good at selling your product. Not all Analytical Planners will be good at refining operations. Style is about preferences, not skill, energy, and experience.

It is a mistake for management style to be the first screening criterion when evaluating candidates for a position.

However, for the reasons described in this book, style is relevant. Some say, "You are hired for what you know and fired for who you are." The implication is that management style and other personality traits are important for success on the job. Consideration of style is important. But I believe that management style should be the third element considered. The first is qualities. Does the person have honesty, integrity, and energy? The second is skills. Does the person have the skills and experience needed to do the job? The third relates to management style. Is the person a good fit for the situation? Does the person understand his or her own biases? Is the person flexible with respect to different modes of operation? This broader set of selection criteria will help you determine if an individual will be a strong addition to your team as your enterprise grows.

Again, the forces driving success over many phases of growth are wisdom, conscious choice, and deliberate and disciplined action. It is the ability to do the right thing at the right time. It is not the result of any single management style or set of priorities.

The following chapters will detail each of the phases of development, their corresponding modes of operation, and the problems you will encounter when changing from one mode to the next. Important elements of these chapters are specifics about the management style for the leader that will impact success in any given phase, along with the optimal structures and priorities for the organization.

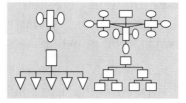

Chapter 3

Concept Development Phase

EVERYTHING IS NEW, FRESH, AND INVIGORATING—A THRILL RIDE EVERY day. The Concept Development phase embodies the excitement, exhilaration, and intensity of bringing a new idea into the world. Start-ups, businesses hoping to rejuvenate their product offering, and enterprises on the cutting edge of insight and innovation experience this phase of growth. For some enterprises, this growth phase will end quickly after a product has been developed around the innovation and validated in the market. They will move on to other growth phases. For others, it may last indefinitely, because of the personal preferences of the team members or because of the nature of the business.

For many growth enterprises, their new business is based on a breakthrough innovation—something that represents a clean break from past practices and will save their potential customers significant time or money or enable them to do something they want to do. But a breakthrough innovation is not a requirement for starting a new business. Offering some advantage over alternative products or services can be enough.

While small companies may be started for different reasons (some based on breakthrough innovations, some not), they typically share a common operational mode at inception: the Innovating mode. For discussion purposes, however, I will present the growth path of an enterprise that is started to benefit from a breakthrough innovation.

These are the typical goals of a growth enterprise in the Concept Development growth phase:

▶ Anticipate the needs of potential customers.

▶ Discover the right combination of features and make the innovation a salable product.

▶ Validate the product and its marketability in a "proof of concept" market segment.

▶ Develop a breakthrough innovation.

▶ Survive as a business.

*S*urvival and validating the product and its marketability are so fundamental to the existence of most new enterprises that they deserve the level of intense leadership focus that we commonly reserve for a crisis situation.

Survival and validating the product and its marketability are so fundamental to the existence of most new enterprises that they deserve the level of intense leadership focus that we commonly reserve for a crisis situation. Late nights and unpredictable workflow are simply part of climbing over the many barriers and hurdles that impede progress during this phase of growth. The need to pay the bills and to invest in product development pushes many other issues into the background. Many enterprises do not have the luxury of worrying about the fine points of such things as compensation schemes, accounting systems, and formal internal controls.

Validation: A Trial-and-Error Process

During this phase, the enterprise must search for validity and discover what form the product will actually take. Validation may involve working out some of the final technical details of the innovation to make sure it actually works. Validation might also involve introducing a new product in the marketplace or placing a current product in a new market.

The first customers you encounter are likely to be independent-minded visionaries in their own right. I will call them *pioneers*. This group of customers and the groups associated with the later growth phases are based on the work of Geoffrey Moore.[1] The customer groups I use are based on Moore's groups, but I have changed the labels to make the customer group labels more distinct from the labels I use for the management styles and operational modes.

1. Geoffrey A. Moore, *Inside the Tornado* (HarperBusiness, 1995) and *Crossing the Chasm* (HarperBusiness Essentials, 1991).

Pioneers[2] are revolutionaries who want to benefit from the novelty of innovation, to make a break with the past, and to start an entirely new future. Their expectation is that, by being the first to exploit the new capability, they will achieve a dramatic advantage over the status quo. They believe in revolutionary change and are genuinely interested in new ideas. Unfortunately, each pioneer customer usually has unique ideas about how to shape the innovation and makes demands that no one else would make. The commercial opportunity presented by these buyers is typically narrower than opportunities with the other customer groups. In addition, each pioneer tends have his or her own vision of what your basic innovation can do and they will see themselves as co-developers of the innovation. These features make this customer group unpredictable.

Typically, pioneers have not yet coalesced into an actual market in which success with one pioneer will lead to easy success with another. Pioneers are independent. They represent a loose collection of partner-like customers willing to give you an opportunity to fulfill *their* visions of the potential of your idea. They like your new ideas, but they have their own visions of how the innovation can be used. They recognize that it may not work exactly as promised and they do you the favor of giving you business but ask for special treatment in return. These trendsetters will want a significant price discount and will ask for special features that no one else will ask for. Products will need to be modified for each customer. But this customer group can keep you in business while you determine how you should grow in the future.

The pioneers are on the leading edge of the technology adoption life cycle and are followed by other customer groups, each with its own characteristics and business potential. The *technology adoption life cycle* refers to the timing of when people tend to accept or adopt new technologies or products. In Figure 3-1, groups on the left adopt early and those on the right adopt late. The pioneers are followed sequentially by the pragmatists, the conservatives, and the sophisticates. Each customer group has different reasons for buying and finds value in different qualities. The business potential of these classes can be represented by the normal distribution curve as shown.

For some products, the shape of the curve is not normal, but this is a good generalization. Although the scale of these customer groups is different for different businesses, the groups with the greatest business potential are typically the pragmatists and conservatives, followed in importance by

The pioneers are on the leading edge of the technology adoption life cycle and are followed by other customer groups, each with its own characteristics and business potential.

2. This group combines Moore's "technology enthusiasts" and "visionaries."

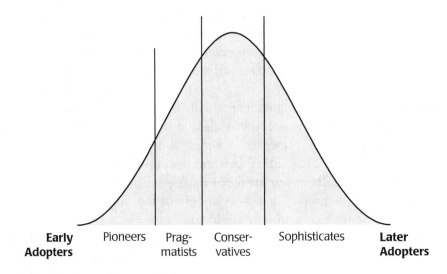

| Early Adopters | Pioneers | Prag-matists | Conser-vatives | Sophisticates | Later Adopters |

Figure 3-1. Technology adoption life cycle

the sophisticates. The pioneers are a small group but are important to your long-term success because they will work with you and help get you started.

To give you a fuller picture of the world of the innovator and his enterprise, I'll tell you a story about Vic Sparrow and Sparrow Inc. Vic is a hypothetical person but represents a composite of a number of leaders I have worked with. Vic is a wise leader and seems to get everything right. The map of Vic's experience is what we should put in our minds as the broad terrain of management circumstances that growth enterprises will encounter.

Like Vic's story, all other stories are real and drawn from our consulting work. In some cases, I've changed details to protect a confidence. But the point of sharing these is to help you gain a sense of the nuances of these phases of growth—including some of the challenges you're likely to encounter—and how others have successfully tackled them.

Vic's experiences have been fairly typical of entrepreneurs working with physical products that embody breakthrough innovations. Vic will take an enterprise within a larger business through several phases, beginning with Concept Development. About four years after Vic founded Sparrow Inc., the company developed its Model 3000. Although Vic's business was already relatively large at that point, he split off a small team to undertake a heroic enterprise. This was actually the *third* time he experienced this phase, but he still felt the excitement of a fresh beginning.

The Thrill of Innovation:
Vic Sparrow Adapts Helicopter Technology

One of Sparrow Inc.'s key customers, Tern Technologies, a manufacturing company using Vic's Model 2000, had great respect for Vic's expertise. They called him in to fix a machine unrelated to the Model 2000. Downtime caused by the failure was costing them thousands of dollars a day. Luckily, this happened just after his son's birthday. Vic had a hunch that the type of mechanism that spun the rotor on his son's new toy helicopter might be able to solve the problem. Vic read up on helicopter mechanics nonstop for two weeks and went to work designing a new part.

Vic called his team into the shop over the next weekend to craft a prototype of Tern's new part. He was like a fire horse after hearing the alarm. Adrenaline was flowing and he felt energized—even though he had not slept well in weeks. He was in his element as he spilled out diagrams across the white board, spoke passionately about the possibilities, and convinced the team that they could work miracles.

Vic personally selected the team of six to develop this new innovation. Four had been with Vic for about three years and had experienced the prior innovations. Two had been hired over the past 18 months.

Oddly, the staff designers largely responsible for the development of the Model 2000 were cut out of the current project entirely. Vic wanted the prototype made immediately and believed the company's standard design process would simply take too much time. Vic also believed that it would not be possible to articulate his vision to the staff designers quickly and completely enough: he did not have a formal design for the prototype; it was in his head. He alone knew the broken machine inside and out, knew why the customer had the problem, and had a strong hunch the solution could be found in helicopter technology. Besides, Vic was an expert designer and machinist, so if anyone could design and supervise construction at the same time, he could.

The team worked diligently over the weekend. Throughout the long hours, Vic moved around the shop hovering over team members to make sure each part was being crafted to fit within the greater scheme. When a fit wasn't quite right, Vic would indicate the adjustments required. All jobs were shared, so that when one team member finished working on a piece, he or she could move to another.

By the end of the weekend, the team had built a successfully working prototype based on helicopter technology. Vic's hunch had been correct.

Early that Monday morning, Vic asked the staff designers, who were smarting a bit from being left out, to identify critical weaknesses in the prototype before he showed it to Tern that afternoon. The staff designers looked at the machine and immediately saw its potential, not only to address their current difficulties but also for other key applications. So did Vic. The 3000 was born.

The Natural Fit: Decisive Visionary

The management style that is best suited to Vic's set of circumstances is Decisive Visionary. These individuals are insightful, creative, big-picture thinkers. They're comfortable starting with blank sheets of paper and making something happen. Because they tend to be intensely focused on a narrow set of issues related to their visions, they readily absorb all relevant information about their primary interests.

I'll mention the characteristics of the *Visionary* component of this management style first, as it dominates all other components. Visionaries typically develop a concept first and then gather information to test that decision or concept. Depending on the results they get, they'll modify the original decision or concept and then go through another testing cycle. In this way, their decision-making process seems circular and diffuse to others. It is not the linear, data-driven decision making that is characteristic of the analytically oriented management styles. In fact, to some, this doesn't appear to be a decision-making process at all.

Being intuitive in their decision making, they gather information from a variety of sources to form their holistic views. They tend to do this best when they receive information from primary sources—when they talk to the prospects, when they personally see what is happing, when they hear comments directly. They have a high level of trust in their own powers of observation. They work best when they are working "at the coal face"—working in direct contact with the outside world. The image of the coal face is apt because it implies the leader is working hands on and getting dirty with the fundamental work of the enterprise.

Visionaries usually have great confidence in their inventions and concepts. They do not require objective evidence to justify their confidence. Their belief is often founded on a view of the world that is somehow different from how the rest of the world sees it. They are able to see the end of the path at the beginning of the journey and simply need to figure out how to fill in the middle. Some of more successful Decisive Visionaries seem to be able to see around corners. They integrate dozens of small cues that indicate what is possible and see emerging truths before other people, particularly those who require defendable facts before changing their worldviews. Their map of the world can be extremely detailed and prove to be quite accurate. But it exists in their minds and they often find it difficult to articulate the complete vision and make it useful for others to use as a guide for their own actions. Visionaries tend to have a high tolerance of ambiguity and uncertainty and a high ability to handle them, which makes it difficult for them to push their ideas to the simplest elements that others require for understanding. The ability to read minds is helpful in working effectively with Visionaries.

Creative ideas alone, however, are not the only important elements of this management style. The *decisive* component of the Decisive Visionary is also important. These leaders are not simply pie-in-the-sky thinkers—they value action. They are not timid about acting on their ideas and concepts and ordering others to take very specific next steps forward. Thus, creativity is tempered with a keen interest in putting ideas into action. This is important to the success of these leaders in the Concept Development phase of growth.

Decisive Visionaries are most comfortable with small, informally structured groups of people. They like hands-on, quick-moving ways of working. They value loyalty and commitment in their team members and prefer to guide the work of others through direct interaction and, they hope, by the power of their compelling vision.

Close communication is important and these leaders get important data and impressions from the team members. Ultimately, the Decisive Visionary leader makes or approves all decisions. What attracts Decisive Visionaries are new and innovative ideas that represent changes from past practices. The bywords are "new," "fast," and "cutting edge."

Every leadership style has weaknesses; the vulnerability for Decisive Visionaries is a low interest in formal long-term planning and long-term execution programs. Decisive Visionaries tend to get bored with the detailed and predictable; they prefer to work with concepts, new ideas, initiatives, and themes. They tend to have great ideas but be poor at executing them. They are distracted by the ever-evolving vision of the world outside them; this makes the consistent execution of a long-term strategy very difficult for them and their enterprises. Despite its weaknesses, this style is remarkably well suited to the trial-and-error development approach that characterizes the need to validate a product and its initial market.

To a large extent, this style is simply the package that breakthrough ideas come in. My research for this book indicates that the high-tech CEOs who personally develop the *high-potential* innovations (those supported by venture capital funding) tend to be Decisive Visionaries, with heavy dominance in the Visionary component. Those viewed as having innovations of lower potential tend to be no different from the general CEO population. If you want breakthrough innovation, this is the nature of the people who can typically deliver.

Every leadership style has weaknesses; the vulnerability for Decisive Visionaries is a low interest in formal long-term planning and long-term execution programs.

We want to draw from the practices of these leaders key elements that model effective leadership in the Concept Development phase:

▶ Their effective use of small, focused, and energetic teams

▶ A preference for primary sources of information—working at the coal face

▶ A clear vision of the ultimate concept

▶ Leading a nimble and cohesive team quickly through a trial-and-error process to discover the form the concept will take

The structures, practices, and priorities that emanate from this type of leader model the Innovating operational mode. They are emulated with great success by many enterprises—even those that do not have a Decisive Visionary as leader. By using these practices, an enterprise can be more nimble and develop a stronger product concept and idea. The ideas may not be as eclectic and fundamentally innovative as those developed by true Decisive Visionaries, but in many cases they are marketable, sometimes more so. A true Decisive Visionary can generate ideas that are remarkably valid but too far ahead of their time and too challenging to execute. Strong enterprises can be built on concepts that are just ahead of their time.

The Innovating Mode

Typical themes of an Innovating organization are:

▶ Build a better mousetrap and the world will beat a path to your door.

▶ If you are not going to do it right, don't do it.

▶ This innovation will rewrite the rules of the industry.

▶ Learn from your mistakes and move forward.

These themes reflect the boldness characteristic of many entrepreneurial leaders who, regardless of their personal styles, are driven by an ambition to change the world or at least a meaningful part of it. While few ultimately achieve such lofty objectives, these leaders' desire to do so propels them and their enterprises far into the business world.

Some may say these start-up entrepreneurs are fooling themselves and others by aiming so high and imply that they should be more realistic. It might be more to the point to view these ambitions as similar to the nuclear fuel that drives a reactor—dangerous if poorly channeled and directed, but the source of immense value if the energy can be harnessed.

During the Innovating mode, products are often customized for anyone willing to give them a try. Effective customization of a product requires you to become completely involved with the customers' uses of it, along with their thinking, emotions, and psychology. Close work with customers allows you think through what they need and want and, indeed, beyond what they are currently able to articulate. You need to know their situation better than your customers know it themselves, or at least from a valuable new perspective. When you have a sense of what might work for them, give it a try and see if it fulfills your vision of what should happen. If it does, go through the same process with another prospective buyer. If not, revise the effort and try again.

Most Effective Structure: Focused Team of Generalists

The most effective organizational structure for innovation is a "focused team of generalists." People with generalist skills or interests are important because they need to play a variety of roles. Of course, the new entrepreneur often must simply take for his or her team whoever is available among friends, relatives, and neighbors. This structure is highly centralized and informal. The team is small enough that every member knows what the others are doing and, more importantly, what they are thinking. There are two basic versions of the "focused team of generalists" structure. The most common is centralized around a "star" leader. The other is a more egalitarian group of peers. Both share many of the same characteristics. I'll discuss the egalitarian version later.

The "star" version is most characteristic of enterprises with Decisive Visionary leaders pursuing breakthrough innovation. In this version of an Innovating organization, the central leader approves or rejects essentially all decisions—regardless of who originally proposes them. A high degree of centralization under this leader is natural and reasonable, as this person often has the strongest relevant technical knowledge, a stronger sense of the ultimate vision, and the most comprehensive view of the current situation. Everyone in the small organization is tuned to his or her vision and depends on it for daily guidance. This structure is diagrammed as shown in the next page, with the leader indicated by a square and employees as circles.

There is little specialization of tasks, with each person performing a variety of functions. All members of the team work together, pitching in to do whatever is needed to move forward, often forsaking personal comfort and continu-

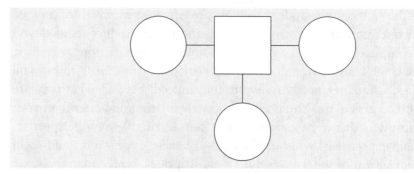

ity with a particular function. One day the whole team might be testing the product in the shop and the next day everyone could be talking to prospective customers. Accountabilities are not clearly defined and they don't really need to be. All team members are working together and moving in unison.

Decision making may feel collaborative because everyone is involved in all decisions, but, in fact, the leader is the main and perhaps sole decision maker. Others are used as extensions of the leader's data-gathering and data-processing abilities, essentially feeding information to the leader. Everyone votes, but only one vote counts. Although there is a feeling of consensus, the leader plays the crucial role of calling a close to a discussion and asserting the decision.

Speed and Flexibility

This focused and flexible structure enables the leader to ensure that every move is consistent with the path unfolding before the enterprise. After taking a few steps, the team may discover that the selected path will not work. They must backtrack and try another. Speed in making these changes is a competitive advantage. The constant contact between the leader and the rest of the staff enables the organization to quickly and easily refine everyone's short- and long-term objectives and make mid-course corrections to the overall strategy. Delegation is not an issue because everyone works together to get the job done. Team cohesiveness and responsiveness are crucial to rapid movement through the discovery process.

The number of people involved in the organization is small enough, usually fewer than ten, that all involved can sit around a table and discuss the issues of the day. Each must know what all of the others are thinking and doing in order to make instantaneous changes in their activities. Little is written down because everyone is there to hear and understand all discussions. The emphasis is on teamwork and innovation, and almost every problem receives the full attention of the whole team.

A loyalty-inspiring vision helps ensure that courses of action initiated by individual team members are compatible. Even though the business situations change quickly, each individual member of the organization can determine, relatively independently, what steps will be compatible with the vision. Each knows this broad vision and can determine if his or her own work is consistent or inconsistent with that. In many cases team members do not need to ask; they can see for themselves that something is amiss and correct the situation. In this way, these focused teams of generalists have a clubby feel in which the members feel empowered to operate independently and in fact are doing so.

Indeed, the members are empowered so long as they are loyal to the vision of the leader—and in many cases to the person as well. In exchange, the leader provides support, employment, and, importantly, his or her personal approval of the members' work and recognition for individual contributions. This bond of loyalty is strong and such an important element of control that loyalty betrayed or abandoned is almost a capital offense. Other forms of control—such as rules, procedures, monitoring, and feedback—are not needed and are, in fact, less effective for controlling the actions of this small team.

The Innovating mode of operation comes together relatively easily and naturally during Concept Development simply by virtue of the organization's size, its focus, and the galvanizing force of its vision and objectives. People tend to like working in this mode and, if the human ingredients are right, it can be very effective in meeting the goals of the enterprise.

Complete Control

Not all enterprises need to be based on breakthrough technological innovations. The product GoDogGo™ was developed by a visionary designer near Seattle. The designer had a flash of inspiration about a ball thrower for dogs. His chocolate Labrador retriever, Hershey, was fanatical about retrieving balls and would not let the designer or his family rest or relax when outside. The designer believed that other people must be in similar situations with their dogs. He talked to the buyers of pet supplies at trade shows and people in neighborhood parks about how they exercise their dogs and if such a machine would be useful and interesting to them. Support for the idea was strong and he found that the idea was particularly attractive to people could not give their dogs the exercise they needed because of a lack of time or physical limitations. He thought that a ball-throwing machine for dogs could have appeal as a cool gadget and some practical benefits.

The designer looked at different ways that ball-throwing machines worked and worked with Hershey to figure out how far and fast the ball should be thrown for dogs. A $4,000 tennis ball machine threw balls at 70 mph and he didn't want to throw something that fast at a dog. Something slower and safer was preferred. He also determined the right height for the machine so most dogs could put the ball back into the machine. The designer personally developed prototypes and design specifications and went to China to determine how the machines could be made reliably and at a cost that would allow marketing it at a price that people would consider spending on their dogs. The designer worked with others to design the mechanics, the product design, and the packaging. But even though others were involved, the designer reviewed every detail. He spent weeks in the factory in China personally reviewing every production detail and every mechanical detail. This was not rocket science, but everything had to come together in a way that fit the initial vision.

The portable, battery-powered, computer-controlled machine operates by remote control or automatically. It throws tennis balls at any chosen distance from 15 to 30 feet and the dog can retrieve them and drop them into the machine for another throw. While the product was developed for other purposes, it is a real benefit to an unexpected group of customers: people with physical disabilities. Service dog owners who are unable to personally exercise their dogs are finding that GoDogGo helps their dogs get needed exercise and play time.

While none of the elements of GoDogGo represents breakthrough innovation, the designer could see the final product when he began and the rest of the process was discovering how to bring that vision into reality. It was a trial-and-error process, but the outcome—the ball-throwing machine for dogs—was never in doubt. The product is not yet a wild commercial success, but this is still just the beginning.

Many businesses are started in this way. An idea, some dedication, and some hard work—all to turn a product idea into a physical product.

The designer could see the final product when he began and the rest of the process was discovering how to bring that vision into reality. It was a trial-and-error process, but the outcome ... was never in doubt.

The Power of Small Teams in Investment Management

Close-knit Innovating organizations are also very important for service companies that must innovate regularly. At the Russell Investment Group, we estimated that about one-half of the investment portfolio management teams in the United States, and well over half of the best investment teams, use the Innovating operational mode. In order to produce strong investment performance, investment teams must develop insight-driven investment decisions every month. They need breakthroughs continually. If they fail to deliver them, the effect is immediate, objective, and obvious: poor investment performance. Individuals and small investment teams tend to produce the best investment performance.

These small informal teams make decisions quickly and their members tend to be involved in primary research in some way. The members, including the leader, work at the coal face of their markets. They look at information that many other people have looked at and see something that others in general do not. When they develop an insight, something no one else is seeing, they quickly take advantage of it by buying the stock. Strong investment results come from seeing opportunities that others overlook and then doing something about them.

This operational behavior fits the drivers of success for investment firms—research depth, insight, and decision-making speed. Indeed, the drivers of investment success do not lend themselves to formal processes and long, deliberate decision-making processes. Strong investment teams implicitly subscribe to the adage "None of us is as dumb as all of us,"[3] and try to keep teams smaller than four or five people. These teams are big enough to have a diversity of insights and present challenging views, but they are small enough that everyone knows what everyone else is doing. The Innovating operational mode delivers benefit for these organizations even though many of them do not have the classic Decisive Visionaries as their leaders; they get benefits by emulating the practices of the management style that is naturally effective in enhancing insight and innovation.

Limitations and Vulnerabilities of the Innovating Approach

The Innovating operational mode has several limitations. It has limited business capacity. There is only so much a small team can accomplish. It works best when it is focused on pursuing a narrow set of objectives; many businesses have broader aspirations than an Innovating organization can effectively support.

---

3. Quote from Despair.com, at www.despair.com/indem.html.

An Innovating organization is very sensitive to the chemistry of the people involved. What each person brings to the team and how the members work together have a big impact on the success of the team. One cannot simply assemble a group of people and realistically expect positive results.

Innovating organizations tend to be one-generation efforts. Partially because of the importance of individual chemistry and partially because of the informal processes and intuitive ways of making decisions, when the initial members cease involvement, the operation and output of the group change dramatically.

A critical limitation of an Innovating organization is the number of people who can be effectively involved in the informal structure. *Nine people should be considered the maximum.* As the organization grows past that size, it will quickly become ineffective: the leader cannot be personally involved in every detail of the organization on a daily basis and the members of the team can no longer coordinate their activities informally. An organization of more than nine people usually requires a more structured and formal organization. To continue growing, an enterprise will require a more formal structure. But this does not mean that a larger organization will bring more success. For some enterprises, staying small is very consistent with business success.

This is a simple but important point: *if your commercial success requires continual insight and innovation, keep your innovating team small and focused.* To keep it small, as the number of different activities increases, carve off the ones that have stabilized and outsource them to another group.

Over the years, many major investment firms have experimented with larger investment teams. They like the performance of the Innovating mode, but do not like its reliance on a few specific individuals. If the key people retire or depart, the impact on the business is significant—it makes a difference which individuals are on the small team. Replacing a key team member affects how the team operates. Large investment management businesses seek to increase their ability to ensure greater consistency of performance across their many investment teams, manage more money, offer more investment products, and reduce their dependence on a few specific individuals.

How do they attempt to accomplish this? These firms create large departments of analysts that support several portfolio management teams, hoping to leverage the work of these analysts more broadly. They also create separate portfolio management teams and instruct each to operate according to a particular process and plan. Unfortunately, as a rule, the results of these efforts to scale up the investment management processes

An Innovating organization is very sensitive to the chemistry of the people involved. What each person brings to the team and how the members work together have a big impact on the success of the team.

have been disappointing. The uniformity of the process means that all portfolio managers are looking at the same or similar investment opportunities; internal competition for these opportunities means lower investment returns. Bigger is not always better.

Defiant Innovation

Let's shift our discussion to a few more subtle dynamics of successful Innovating organizations—dynamics that need to be managed carefully over time. In the Concept Development phase of growth, these can be useful, but if they are left unmanaged, the downstream effects can be quite negative.

The first is a cultural bias that we call *defiant innovation*. This bias usually emanates from the leader's own attitudes and from the reality that a truly innovative product is indeed alone in the marketplace. Defiant Innovation is a disdain for current industry practices and often for customer preferences. The belief is that the customers do not know yet what they truly need or want and, further, that the Visionary leader has identified a market need that the marketplace has not yet articulated. These are attitudes that drive many enterprises bent on developing a breakthrough innovation.

Because its driving vision is often bold and far-reaching, at times a small enterprise will come to believe that its industry and potential competitors are not likely to be doing anything worth knowing about. This organization will conclude, sometimes correctly and sometimes erroneously, that it is a waste of time and effort to keep up with what other companies are doing. The team members conclude that market research is not really important because they are way ahead of the market. For a time, this makes sense, because at first there are frequently no competitors and then, when they do emerge, often they are far behind. So when the organization needs to develop strategies, it looks to broad and creative concepts and paradigms and the leader for direction, but not market research.

While it may be reasonable to come to these conclusions in the early phases of growth when there is no market to research, this attitude of defying conventional wisdom and market research becomes embedded in the team's culture and in its belief system about how the team should operate. These conclusions live on and express themselves in later phases of growth. Later, problems develop when circumstances are different: the innovative product has been copied and is no longer so innovative. The former potential competitors have become real competitors. And customers, once grateful to get any product, are demanding a range of features that reflect their

53

interests, not yours. How defiant innovation becomes defiant isolation is discussed in Chapter 8.

Leadership Allelopathy

Having a singular vision during the Innovating mode is extremely important. Decision making and planning are informal and intuitive in this stage; an organization with multiple, competing visions wastes precious resources trying to reconcile and consolidate them. During the trial-and-error process of discovery, effective leaders often populate their teams with energetic and loyal implementers rather than independent, visionary decision makers.

This is especially true of the more centralized "star" organizational structures. Team members who insist upon being completely independent decision makers often introduce more distraction than strength during this phase. Their independence from the vision of the leader inhibits them from keeping up with the day-to-day refinement of the strategy. Thus, the focus and resources of the organization are diluted. For these reasons, it is often best to follow essentially one visionary during this phase. Energy, loyalty, and dutiful implementation of instructions, therefore, become relatively more important qualities than an ability to strategize or to make decisions independently in this phase of growth.[4]

The benefits of following a single visionary are so great that there is a discernible effect within successful Innovating organizations that we call *leadership allelopathy*. This is the second dynamic that these enterprises may encounter that serves a useful function early on—but may create problems for organizations downstream, in later stages of development.

Allelopathy (pronounced u-le´-lu-path-e) is a term borrowed from the field of biology that refers to the growth-inhibiting influence of one living plant upon another. Some species of plants have evolved over time to possess a capability that helps promote the success of the species. When one individual of a species with allelopathic capabilities germinates, it emits toxins into the air and soil that inhibit the normal development of other seedlings of the same species. Thus, other seedlings sprouting later are stunted in their development and the first seedling is able to garner most of the water and soil nutrients and become the dominant individual.

---

4. Multiple visionaries can be accommodated within the organization if one is clearly dominant by virtue of age, personality, or some other feature that prevents direct competition.

Once the dominant individual is well established, it stops emitting the toxins and the other seedlings resume normal growth, albeit at a step or two behind the dominant individual. The species benefits from reduced competition for water, sunlight, or minerals that may be scarce in the area. Should these resources be depleted, the larger, better-established individual has a greater chance of surviving and maturing enough to produce seeds for the next generation. Without the allelopathic effect, the entire population of equally developed individuals may perish if resources are depleted.

A similar effect is found in successful innovating organizations. The dominant leader sometimes undermines others in order to remain the dominant visionary or to become more dominant. *Dominant* does not necessarily mean *domineering*. It simply means that decision making is guided and coordinated by that individual.

Even team members who are not competing visionaries are affected by leadership allelopathy. Visionary leaders tend to avoid other independent thinkers and hire individuals who can be loyal to their vision. The organization's culture, decision-making structure, and compensation practices often encourage loyalty to the leader's view. With only one real decision maker in an innovating organization, the other members are not given the chance to develop as independent decision makers. These forces are often so powerful that even people who in other circumstances would be independent thinkers and doers do not develop those characteristics. They are encouraged and rewarded for respecting the dominance of the leader.

The dominant leader sometimes undermines others in order to remain the dominant visionary or to become more dominant. Dominant does not necessarily mean domineering. It simply means that decision making is guided and coordinated by that individual.

Hunting for Birds by Watching the Dog

Another factor that contributes to leadership allelopathy is the intuitive aspect of the leader's Decisive Visionary management style. The members of the organization must pay close attention to the leader in order to track his or her moves. The thought processes and actions of innovative leaders are not linear and predictable and are not tracked easily. One moment they are thinking and talking about one subject and then instantaneously shift to another, leaving the staff to mentally scamper to the new topic.

Tracking an innovative leader is like going grouse hunting with a bird dog in tall grass. The innovative leader is like the highly sensitive dog sniffing out the game. One moment the grass rustles on the left, the next on the right. When the dog finds game, it flushes the game out of the brush. The hunter can try to do the same but is disadvantaged because of the dog's superior sense of smell. The hunter quickly learns that tracking the dog is a more successful than trying to personally find the grouse.

This system works for all as long as the dog stays interested and involved. If the dog is taken out of the picture, the hunter will be ill prepared to find game on his own. In fact, he is less prepared *because* he developed the expertise to follow the dog, not hunt for grouse. He has relied on the dog, but the dog is gone. Members of an Innovating organization often focus more on predicting what the leader will do next rather than what the market will do next. If the leader becomes bored or distracted, the team quickly loses direction—a key risk when building for long-term success.

By now, you know where this is heading: once the business is established, staff should be trained to read the market—or hunt grouse—on their own. However, even if the Visionary leader pulls back on the allelopathic effect by encouraging the development of truly independent decision making, the fact that it has taken place sets the stage for some weakness down the road. Decisive Visionaries hire loyal implementers with generalist skills. These individuals in turn tend to hire highly skilled people with very narrow fields of expertise. When the Visionary leader is taken out of the picture, the loyal implementers are quickly overtaken by the skilled specialists, yet the skilled specialists lack the generalists' perspective. With these concepts in mind, we are not surprised when we read of a Visionary leader whose failing was that his or her second string of leaders and managers is not as strong and independent as the leader. At one point in the development of the enterprise, this hiring practice helped the enterprise remain focused and agile. However, as the enterprise developed, this practice shifted from and advantage to a disadvantage.

Small Team of Peers

The egalitarian version of the Innovating mode is similar to the more centralized "star" version in terms of cultural priorities on working at the coal face, insight, agility, and coordinated teamwork. It is similar in its sensitivity to the number of people on the team and the organizational structure can still be called a team of focused generalists.

The big difference is that, instead of one central leader who has meaningfully more expertise than the other team members, expertise is spread more evenly across the team. The team members operate more as peers and the allelopathic effect described above is less pronounced. But the sensitivities to team size and other preconditions required for effectiveness hold true for both versions of an Innovating organization.

Preconditions for the Innovating Mode

The result of an effective Innovating mode of operation is successful Concept Development, and success often brings growth. This mode of operation will remain effective until the preconditions for using it successfully are no longer valid. So long as they remain valid, the Innovating mode can remain the ideal operational mode. The following are the preconditions.

Insight and innovation drive business success. In many new businesses, some initial insight about a new opportunity is needed as the first step. The insight is a breakthrough innovation that will cause major changes in the world. For some, it will be an innovation of lesser magnitude, but one still worth pursuing. Once the innovation has been developed, growth will be driven by other phases and operational modes. Some enterprises, however, require insight and innovation on an ongoing basis. For these, the Innovating mode will continue to be appropriate.

Fewer than ten people are involved in decision making. This precondition is important because the success of this mode of operation is very sensitive to the number of people involved. The suitable team size can be the result of either the newness of the enterprise or a conscious choice to limit the size of the team.

A small number of overriding issues command the attention of the team. The Innovating mode is very effective when the objectives are few and focused. A high number of objectives requires a more complex organization. The simplicity of the objectives can be the result of the natural circumstances or a conscious choice to limit the complexity of the management situation.

Decision makers maintain direct contact with the external environment; they work at the coal face. An Innovating organization is simple and can produce great results as long as the decision makers are not insulated from external information. This is particularly important for people with a conceptually oriented management style, like the Decisive Visionary. Confronting external information helps keep them current, grounded, and practical.

Organizational growth and the stabilization of your product in the marketplace will begin to negate these preconditions and require you to change your mode of operation. Growth will push your enterprise into facing more complex issues that will require attention over much longer periods of time. As your business begins to grow beyond the capacities of an Innovating organization, a change in the way it operates will be required.

Vic's Model 3000

As Vic's team sat around the prototype of the Model 3000, they felt a mixture of exhaustion and euphoria. Like its predecessors, especially the model 1000, the 3000 version broke new ground and, they believed, set new standards for the industry.

Only the old-timers tempered their excitement. They had experienced the thrill of breakthrough innovation before and had seen that innovative ideas don't automatically guarantee industry leadership. Vic knew that his firm's potential customers would not only have to find out about the 3000, but also have to modify their practices in order to use it. This created a high barrier to its rapid adoption and to growth for the company. Staff who had joined Vic over the last 18 months, however, had boundless enthusiasm for the future.

Regardless of how they felt, they did have a new opportunity for growth and a shot at industry dominance. With the sales of the 2000 combined with those anticipated for the 3000, they could grow with confidence.

Vic knew a shift in their thinking would soon be required. He prepared himself for the change and also began to signal to others that a phase was coming to an end. He encouraged everyone to celebrate their successes. He also encouraged them to talk openly about what they would have to do differently to continue to be successful.

The Transition

The transition out of the Concept Development phase is often the most difficult transition a new enterprise will experience. People will resist changing modes of operation. It is exciting to be part of an Innovating organization. There's a bit of a sense of romance to it: it's a time of collaboration and discovery, a time when the team members work well together and all efforts are focused on the Herculean task of developing and validating the vision and turning it into a product.

All team members identify at a very personal level with the path they have taken during the Concept Development phase, regardless of how many unneeded bends and turns there can be in the path. The path remains an important element in people's concept of who they are and the role they play in the organization. Their current success asserts that the path was ultimately the right one.

Reluctance to Demystify the Magic

Some of the most trying problems a business can face are those rooted in practices that have been successful in the past. For an enterprise that has recently just experienced a successful Concept Development growth phase, a common undesirable legacy is a reluctance to demystify the magic that created the breakthrough innovation and all its supporting activities. When this happens, prior practices and procedures are maintained, even enshrined in the lore and culture of the enterprise. Growth is pursued by simply doing more of what has been done in the past.

It's only natural that members of any organization will feel good about the success of earlier efforts—and they tend to develop a strong attachment to the actions they took to produce that success. However, they may view past successes as a function of their good judgment and experience and resist suggestions that they need to restructure and simplify what they do in the present. They assert that they have a complete understanding of the various steps they need to take to accomplish their work. They will also believe that all steps they take have value; otherwise they would not be taking them.

Neither is true. The problems associated with these false understandings start without much notice. When there's more work to be done, people on the team work longer hours and more people get involved. When new goals emerge, they are added to the current ones. People work longer and longer hours and become more focused on getting just their own jobs done. They gradually stop paying attention to how others are doing their work. There are more people, too many people to track effectively, and everyone is busy doing more work just to keep up. Tasks become less coordinated very quickly. Extra time is required to coordinate workflow, but this takes time away from actually doing the work. Because everyone has been a generalist, there's no groundwork for a logical way to assign new tasks. Whoever volunteered to take a job years ago is still doing it. Important task begin to fall through the cracks. Mistakes are made. More and more time is used up in correcting mistakes.

Without rationally structured job responsibilities that enable a wider range of people to participate, quick delegation of tasks is not possible. People who have not grown up with the practices as they have evolved will rarely be effective in an amount of time that addresses immediate needs. Training becomes more costly than having the staff members currently responsible work longer hours. The hours get longer and longer.

"The way we do things" is protected and enshrined in the culture and lore of the enterprise: "The all-for-one attitude made the company strong." But the increasing workload is becoming unmanageable. The leaders are devoting more of their time to internal issues. The enterprise is doing 9,000 rpm in first gear. The engine is whining and pumping more fuel into the engine is not making the car go much faster. The engine is hitting its limits. The steel, lubrication, and connecting bolts making it work are getting hotter and hotter. Without a change in operations, the engine will blow apart.

This situation can be traced to the highly effective ad hoc processes that helped the enterprise get through the trial-and-error process quickly. The path of trial and error is rarely the shortest distance between beginning and end and this original path should not be formalized into routine practices. The enterprise must arrange the essential steps in an efficient, logical sequence. Failure to straighten out the path will result in costly inefficiencies that will be built into future practices. But the interesting thing about all of this is that the process is self-reinforcing. Here's an example.

Rationalizing existing steps for an existing process is very different from discovering the steps that make something happen for the first time. Discovery is a creative process; the subsequent rationalization of steps is an analytical process. Both approaches have their place. At Egret Analytics, everyone was amazed that the process worked at all in the early days. They all felt a legitimate sense of accomplishment that their journey of innovation had met with success. They continued for a number of years dutifully following what they believed to be an innovative but inherently expensive and highly customized process.

Egret Analytics: Learning to Let Go of Past Practices

Egret Analytics, a scientific laboratory that analyzes soil for traces of uranium, had a proprietary process for testing soil samples that was reliable and priced much lower than competing techniques. The firm achieved early success because of its innovative technique, but after about two years of production it had trouble increasing the capacity of the process. The firm charged $20 to analyze each soil sample, but each sample cost the firm about $16 to run.

Prevailing sentiment within the firm was that the lab needed to double the size of its machines. An analysis by someone new to the firm, however, revealed that streamlining the workflow could increase capacity.

The firm was still using a process very similar to the one it had used to validate the theory. It was a labor-intensive process that required the judgment of experienced staff to ensure that the process was proceeding as intended. With these experienced workers involved, no procedures were written down because everyone knew the process inside and out. The temperature of the heating oven, the duration of the plating process, and the sample-handling methods needed to prevent contamination all required high expertise.

Many of the less sophisticated steps at Egret had also remained unchanged. Each soil sample was unpacked near the rear loading dock, carried to the front of the office for logging into the record book, and carried back to the rear of the lab for sifting and processing. The analysis results recorded in the front office were sent back to the customer near the loading dock. This too was much the same flow of activity as used when the process was developed. However, the process then had handled 25 samples a week, whereas the weekly volume now had become 500.

The experienced team members were unhappy because the thrill of discovery was over and they were overqualified for the work they were doing. They were getting bored, but each thought his or her job was important and could think of dozens of reasons why it just had to be done the same way as always. Also, each was tied to a process that was making money and the enterprise needed the money. Every team member thought that if they doubled the size of their operation by buying bigger machines, they could afford to hire and train people to help them out.

The newcomer, however, asked the staff to write down everything that they did to process the samples, including all the preferred temperature settings and any indicators that the preferred settings might not be appropriate for a particular sample. This was not a pleasant task because it seemed very clerical to these scientific experts. They thought that all the education and expertise they used to judge the correct temperature setting could not possibly be distilled into a few simple steps or guidelines. Nor were they happy that someone who was not part of the early development was suggesting changes; an outsider could not possible understand all the finer points of the process.

With some encouragement, they compiled all the relevant information. Then a team was formed to identify bottlenecks that kept capacity low. These professionals streamlined the process by relocating the machines to fit the physical flow of the samples from the loading dock through the lab to the office where the results were recorded. They also found that less judgment was required for the temperature setting if they did a more thorough job of sifting the sample before it was heated. They dropped several superfluous steps. Ultimately they reduced the costs from $16 to $3 per sample. In addition, reliability and consistency increased because the procedures were standardized. Staff members felt more satisfied because they were released from jobs that had become routine and could focus their attention on more interesting issues.

Phase of Growth—Summary Table

Phase of Growth	Concept Development
Goals	• Creation of breakthrough innovation • Survival of the organization • Validation of business and product concepts
Mode of Operation	**Innovating**
Preconditions	• Fewer than ten people are involved in decision making, due to the newness of the organization or a conscious choice to limit the size of the group. • A small number of overriding issues command the attention of the team, with no critical need to attend to others, due to a dominant critical issue or a conscious choice to limit the complexity of the management situation. • Direct contact between the decision makers and the environment ensures that people are not insulated from external information.
Primary Controls	• Supervision of the leader • Business vision
Organizational Structure	• Team of focused generalists
Expertise Profile of Team	• Allowing members to use their own discretion to determine the best course of action
Cultural Priorities	• Insight, new ideas, action, agility
Product Strategy	• Custom and innovative products developed for a small number of partner-like customers
Inherent Weaknesses	• One-generation activity • Sensitive to the chemistry of those involved • Limited business capacity
Beneficial Legacies	• Innovative business product • Toehold in a key market segment

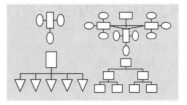

Chapter 4

Classic Indicators That It's Time to Shift Gears

*HOW DO YOU KNOW WHEN IT'S TIME TO SHIFT GEARS? THIS CHAP-*ter describes five classic indicators that an enterprise is exceeding the limitations of the Innovating operational mode and must enter a transitional, Foundation Building phase. Most entrepreneurial ventures encounter these challenges to some degree, even the very successful ones. Experienced singly, some of these may not be life-threatening problems, but you should be alert to them as indicators of deeper shifts. They will help you enter the transitional, Foundation Building phase early and do it quickly.

1. Battles over Turf and Titles
2. You Had to Be There at the Beginning
3. The Office Manager Crisis
4. The Crisis-and-Rescue Cycle
5. Snowflakes in Waiting

Because these are classic indicators that an Innovating organization is ready to enter a period of Foundation Building, the solution to most of these situations is to operate more strongly in a Foundation Building mode. While that may sound simple enough, the challenge is to tune your senses to identify when an indicator is actually a subtle warning sign that major changes are needed.

Battles over Turf and Titles

Tempers flare and members of the enterprise become territorial. Although the organization is still small, usually with one to two dozen people, key people claim the roles and responsibilities of someone else in the organization. Political and personnel problems begin to take more and more management time. The leader spends an increasing amount of energy refereeing squabbles over who should do what and who is responsible for what. People become extremely sensitive to titles and new titles are doled out to add some structure to the complex web of relationships, to reward past achievements, and to motivate staff for the future. In addition, some employees are overly possessive about their connections and contact with the leader.

The organization's structure also develops haphazardly as employees begin to fend for themselves and become protective of their information and influence. As a result of these problems, factions develop and the still-small organization begins to move in a surprising number of directions. Increased staff in-fighting distracts the organization from exploiting external opportunities. Although Battles over Turf and Titles may initially seem like a superficial problem that can be addressed case by case, these are symptoms of deeper underlying problems and can be a good early warning indicator that more comprehensive changes are needed.

This situation is a result of using direct supervision as the primary control lever during the Innovating mode. When the leader was able to daily regulate what everyone was doing, it was easy to define the roles and boundaries of every individual. As generalists, everyone was involved in every detail, and constant adjustments and refinements could be made to ensure that the organization was agile and innovative. This approach worked well as long as the organization was small. As the company grows, not everyone can have direct contact with the leader or with each other. Other control levers have not been developed.

A good indication that a company has exceeded its capacity to manage informally is that there are more people than can sit around a small conference table.

A good indication that a company has exceeded its capacity to be managed informally is that there are more people than can sit around a small conference table. While a seven-person team, for example, can be self-regulating informally, a larger team cannot. The time it takes for each person of a 15-member team to find out informally what everyone else is doing is more than most people in a business organization are willing—or can afford— to spend.

When the leader no longer knows the details of every person's activities and the team can no longer regulate itself, a "control vacuum" develops. Team members are left to define their own positions, accountabilities, and responsibilities.

People naturally become territorial and stake claims to areas they consider to be theirs and areas that will carry them forward in their jobs and careers. Few of the members have the breadth of vision of what everyone is doing to define their roles and others on an ad-hoc basis. As a result, in relatively small organizations (only 15 people, fir example) there will frequently be two or three people performing activities that overlap significantly or are completely at odds.

The role of the leader quickly changes from one of supervising individuals as they work together under a common vision to refereeing small groups of people who are pursuing their own agendas or second-hand interpretations of the business vision.

Conflict at Caribou Co.

Caribou Co., a Vancouver, Canada-based paper company of 14 employees, had just hired three people to assume some of the workload of the current staff. Charles, the CEO, is in his office and is being confronted by three long-time employees—Carl, Connie, and Bob.

"Connie is doing what I am supposed to be doing," Carl complains. "The system producing the reports must be run during the evenings, when the other systems are down. And anyway, she is not doing the report right. I have been doing it for three years and I know how it should be done. I simply have not had the time to get to it this quarter."

"But Carl was late getting started," Connie responds, "and it must be done by the end of the month. Besides, I should be doing this because it takes me far less time to get it done because I am already working on the system that produces the reports. I ran these exact same reports for my prior employer."

Charles silently assesses the situation and concludes that Carl feels threatened by Connie, a relative newcomer. It is clear that Carl can do a good job and it would be a shame to lose him. But Carl is pretty busy these days: he is doing most everything that needs doing.

Carl interrupts these thoughts. "I work late nights keeping all these systems going and there are few problems when I run these reports."

Connie is new and aggressive, Charles concludes. Perhaps I need to give Carl more recognition for what he has been doing.

"Carl," Charles announces, "I'd like to give you a new title in recognition for all you do here. You now have the title 'manager'!"

Bob, who has not yet spoken, makes a mental note about Carl's promotion. Work hard and take on responsibilities—that is how you get ahead.

Connie is silent. She too makes a mental note. Her efficiency argument didn't resonate with Charles. Getting ahead will require her to get her name on lots of different tasks.

Carl, Connie, and Bob leave Charles's office.

The scene happens often and may not turn into anything larger than what was described here. But these are the types of conversations that can let you know that some deeper changes will soon be in order. Incremental changes to job responsibilities will soon be insufficient. The changes may be difficult as generalist capabilities, training, and interests of many members are no longer as important as they once were. Many successful Innovating organizations are staffed by generalists, so everyone can lay claim to multiple activities with some legitimacy. Sorting out the appropriate span of control for each member is difficult because it truly cuts into what a generalist does. It also affects the power and stature of those involved.

Addressing these issues is the essence of a Foundation Building mode: a difficult period, but fortunately only temporary. It is for this reason that the management style of the Collaborative Planner is most effective. This leader can approach the fundamental problems methodically by considering the views of everyone to work out objective, fair, and logical solutions.

You can make the transition smoother by encouraging staff to take a close look at what is really going on—and supporting their efforts to make their work more structured, systematized, and efficient. Instead of delaying and prolonging the needed changes by making incremental changes here and there, you need a comprehensive review and comprehensive solutions.

You Had to Be There at the Beginning

New team members take an unacceptably long time to understand the enterprise and to become effective. They are dependent on those who have been with the company since the early days. Many of the work processes and procedures evolved organically as the business formed and developed and have not been made more transparent and rational. In many instances there is nothing written on procedures and processes for new people to study. Suggestions for change are strongly resisted. To understand the business, the organization, and how things get done, one almost has to have been there since it began. The original staff enjoys a special camaraderie that can appear as a clique closed to newer members of the enterprise.

This legacy typically appears after the Concept Development phase as the "second generation" of members is hired and tries to become productive. Future growth will be influenced by how quickly new staff can become productive. Longer training periods can put an increased burden on the "first generation" members, energy that could be better focused on being productive.

The first successes of an innovation-driven enterprise come from doing new things or by doing existing things in a new way. Trial and error is prevalent and little is documented about how things are done. Documentation is costly and time-consuming—and why would you document the details of some trial that may not work? Also, documentation is simply not a priority. When the winding path that finally proves to be the right path is discovered, the top priority quickly becomes running up and down that path as fast as possible to generate business. The path is not straight, it is not the shortest distance between beginning to end, but those who discovered it know it like the backs of their hand. Finding the way along this path becomes part of the tribal lore—the stuff of stories and anecdotes. To travel this path efficiently, "you had to be there at the beginning." Only those who were there know exactly how it should be traveled.

The first successes of an innovation-driven enterprise come from doing new things or by doing existing things in a new way.

It is important to recognize that this situation maintains the power and work patterns of the "first generation" as the organization grows. They know the ins and outs of getting things done and are therefore entitled to their more senior status within the organization. Transparent and rational processes are often a threat to them. As generalists, they may not have the deep functional expertise, but they know how this organization works. Suggestions to change the situation to enable anyone to understand the inner workings will undermine their positions and are quickly rejected.

The result is that employees who have not grown up with the firm and experienced firsthand the trial-and-error process have little hope of becoming productive quickly. New employees have to learn by osmosis—simply by being around people who were there at the beginning.

When enterprise leaders do not take the initiative to make the work processes more transparent and rational, training new staff efficiently and quickly becomes more difficult. If growth is an objective, the lack of transparency and rational processes threatens your success in meeting that objective.

Lore and Legend Fall Short

Wise Owl Investments, a money management firm in Denver, developed an innovative way to research small companies. The research process was conducted by five analysts who each analyzed companies in many different industries. The process worked very well for many years. It was clearly the foundation of the firm's investment success. As Wise Owl attracted new clients, it hired additional analysts to help perform the research. Because the firm had more business, it could hire analysts with stronger academic credentials. Because no manuals existed to describe the proprietary research approach, all learning was done at the side of experienced analysts. War stories and personal philosophies conveyed the general process, but none of this information was in the form of objective and unambiguous rules for making decisions. The new analysts had to experience the process and undergo an extremely lengthy informal apprenticeship before they could be trusted to evaluate companies independently. The hesitancy to trust the new analysts was justified, as they truly had not absorbed the essence of the approach.

Unfortunately, even-measured business growth left Wise Owl no choice but to depend more and more on analysts who were not fully indoctrinated. Because the essence of its investment approach was still embodied in lore and legend, the new analysts were not able to operate as effectively as needed. Inevitably, their research was inadequate and the investment performance of Wise Owl's funds suffered.

The approach used by Wise Owl could have been made more rational and transparent and the transitional, Foundation Building phase for this group would have been successful. But, as mentioned earlier, some business processes do not lend themselves to being made more formulaic. One must review carefully which processes should be made rational and which ones should be left informal. When in doubt, err on the side of being more rational and transparent. our experience indicates that business processes are suitable for being transformed than are actually transformed.

A key sign that the transition out of Concept Development has been successful and Foundation Building has been complete is that someone new can come in and be effective in a reasonable amount of time.

A key sign that the transition out of Concept Development has been successful and Foundation Building has been complete is that someone new can come in and be effective in a reasonable amount of time. Practices and procedures that are codified become more transferable. If this is done early and in time for the more experienced and generalist staff to work their way into more specialized roles that fit their skills, the enterprise becomes more fluid and flexible.

The Office Manager Crisis

The office manager in this scenario represents any employee who serves as the leader's "right hand" and manages the many tactical and administrative issues the innovative leader often readily delegates. The typical new entrepreneur, being more concerned about innovation and big-picture issues, often hires an office manager to handle the administrative and incidental tasks. The office manager is usually one of the first people hired and is a loyal generalist who is capable of performing a variety of activities. He or

[handwritten: Example is HRD The office mgr was Donna E]

68

she is typically flexible, loyal, and a jack-of-all-trades. The office manager grows up with the firm and knows it in rich detail. He or she becomes so enmeshed in the inner workings of the company that, eventually, no decision can be made without consulting him or her. The office manager becomes a proxy for the actual leader.

However, as the enterprise grows, the office manager becomes more and more overworked. The office manager performs the Herculean job of keeping track of all the details pertaining to the past and current operation of the business. He or she is, in effect, regulating the organization with the implied authority of the leader.

Quiet arguments involving the office manager begin to develop. New members trained in accounting are dependent on him or her to locate and interpret needed records that no one else knows about, a dependence that slows their work.

Detailed information about past customer relationships resides only in the head of the office manager. Changes to the production system must be reviewed by the office manager to scour for any potential conflicts with acceptable practices and procedures and legal matters. The production department slows.

The office manager corrects new staff for violating tenets of corporate culture that are so specialized that only a long-time employee could know them.

These are all sources of tension that the leader who has empowered the office manager fails to see early. No one wants to upset the office manager, who is a trusted and loyal supporter of the leader and has that top person's ear.

Initially, there is little apparent need to change this situation, as long as the office manager is constantly involved. But this situation inhibits the normal development of other staff and the organization as a whole. Eventually, the office manager's capabilities hit a ceiling and the situation becomes a true crisis. The office manager becomes indispensable to the day-to-day operation of the firm but unable to provide the breadth and depth of specialized knowledge and skills it requires to operate. The leader is usually last to recognize the problem.

An innovative leader often assumes that everyone, including the office manager, will mature naturally along with the growing complexity and magnitude of the job. However, the responsibilities normally delegated to this person at the beginning of an organization's development change dramatically over time. It is not realistic to assume that the person hired when the business began will be able to keep pace with the changing technical requirements and greater focus that will ultimately be required. Nor is it reasonable to assume that someone who is motivated and energized by generalist activities will be satisfied by more narrowly defined tasks later on.

With these well-intentioned but faulty assumptions, the leader often delays providing the organization with the specialized competence it needs as it matures. This delay only widens the gap between what the situation requires and what the office manager can provide, regardless of his or her skills, hours worked, and dedication.

Left unmanaged, the situation becomes a crisis because the enterprise cannot operate a day without the office manager—but it cannot grow without deeper expertise. The Office Manager Crisis is often painful and time-consuming to resolve. It affects a loyal, long-term employee who has been essential to the daily operation of the firm, the development of other staff, and the progress of the organization as a whole. This situation is the first main test of how an entrepreneurial leader will manage the issue of personal loyalty vs. technical proficiency—one of the most trying issues to resolve.

When "Invaluable" Is an Impediment to Growth

A San Diego software development firm started with just a few employees. Among the first administrative people hired was Mark, an energetic young man who was willing to undertake any task. He started with bookkeeping and then was promoted to head of administration. Due to his energy and willingness to work long hours—and because the organization was small—Mark was involved in every aspect of the company's operations. He eventually had three people working for him who performed tasks suitable for entry-level staff. He became so entwined with the company that the president said that Mark was actually the true president and that if something had to be done, Mark could get it done. This did not sit well with others.

Mark maintained strong control over his team and did not allow them to progress to higher-level tasks. In addition, he felt threatened by people elsewhere in the organization who were developing greater competence and he withheld information that would enable them to act independently.

Somehow every decision had to involve him. If someone cut him out of the loop, that person did not get the information he or she needed. Then, if that person failed, Mark would step in with what was required to reaffirm that progress was more certain with him than without him. For the most part, this actually was true. When Mark wasn't involved, things didn't go as smoothly or quickly. Although this may sound as though his intentions were bad, that wasn't the case. He insisted upon being involved in everything because he believed that he really did have all the solutions at hand, which was the key to Mark's early success. He was also seen as a parent figure to many in the organization and was a tremendous resource. He resisted change simply to protect the practices and cultural values he felt had been responsible for the firm's successes.

However, the growth the firm was experiencing required greater functional expertise than any generalist could provide, regardless of his energy. In this case, the leader was among the last to realize that the office manager's role had become an impediment to growth. Mark's intense bond of loyalty with the firm made it difficult for the leader to see the broader picture and longer-term business needs—or that the real needs of the company in specialized areas like accounting, personnel, and production had progressed beyond what Mark, as office manager, could provide. Once Mark's job had been separated into its different functions, he was not suited for any specialized area. Mark ultimately left the company.

With Mark's experiences in mind, the way to avoid this debacle is clear: make a special effort early on to plan a career path for your firm's office manager. Provide the training he or she needs to become more of a specialist. As leader, you can initiate this plan before your organization has developed too far in terms of requiring technical specialization. This individual can then specialize in an area well suited to his or her interests and capabilities and to the organization's needs. If you do recognize the short life of this role in a growing company, you can avoid the Office Manager Crisis. Move through the transitional Foundation Building phase early and quickly.

Unfortunately, many office managers find the narrower focus and the requirement to develop a greater level of technical expertise to be beyond their interests. What they like most may be the breadth of activities and the exposure to all aspects of the company.

The situation in this undesirable legacy may not reach a crisis level if the business environment and enterprise are strong enough to support the office manager in a more generalist role that still allows other staff to develop. The economics of your situation may not allow this option, but it is often preferable to losing the manager's experience.

The Crisis-and-Rescue Cycle

The entrepreneurial leader continues as the primary mover and shaker in a young company. However, the leader begins to be overwhelmed by the numerous responsibilities that continue to expand as company growth picks up. Someone suggests that delegating work to others is the answer. So the leader immediately delegates work and responsibilities to other members of the team.

The situation deteriorates shortly after delegation takes place. Details are overlooked, errors are made, and the essence of the vision is not fulfilled. Eventually the leader must return to the scene in a rescue operation. The leader's return reinforces the idea that he or she is absolutely indispensable to the day-to-day activities of the business. And some time later, once again, the leader becomes overwhelmed. Delegation appears to be the best solution. The cycle is repeated.

This Crisis-and-Rescue Cycle prevents the leader from addressing new issues; it also hinders other members of the enterprise from developing their capabilities. Throughout this cycle, the organization makes mistakes, people overlook details, and execution of decisions is poor. Systems that have been initiated do not become operational. The leader cannot devote attention to other matters and must fight rear-guard action on internal issues rather than being focused on the new battles for business growth that lie ahead.

The Crisis-and-Rescue Cycle prevents the leader from addressing new issues; it also hinders other members of the enterprise from developing their capabilities.

This undesirable legacy is based on the informal nature of decision-making and the use of supervision as the main method of control during the Concept Development phase. Responsibilities and accountabilities are not well defined. Infrastructure is lacking in important areas such as accounting, decision-making, and planning. In addition, employee responsibilities are not specialized enough and the process for doing the work is overly complex. All these factors make it difficult to delegate successfully.

It also often happens that an entrepreneurial leader gets bored with the day-to-day running of the business and wants to start something new. He or she likes to believe that the loyal team can handle the future. Instead of shepherding the business through a Foundation Building phase that will enable the team to operate more independently, the leader suddenly decreases involvement. The natural distaste that successful innovative leaders have for Foundation Building makes this scenario all too common. Mundane business issues and management do not hold their attention like pursuing a new innovation.

I mentioned in the last chapter that a common refrain is "Entrepreneurs don't delegate." In fact, they do delegate and do so frequently and repeatedly. Unfortunately, they tend to delegate abruptly and with little preparation. All else being equal, Decisive Visionaries favor either complete personal control or complete delegation: it's all or nothing. The individual to whom they delegate is typically not adequately prepared for that autonomy. They go from gathering data to making decisions in the blink of an eye. Without a support structure and a logical method of achieving objectives, the delegate is in a no-win situation. Inevitably, he or she makes poor decisions and bad judgments and the leader must come to the rescue. Finding that decisions have not been made the way he or she would have made them, the leader then takes back all of the decision-making authority and control.

This sequence of events reconfirms to the leader that he or she really shouldn't have delegated. Faced with an organization out of control, the leader puts forth a super-human effort and tries to repeat the success of the early days by reasserting tight central control.

However, it's not possible to maintain tight personal control in a large organization over long periods of time. The leader soon tires and decides to try delegating again, particularly after a period without any problems. However, without real preparation for delegation, another crisis develops and another rescue is necessary.

"Chronic" Crisis and Rescue

Audrey was a hands-on leader who thrived on the thrill of start-ups. About three years after starting one business, she believed that her team had learned the ropes. They had worked together all that time and, although there was no formal training (because everyone had seen every part of the business), she thought that any one of her staff could replace her. The truth was that she was getting a bit bored and dreamed of the start-up phase.

Audrey decided to launch another business. Once the decision was made, she felt the rush of excitement as she contemplated the new strategy. As soon as this occurred, however, she was completely absent from the first business.

The remaining team members attempted to keep the first business going. They were successful for a while. They tried to make decisions in a way that was consistent with their absent leader's views, but they were simply guessing about what she would have done and tried to keep doing what had been done in the past. Unfortunately, none of those remaining intensely held a vision of the organization's purpose. Most of their experience had consisted of following Audrey's guidance, not working independently. While they kept doing what they'd done in the past, they lost track of the reasons for doing things that way. Because of this, the team had no way of knowing how their internal practices should be revised in response to the changes in the business. None had been in a position to see the overall big picture.

Ultimately, business problems emerged. Seeing the situation, Audrey returned to the scene to guide the organization through the difficult period, setting a bold new vision to focus her people and to guide their activities. She again became involved in every detail. But when the short-term problems were solved, she disappeared from the business and the cycle began again.

Because Audrey was committed to the success of both efforts, the problems experienced by the firm never became critical. However, while both businesses were just successful enough to stay in business, the Crisis-and-Rescue

> Cycle became a full-time preoccupation. Audrey did not have the time to address the fundamental problems of either business and neither grew. The leader and her companies were trapped in a perpetual crisis-and-rescue cycle and could not prepare for future growth.

The Crisis-and-Rescue Cycle can be broken. When there is no crisis at hand, the leader should adopt the Foundation Building mode. This enables him or her to identify decision-making resources, requirements, and objectives and to deliberately set the employees up to succeed rather than fail.

Snowflakes in Waiting

Just as water molecules gather around a speck to create a snowflake, the leader acts as the object around which the members of an innovating organization gather.

A speck of dust or pollen is often needed to form a snowflake. Without something to crystallize around, the water vapor fails to form into snowflakes and remains vapor. Just as water molecules gather around a speck to create a snowflake, the leader acts as the object around which the members of an innovating organization gather. If the leader opts out of this role for any reason, there is no force or vision to bring a discussion to the point of making a decision.

Without the leader, an organization that was once decisive and responsive stagnates. People avoid making decisions. All required information is collected and assembled, but no one brings the issue to a point of resolution and determines who will do what to make something happen. Weakness arises not so much because wrong decisions are made but because no decisions are made and little action is taken.

This situation is related to the leadership allelopathy of the Innovating mode. As described earlier, leadership allelopathy refers to the beneficial way an Innovating leader helps maintain the singular vision of the firm by seeking people who are loyal and support it—as opposed to having independent visions of their own. These members of the organization are rewarded for their continued loyalty to the leader's vision. Allelopathy can be positive as long as the effect is reduced once the vision has been validated.

In the Innovating mode, everyone has a vote, but the only vote that counts is the leader's. Everyone participates in the process and there is a sense of consensus decision making, but there is just one decision maker. Others are loyal to the vision of the leader, gather information, and participate in discussion, but only the leader calls for an end to discussion and authorizes action.

When the involvement of the leader decreases, he or she no longer plays the role of the speck around which information gathers in order for the decisions to be made. Everyone performs just as before, but the decisions do not get made as quickly or effectively.

Hired for Loyalty

A New York City money management firm had experienced several years of strong investment performance, had taken on new, large accounts, and now managed several billion dollars. The founder, Matt, was an aggressive and charismatic leader who had created the firm four years previously and had personally hired key staff. Each person was a generalist and they all participated in all decisions and openly shared their views about what should be done. Because of the firm's success, Matt decided to develop a new investment product to take advantage of clients' interest in similar services offered by a competing company.

The current team members took over primary control of the existing investment process. Because the investment disciplines had been fully developed, Matt believed that it was time to step aside and let some of the other members of the organization assume stronger roles in order to pursue their career interests. He reduced his involvement, but there were few other changes. The staff and the leader continued to have meetings every week to discuss recent economic news and its impact on which stocks they bought and sold.

Unfortunately, as time passed, the company's performance began to deteriorate. When the team studied the situation more closely, they realized that their decisions were "safer" and less bold than they had been in the past. They were slower to make decisions and any decisions they made quickly tended to be conservative. Competing firms were simply faster and more insightful.

To promote faster decisions, the firm's management agreed that one person should be the central decision maker. They believed that strong central leadership was needed. But it was difficult to determine which of the four peers should be promoted above the others to become leader. People who had enjoyed being peers and having the same role in decision making resisted this change. Unfortunately, Mike, who was selected to take on this responsibility, had a temperament that didn't lend itself to a visionary role. Mike was uncomfortable asserting a view and instead tried to be as collaborative as possible so that others would support the process.

Despite all attempts, the organization could not operate effectively without Matt, the original central leader. Not only did attempts to improve the decision-making structure go against the one-for-all culture that was so highly prized, but the improvements also seemed to require more independence of thought than the staff could provide. They had been hired for loyalty to the vision of the leader and had developed in an era of leadership allelopathy, which had diminished their ability to function as independent decision makers.

There are three primary ways to avoid the phenomenon of Snowflakes in Waiting.

The first is to determine that the Innovating mode is the right one for your business at this time. If this is the case, decentralized decision making is not appropriate. Under this scenario, the leader should stay involved and the organization should avoid growing. Outsource as many activities as possible to maintain a narrow focus of efforts. Avoid adding new products.

The second way to avoid this legacy is to carefully reduce leadership allelopathy. Over a period of time, you should allow staff to develop their own capabilities as independent decision makers earlier than needed. It is important to remember that, overall, allelopathy is good for an early-phase entrepreneurial venture. It enables a young firm to be highly focused, innovative, and responsive to quickly changing opportunities. However, as soon as an innovation is developed that will support extensive growth, allelopathy should be reduced. As you begin to see that the Concept Development phase and the Innovating mode are no longer appropriate for your business, begin to hire people who are more independent, as opposed to those of high loyalty.

A third way to avoid the Snowflakes in Waiting scenario is to begin early to develop formal processes that will guide decision making without your close supervision. Begin to differentiate the roles of members of your organization early to allow for greater specialization and depth of understanding. Assign accountability and authority in unambiguous terms early, before you step out of the picture, so everyone can become accustomed to the new roles. Then, let your top managers make decisions. Even if you don't entirely agree with some of these decisions, your managers need to operate with a degree of independence.

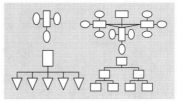

Chapter 5

Shifting Gears

I F YOU ARE LIKE THE LEADERS OF MOST ENTREPRENEURIAL ENTERPRISES, THE biggest leadership mistake you make will be right here. At first, you may sense that things are changing and pass this off as "growing pains" or as your enterprise's adolescence. You may dismiss subtle signals that a deep fundamental change is needed and continue forward in a business-as-usual manner, saying, "We will outgrow this." You may dismiss the whine of the engine as it revs at 9,000 rpm as the sound of success. But this is the wall in the darkness.

The effects of this leadership misstep may not be evident for a while, but this is when it happens—and its impact can be immense. If you're able to see the signals and act on them early, you can dramatically increase your chance to climb over or go around the wall and develop a sustainable and successful enterprise.

Somewhere between having seven and 17 people (the higher number includes staff members in supporting functions) involved in core activities of the enterprise the change will take place. Keep your wits about you. Realize that the purpose of this transitional phase is to make the concept on which your enterprise is based more rational and objective, its processes more transparent, and, importantly, its main product more widely accepted. Remind yourself that the key to survival lies in wisdom, conscious choice, and deliberate and disciplined action. Step back and try to see what the real impediments to continued growth and success are, just as Vic did.

Vic Shifts Gears

Vic's Model 3000 is now on the market. Sales are increasing and putting a strain on operations. Tern is a major customer and has bought 12 Model 3000 units. Finch Enterprises, a rival of Tern, has purchased seven units, but these required modifications. These customized changes made it less imperative that Finch Enterprises change its practices to use the 3000. Vic had obliged and, in fact, was pleased to do so because it enabled his company to satisfy a prominent customer. With these major customers and about a dozen others, the company is providing the 3000 with many specialized features. This model began with certain standard features, but Vic and the customers have jointly designed each unit, so no two are alike.

As a result of all these special modifications, production and customer service are quickly becoming a nightmare. "I'm not going to step in this time," Vic thinks to himself as he listens to his production manager, Pat (a Collaborative Planner), describe a production bottleneck. "The production team complains of being overworked," Pat reports. "They're working late nights and weekends, and they're making too many mistakes. Everyone seems busy, but I don't really know what many of them are doing. To make matters worse, everyone seems to resent that I was made supervisor," he laments. "Every time I ask them to do something, they ask, 'Does Vic agree with this?' or 'Is this the way Vic wants it done?'"

Vic realizes they're going at 9,000 rpm in first gear. Vic resists the temptation to step into the production room to troubleshoot personally, even though he could solve the immediate problem quickly. Before this, Vic had intervened to solve such problems, but he soon found that by doing so he was undermining the people he had assigned to take responsibility for solving problems.

A key difference this time is that he promoted one member of the team, Pat, to supervise the others. In the past, no one had responsibility for overseeing production; it seemed odd to fabricate a management role when everyone involved had been there since the business began. Unfortunately, without the oversight, problems were not detected until they became a crisis and therefore represented significant business risks, which absolutely required that Vic step in. The problems coming up now, however, are not urgent and his new managers have the time to work toward a permanent solution and for everyone to get accustomed to the new structure.

"Pat, let's talk about this in the weekly operating committee meeting," Vic responds.

Vic had formed an operating committee consisting of the new heads of the production, accounting, sales, and design departments. The whole company consisted of only 18 people and it was tough to exclude people from the meetings who had always participated in the past. But Vic wanted a small group of key people to resolve internal coordination problems, advise him on policy issues, and communicate back to the rest of the members. At first the committee meetings were used to exchange information and Vic still made most decisions. As time went on, the committee made more decisions. It is important to him to get agreement among those who are informed on key issues.

After discussing the production bottleneck at length, Pat gives the operating committee some ideas about how to approach the problem. He meets with each production staff member to review what he or she did and what that accomplished, then solicits suggestions for how to improve the process. In addition, he involves the sales department to determine if the number of versions of the 3000 can be reduced. The committee discusses the proposal and agrees to it.

To Vic, this life is dull. The number of meetings seems endless and soliciting ideas for incremental improvements holds no excitement for him. He realizes, however, that if improvements are to be made and business scale is to be achieved, the team has to go though this process and he needs to be involved. He must be in a position to endorse the changes. He recognizes the impact of his endorsement on how things get done.

Vic asks everyone to keep track of all steps they're taking to accomplish certain tasks, the amount of time each step takes, and any costs involved. He also creates a more detailed business plan and a mission statement and posts the mission statement in the employee lunchroom. The operating committee updates both every six months. The objective of all these measures is to make activities and decisions more visible and involve more people in making decisions—and it seems to be working.

The Transitional Phase

Done correctly, the first Transitional phase is the time for quiet revolutions. Internal management priorities, work processes and practices, product strategies, and structures that have been successful in the past are dismantled and the useful pieces are reassembled. For most enterprises, this quiet revolution should begin when there are more than about five people meaningfully involved in decision making within the enterprise. This is typically the point at which not every person can be involved in every effort and not everyone can be accountable for everything. The timing depends on circumstances, but there are few instances when it is appropriate to begin this phase with more than ten people involved.

While the Concept Development phase of growth was a hands-on phase, with the leader directly involved in every aspect of the organization, the first Transitional phase is a hands-off mode. Real delegation begins to take place. If it is done early and effectively, almost everyone can stay connected. But some horse trading will be necessary—almost everyone involved will need to give up some duties, responsibilities, and working relationships. This is a phase of internal realignment and change and it will be facilitated by creating a secure situation for team members. All must be convinced that the changes are not an indictment of their past efforts or solely a threat to their jobs. If this process begins early, there is a better chance of avoiding staff cuts. If the transition is delayed, more staff must be added to achieve growth—staff who would not be needed if they were coming into more rational work processes.

Preconditions

Three preconditions should be met prior to entering a Transitional phase. You need to answer yes to each question before moving on.

The first and most important is *Do you have sufficient business momentum to carry you through a period of internal restructuring?* You'll need to turn some of your attention away from getting new business and direct it toward solidifying the gains already made. If you are too early in your development, you may not have enough solid customer relationships to give you the opportunity to focus on strengthening your internal infrastructure. If you are early, getting the Concept Development phase right may truly be the most important objective. Building a foundation for the future may not be advisable because you may not have a good enough idea of the essential elements of your business.

If you are too late, the stresses of going 9,000 rpm in first gear will have worn you down and your business will be beginning to sputter—and you won't have the momentum to carry you through this transition. If this is the case, you may need to pare back your business to a smaller, more manageable scope and gain some business successes before trying this.

The second precondition that requires an affirmative answer is *Are some or all of your business concepts and processes suitable for being made more formal and routine?* Some businesses that depend on a steady flow of creative ideas, such as design shops and some investment management firms, depend on processes that cannot be reduced to a formula. When these enterprises try to reduce them, they lose their innovative and insightful edge and their business performance suffers.

Other businesses are driven by processes that are suitable for being made more logical, routine, and transparent. Examples of these are companies that make physical products (computers, food items, etc.). Even the delivery of some services can benefit from being made more transparent and rational. Among companies such as investment firms and design studios whose primary processes are not suitable for transformation, there will be some ancillary business processes that will require it. Only one segment of these businesses may be an Innovating enterprise indefinitely; other segments may move on through this Transitional phase. Because there are routine business functions in almost every company, each should pass through this phase to some degree or another.

The third question is *Have you identified a suitable target for future development?* In other words, as you build the foundation, do you know what type of structure it will be supporting in the future? This is important because different structures require different foundations. This is a more flexible precondition because you must make this assessment in the later part of this developmental phase. Chapters 6, 7, and 8 are intended to help you visualize the different phases and be more effective in making this decision.

The Naturally Effective Style of Management

The naturally effective management style during the first and subsequent Transitional phases is Collaborative Planner, a combination of the Analytical Planner and Collaborative Facilitator style components. The Analytical Planner component of this management style prefers to gather information *before* making decisions. This component likes analytical rigor in assessing a situation and a systematic evaluation of practical alternatives. The Collaborative Facilitator component has a strong interest in the views of others when making decisions and is concerned with the welfare of the enterprise's members.

Together, these components make Collaborative Planners interested in promoting effective communication among staff members, with customers, and among the various constituents of a growing enterprise. They are predictable managers and can patiently work through the personnel issues that are common during this phase. They tolerate many meetings and detailed, thorough reports. They listen, analyze, and seek to make processes more logical and rational. They want people to be accountable and will change

The naturally effective management style during the first and subsequent Transitional phases is Collaborative Planner, a combination of the Analytical Planner and Collaborative Facilitator style components.

reporting relationships to make this happen. But they also want to create a sense of security and unity in the pursuit of common goals and interests.

The downside of this management style is a focus on internal preparation. Collaborative Planners place a high value on being prepared with processes and procedures and also the human side of the enterprise. At an extreme, they will sometimes "wait for all the traffic lights to be green before leaving on a trip."

The attributes that look and feel successful to a Collaborative Planner are a logical arrangement of tasks, clear accountability, efficient processes, and general awareness of plans and acceptable practices. This style of management models the goals, practices, and priorities embodied in the Foundation Building mode of operation.

The Foundation Building Mode of Operation

Typical themes of a Foundation Building organization are:

▶ Develop and use a range of control levers.

▶ Delegate.

▶ Fix it, even if it isn't broken. (Solidify and rationalize existing work processes.)

▶ Build for the future by selecting a kingpin market segment or niche.

▶ Initiate development of the most appropriate next operational mode.

Using the Foundation Building operational mode, the organization and its leader must focus for a period of time on the internal issues of establishing an infrastructure that is efficient and rational and accommodates multiple decision makers.

Using the Foundation Building operational mode, the organization and its leader must focus for a period of time on the internal issues of establishing an infrastructure that is efficient and rational and accommodates multiple decision makers. The goal is to begin to differentiate and systemize the tasks done by various people and regroup these tasks in a way that makes sense for the future and lay a foundation that will support the future growth of your organization and production of your product. During this mode, you must begin to consider a broader range of issues. These red-tape issues will seem less dramatic and exciting than the issues of the previous phase. You must develop a more formal communication system and decision-making structure, keep records, develop accounting procedures, and establish control and monitoring systems.

Foundation Building is big job and one that carries some risk. In one sense, the term "Foundation Building" does not represent what's going on.

When you build a house, the foundation comes first; it is not usually added to an existing structure. But in a growing enterprise, we have built a structure on a makeshift foundation, using whatever materials were readily available at the time we built it. While the foundation and structure have served their purposes, we now need a stronger foundation that's better suited to current needs and what we expect to happen in the future. But since we're already using the foundation, we will need to retrofit it while the structure is still in use. And before we remove or rework the old ad hoc foundation, we have to put up other support to keep the structure useable.

Initiate Broad Controls

Remember that in an Innovating organization the leader personally and directly controls the activities of members of the organization. Of course, as the organization grows, it is neither possible nor advisable for a leader to personally control all activities. Delegation must take place. Some say that entrepreneurs cannot delegate. While we can understand why this is said, I see the situation differently.

Entrepreneurs typically have two approaches to delegation: zero delegation and 100-percent delegation. They delegate very little, and this can be acceptable in the Concept Development phase. When an entrepreneur is convinced that delegation is appropriate or is forced to delegate, he or she delegates everything all at once. Abrupt delegation has a poor chance of working; the issue being delegated is usually too large and complicated and the people to whom it is delegated are usually ill prepared. Few entrepreneurs purposely and systematically prepare their teams in advance for a greater level of delegation of responsibility. They typically want complete control or no part of the control.

Entrepreneurs typically have two approaches to delegation: zero delegation and 100-percent delegation.

Preparation consists of developing intermediate controls prior to needing to use them. Direct personal control must be replaced with other, intermediate forms of control that the leader can use to indirectly influence others. I will focus on seven control "levers," listed in Table 4-1. These include such controls as organizational structure, performance monitoring and feedback, and cultural priorities.

Seven Levers to Control Your Organization

The idea behind the seven levers is that, as leader, you have seven primary ways to guide the people and activities within your organization. *Your enter-*

Control Levers	
Supervision	Personally guiding and supervising others' activities
Business Vision	A compelling and loyalty-inspiring forward vision for the enterprise
Cultural Priorities	Informal priorities within the organization
Organizational Hierarchy	Responsibilities and authority determined in the organizational structure
Formal Plans and Processes	Clear plans, instructions, and rules for how the work should be done
Expertise of Team Members	Actions guided by the individuals' own judgment
Formal Feedback and Evaluation	Comments on individual performance to help individuals self-correct

Table 4-1. Control levers, Foundation Building phase

prise should be 100-percent controlled 100 percent of the time. When you reduce the impact of one lever—for example, reducing the impact of your personal supervision as a control when your organization gets too big to control personally—you must depend more on other levers. Thus, the positions of these levers must change as you move from one mode of operation to the next. If you do not use them, your business will not be adequately guided and controlled.

An important control that is not explicitly included in this list is budgetary control. Yet, for our purposes here, budgetary measures are used to develop the other controls. People are hired for the structure, an investment is made in systems and processes, and leadership time is spent shaping the culture of the organization, training staff, and developing broad visions and formal plans and procedures. All of these are influenced by budget issues.

Levers are a bit like calories. If you cut something out of your diet, you're probably going to go hungry if you don't substitute an equivalent foodstuff. In a similar way, problems arise when the intermediate controls needed for the next mode of operation aren't enough to make up for what's been taken out of the picture. The organization then begins to lose focus and control and, as a remedy, the leader often reasserts the controls effective during a past mode of operation. This causes to development to lose steam, regardless of how the external business opportunities change.

Recall that an Innovating organization is controlled primarily through direct interaction of the leader. Let's say this controlling force represents over half—about 60 percent—of the total controlling force affecting the operations of the enterprise. This day-to-day, direct interaction with the leader ensures that the efforts of every member of the organization are coordinated and appropriate for the issues at hand.

The next-biggest impact is the loyalty-inspiring business vision espoused by the leader. The vision is interpreted by the members of the organization, who determine their own actions.

The cultural priorities of the organization, regardless of where they come from, also have an impact. This profile of control is so effective in a small organization that the entire organization (albeit small) can change direction almost instantaneously—an ability that drives success during Concept Development.

The profile of control levers in Table 4-2 is generally reflective of how Innovating organizations are controlled, based on our work with many enterprises. The greater the weight, the more important the control is as a way of influencing the activities of the organization's members.

Using this framework of control levers, we can define key characteristics of each operational mode. This profile helps define the nature of the mode and highlights which controls will need to be built in order for the organization to remain adequately controlled in a future phase.

Phase	Concept Development	First Transitional Stage
Mode of Operation	Innovative	Foundation Building
Control Levers		
Supervision	60	20
Business Vision	25	10
Cultural Priorities	5	10
Organizational Hierarchy	0	20
Formal Plans and Processes	0	20
Expertise of Team Members	10	10
Formal Feedback and Evaluation	0	10
Total Control	100%	100%

Table 4-2. Relative influence of control levers

During this first Transitional phase, the control levers that have not been used in the past are initiated. The most influential during the Transitional phase are "Organizational Hierarchy" and "Formal Plans and Processes." A set of reporting relationships must be established and respected, especially by the leader. During the first Transitional phase, other reporting relationships are needed. Formal rules and guidelines for performance, while they may seem legalistic, allow members of the organization to begin to make decisions more autonomously. This is part of managing the ebb of leadership allelopathy (the effect of the central figure hindering the growth of those around him or her).

Additional formal methods of control that begin during this phase are personnel evaluation systems, company philosophies, and mission statements. As formal plans are made, several people can begin to make decisions independently. Most of these efforts are largely in preparation for even greater emphasis in future operational modes. These methods become operational during this phase, but only at a low level.

Once these controls are in place, it is important for the leader, who had little need for formal intermediate controls in the first phase, to come out and say, "These controls are important." This endorsement will have a far-reaching impact on everyone in the organization. If the leader is seen to dismiss or depreciate the various controls, they will have little impact. This is a tough balancing act: to stay involved enough to guide the fledgling controls and endorse their use while staying out of the picture enough to avoid undermining them.

Some people ask us if it is best to fully build all the control levers in a detail and completely during this phase. No. Doing so is not advisable or practical. There is a cost associated with building each one and most small enterprises do not have the resources to fully develop them at this point. But even if an enterprise did have the resources, it still would not be advisable. At this stage, one usually does not know the exact forms the control levers will need to take over the long term. Also, as the term "control levers" implies, you will use them differently during different phases. Initiating them during this phase is important, but they need not be operational in full force.

Solidify and Rationalize Work Processes

In order to make more rational and efficient the work processes already in place, you have to pause and consider them. During the Concept Development phase, your processes developed in an ad hoc manner. Now

Once these controls are in place, it is important for the leader, who had little need for formal intermediate controls in the first phase, to come out and say, "These controls are important."

that they're more established, streamlining them will allow you to work more efficiently. Look back to see where you have come from since the very early days to reach the present point. Appreciate the winding and circuitous path for what it was, a path of discovery. There are probably many parts of that path that are not necessary; before the path becomes a well-worn highway, straighten out some of the curves. There is no longer a need to take the detours that were so important to the process of discovery. Consider this adaptation of an essay by Charles Lamb, "A Dissertation Upon Roast Pig":

> Centuries ago the great culinary delicacy of roast pig was accidentally discovered in a small village. One morning, a fierce fire burned down all the buildings in one part of the village. Later that afternoon, as the residents picked through the debris to salvage what they could, they discovered a pig that had been trapped in one of huts. The discovery took place about dinnertime and the villagers decided to eat the pig. To their surprise, it was cooked perfectly and tasted quite good. It provided a feast for the evening and quickly became one of the most popular delicacies of the region. Roast pig was frequently prepared for special occasions. The only drawback was that every time they wanted roast pig, they had to burn down a hut.

This is a story made to order for many entrepreneurial ventures. Once something is discovered, the participants feel quite gratified about their marvelous creation—but they keep repeating the same original process to get it. Ad hoc, informal, and intuitive decision-making processes become embedded in the firm's culture. The legacy negatively impacts the firm well into the future. While the visible downside for most enterprises is not as dramatic as a hut in flames, the long-term effects can be far more serious:

▶ New employees will require a great amount of time to understand what is going on and how to be productive. The organically developed work processes are not transparent and logical and the newcomers will need to sit by the side of an old-timer to listen to the lore of why things are the way they are.

▶ New employees will fail to develop the needed expertise. They lack personal experience with the product and its production techniques. This makes delegation of responsibility unwise. Old-timers will feel empowered.

▶ Decision making will need to remain with the old-timers. With the greater workload and an inability to bring on new decision makers, decision making will be slow and remain more centralized than is appropriate for a larger organization. In addition, the work may not be done with the higher level of expertise a larger enterprise needs, as the old-timers tend to be generalists.

▶ Selling your product and its benefits will take more time. The various permutations of the core innovation that have been sold to your proof-of-concept customers typically make an unwieldy product line: newcomers must master its many versions and differing features.

▶ Manufacturing practices suited to produce a small number of customized products will strain under higher volumes. The extra bells and whistles needed for the proof-of-concept customers make mass product more difficult and costly.

These weaknesses and others (profiled in Chapter 3) are key indicators that deeper Foundation Building practices are needed. If these weaknesses and their more fundamental underlying causes are not addressed, their effects will hinder future business growth. You must rework every element of the business. You need to get it ready to turn it over to complete strangers—your new employees. Michael Gerber[1] likens this to developing a business format franchise. Put everything in a manual and make sure everyone has a manual—and follows it.

Remember to assess which practices are suitable for this formalization and developing an operational mode other than the Innovating. Some investment processes are not suitable for large groups. Some investment teams that seek to become more institutionalized and less dependent on one person go through a period of formalization and foundation building. Yet, they often delegate key decision-making responsibility to recently hired staff too quickly. Doing so looks like a good step to some because more people are involved and formal roles have been defined and others are brought into the decision-making process. Yet for many investment teams, decision making can become excessively collegial and weaken decision-making effectiveness. It is too slow to produce strong investment returns. In addition, the individuals to whom decision making is delegated are typically less experienced than those who are giving up some decision-making responsibility.

While it may seem odd for investment firms to delegate excessively, the demographic pressures within the team become very strong and delegation

---

1. Michael E. Gerber, *The E-Myth Revisited: Why Most Small Businesses Don't Work and What to Do About It* (Ballinger Publishing, 1985).

becomes almost unavoidable for some firms. When junior professionals are hired to support the senior professionals, they are satisfied with that role. But four or five years later they want to progress in their careers. The investment firm wants to keep the staff that it has trained and delegation of responsibility is almost inevitable.

Initiate Hierarchy

To create a hierarchy sounds like heresy to most entrepreneurs, but if you don't do it, your organization may be too dependent on you for guidance and control in the future. If you do this now with the parts of your business that need it, you will not have to attempt it later when outmoded habits are harder to break.

In contrast to the Concept Development phase, in which there was essentially one decision maker, you now need multiple decision makers and formal decision structures to handle future growth of the business.

The first Transitional phase is a time for many meetings to exchange ideas about how to restructure effectively. Each person has direct knowledge of what he or she has been doing. Take inventory of what each is doing and group the tasks into general categories. Make sure the person best equipped to handle the tasks is responsible for doing them. Seek logical structures and separations for each person's responsibilities. The diagrams in Figure 4-1 show the sequence of structures as the organization grows from the early Innovation mode through the Foundation Building mode. The squares represent independent decision makers and the circles represent their group members.

This chart shows the typical progression within an organization during the initial phases of growth. At first, each person has a direct reporting relationship with the leader. Eventually, the leader's ability to manage the rapidly growing functional areas is exceeded. Once there are more people or functions than can be managed by a single decision maker, you need to regroup by function and shift decision-making responsibilities.

*W*hen junior professionals are hired to support the senior professionals, they are satisfied with that role. But four or five years later they want to progress in their careers.

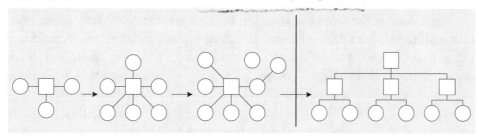

Figure 4-1. Structure: from early Innovation mode through Foundation Building mode

Greater Specialization of Expertise

This first Transitional phase is the time to introduce greater specialization of work for your organization. Once an initial hierarchy is in place, rather than having every member work on everything, have them begin to focus their efforts on a narrower set of activities. The organization is more stable now, yet its problems have become more complex and require deeper expertise.

You need people with specialized expertise to address issues like accounting, marketing, and production. This, too, is difficult because in the past everyone has seen every part of the business and they all must now pull back and begin to specialize. This transition can be especially difficult because many of the people were hired for their generalist abilities rather than their specialist capabilities. One person with many hats was a benefit early on, because this skill enabled the organization to be responsive to many types of challenges. But that situation has been changing.

A functionally segmented team is most effective for the Foundation Building mode. With this structure, you reduce the span of activities for the generalist staff and assign clearer accountability, responsibility, and authority. You should make decisions in roundtable discussions consisting of the heads of the functional groups. You will need to exclude some members of the organization from the central decision-making body in order to keep the number of participants at a manageable level. The focus of the group is on coordinating efforts and problem solving.

A functionally segmented team is most effective for the Foundation Building mode.

In the Concept Development phase, people all worked together and were fairly equal in stature within the organization. During the first restructuring, you'll need to promote a few people. They will begin to supervise and to take responsibility for the activities of others. This is a very difficult step for most ventures. In the past, everyone pulled together as one team. Some of those team members now have to rise above their peers and take management roles. It's difficult for people to rise above their peers, and it's difficult for the others to see someone else get ahead.

Also, during the Concept Development phase, everyone had direct contact with the leader and could seek guidance one on one. Everyone could feel self-esteem, power, and influence by having direct access to the leader. Such access is now more limited. There are simply too many people within the organization for the entrepreneur to have direct contact with everyone.

To many successful leaders of Innovating organizations, this phase is unpleasant and, more importantly, boring. Many entrepreneurs avoid it altogether or do not give it the emphasis it requires; as result, a decision-making vacuum ensues. The leader tries to control the organization by using the informal controls and intuitive planning that were successful in the past. In this vacuum, some forms of structure and methods of control will begin to take shape. Unfortunately, without central coordination, they will not develop in a comprehensive and coordinated manner. Most likely, they will be ad hoc and cumbersome and will reflect the vested interests of their various architects. These ad hoc internal structures are often fiercely protected because they were the result of someone's earnest personal efforts to address a real problem. Dismantling these systems and then rebuilding takes longer than building them right at an earlier time.

A larger organization is more difficult to restructure. A rational and effective business infrastructure is a requirement for growth, and it will never be easier to build one than when you have between six and 12 people directly involved with the changes.

Select the Kingpin Market Niche

During this phase, it is important for you to identify one or two of the most attractive market segments or niches that need what you offer. Even a small market, if handled successfully, can trigger sales in other, larger segments. Geoffrey Moore[2] focuses on the marketing and product strategies of technology-related companies and develops a useful image of this niche selection situation. The goal is to identify a set of market niches that are related but among which there is one particular niche you can dominate. Try to anticipate the relationships between success in this first niche and how other niches might respond. Moore uses the analogy of bowling here: you knock down one niche, which in turn impacts others.

A rational and effective business infrastructure is a requirement for growth, and it will never be easier to build one than when you have between six and 12 people directly involved with the changes.

This is a useful way to conceive of the process, even outside of high tech. In the Concept Development phase, your customers picked you. They were interested in what you had to offer and would sit through your unpolished presentations and tolerate product errors in exchange for the product and the custom fitting you would do for them. This was your proof-of-concept market segment. But now, try to select a niche of potential customers who will take your product without the custom work—a segment (more than a handful of customers) that will value what you offer. Rework your product to address their needs for the product and how they will use it. Success with them will make it easier to penetrate neighboring segments.

---

2. Geoffrey A. Moore, *Inside the Tornado* (HarperBusiness, 1995).

Strategic thinking can overcome size and strength. But this strategic view is different from the strategic thinking of the Concept Development phase. Rather than change the world, in this phase you want to change the minds and buying habits of a specific segment of potential customers. This requires not a breakthrough innovation, but research into what those potential customers want and how the segment works: what they buy, how they buy it, and whom they talk to before buying. Any defiance of what the market wants will slow your progress during this phase. It is time to change gears.

Pioneering customers who gave you the opportunity to understand their needs and to test your product enabled you to get where you are today. However, these customers, as early adopters, may not represent the bulk of the customers who could benefit from your product. Pioneering customers expect special features; it is challenging and costly to meet all their needs.

Standardizing Your Product or Service

You may want to incorporate into the basic product some of the features originally requested by these customers for use by all your consumers. Now is the time to simplify your production processes by standardizing the product.

*A*ny defiance of what the market wants will slow your progress during this phase.

To standardize your product, go out and ask customers what they like about it. Find out what the common opinions are across your customer base. The tricky part of this exercise is to then identify the most basic product that will both reflect the essential elements of your innovation and serve the largest potential market. Instead of adding features for each customer as you did during the Innovating mode, simplify your product to its essential elements in a form that can be produced in high volumes. If you have truly developed a breakthrough innovation, the market is likely to accept the standardized version and perhaps pay a premium for the product. The goal is to define the simplest product with the fewest parts that provides the core benefits of your innovation.

Appreciate that you are able to sell the product widely, giving it the possibility of becoming the industry standard or the preferred brand or type. This process will take some time and should be done concurrently with your effort to build your business infrastructure.

The Foundation Building Mode Is the Opposite of the Innovating Mode

The Transitional phase that comes after a successful Concept Development is particularly challenging because of the tasks that must be accomplished

Concept Development Growth Phase	First Transition
Decisive Visionary	*Collaborative Planner*
They develop comprehensive visions of the possibilities and then gather data to test their visions. They revise visions based on new information, but the data does not drive the development of the possibilities.	They collect data before making decisions. Data is analyzed logically and systematically. The results of this analysis drive the decision.
Their convictions are strongly held and they are comfortable defying the conventional wisdom that says their vision is not possible.	They solicit the views of experts and others who have had similar experiences and will consider these views in the development of strategy going forward.

Table 4-3. Biases in naturally effective management styles

and, more importantly, because the leader has to reverse many of the successful practices of the past. This change is seen in the management styles that model effective leadership (Table 4-3).

These differences in management style are reflected in key differences between the modes of operation effective in each phase (Table 4-4).

Clearly, the challenge for those in the first Transitional phase is to adopt a completely different mode of operation than what has been used with great success in the past. The Foundation Building mode would not have been effective in the Concept Development phase of growth. The Innovating mode will not be most effective in Foundation Building. Aligning the right operational mode with the current phase of growth is important. Making this change requires the perspective and discipline to know how to operate in the current circumstance.

Stages of Awareness

Change will be especially difficult if the key elements of the Innovating mode of operation have been enshrined in the organization's culture and if the leader is personally more of a Decisive Visionary than a Collaborative Planner. The typical leader goes through the following four stages of awareness of the need to change:

▶ Disregard

▶ Disinterest

Concept Development Growth Phase	First Transition
Innovating Mode	*Foundation Building Mode*
Creating bold new products	Simplifying existing ideas and products
Following intuition through a trial-and-error process of developing an innovative product and business practices	Reviewing market data and evaluating alternative scenarios before taking action
Defying conventional wisdom	Seeking the views of others
Customizing for each customer, adding special features	Paring down to a limited number of product features
Hiring generalists with an ability to handle various (often unforeseen) issues	Hiring specialists with competence for specific tasks that will be required regardless of strategy pursued

Table 4-4. Modes of operation and management differences

▶ Delusion

▶ Denial

Disregard. At first, the growing complexity of the enterprise is not noticed. Where once there was one focus (launch of a single product), there are now many products. Where once there were five people sitting around the lunch table, there are now 15. Where once there were a handful of customers the leader knew on a first-name basis, there are now 40 unfamiliar faces. The greater persistence of problems that need management attention is not usually noticed. In the early days, survival and the validation of the concept superseded all; now parts failures, payroll taxes, insurance, call centers, production lines, accounting rules, legal matters, systems development, human resource issues, and marketing research crowd the minds of the enterprise's leaders.

The seemingly mundane nature of these tasks does not usually register them on the list of issues requiring top leadership attention, at least initially. Yet they are important and require explicit leadership attention. Unfortunately, the leaders often overlook them because their attention is on slaying dragons. These changes in the nature of the important issues requiring leadership attention require your enterprise to operate differently, but the change is gradual. Like the frog that will sit in cool water as it is heated and brought to a boil, most leaders disregard the need for change.

Disinterest. When these issues do crowd into the consciousness of a leader, he or she handles them in short bursts, much like firefighters upon hearing the alarm. But when the crisis passes, there are no lasting fixes. Why? Because creating the fixes is not interesting. After many years of evaluating the way organizations operate, I am convinced that the most powerful forces driving success and failure are interest and boredom. Basically, we do what we like to do. If we are not interested in it, it gets light treatment. Many of the processes coming naturally to a Collaborative Planner that produce success during Foundation Building are not interesting to the Decisive Visionaries effective in Concept Development. The Foundation Building processes are not wildly creative nor are they quick. Formal meetings (with agendas) are an inevitable part of the restructuring process. Leaders successful in the Concept Development phase enjoyed the early days and say, "Let's keep doing what works."

Delusion. In the next state, leaders acknowledge the situation and commission superficial solutions. Consultants are brought in, nice PowerPoint presentations are made, and some titles are bestowed. This is, in some ways, the most dangerous state because making superficial changes relieves the sense of urgency, but little thought is invested in making fundamental changes in how the enterprise and the leader operate or in building work processes for a larger, broader business footprint. Old habits continue.

Denial. As the leader does get a sense of what must be done and the new direction ahead, he or she will often reject it and say, "No way. Those are the reasons I left Big Bureaucracy, Inc., to form my own company." The leader will assert that he or she is building a "flat organization" and takes pride in the informality of the early days. This state is more positive because there is recognition of the depth of the changes being entertained—they go to the essence of the enterprise.

If disinterest progresses to denial, the enterprise is most likely being harmed. The work load is overwhelming the inefficient work processes and decision-making structures and business momentum is slowing. The larger business has more to lose by taking a restructuring time-out, and the time required for adequate restructuring is greater for a larger business. The cost of building the structure needed for a larger business is also greater, as there are more people to retrain and more work to redirect. Delaying Foundation Building means prolonging Foundation Building.

The key to progressing from this point on is recognizing that the Transitional phase requiring Foundation Building is only that—a phase that will come to an

The key to progressing from this point on is recognizing that the Transitional phase requiring Foundation Building is only that—a phase that will come to an end.

end. The strong negative reaction to fundamental change is moderated significantly by the understanding that when the enterprise has met the objectives of Foundation Building, it will move on. Indeed, it must move on to survive and grow because Foundation Building consumes business momentum.

Getting over the Wall

Don't overreact if you feel personally out of sync with the enterprise—or as if you're missing external market opportunities as you begin to build infrastructure. If the breakthrough concept that you validated in the first phase is truly valuable and you restructure early, the momentum of that idea and its success will carry you through the period of time it takes to restructure. See the need for change early and act early. *The priorities set by the leader represent the most significant barrier, but it is also the easiest to overcome.*

The second most significant barrier is the other members of the enterprise. Changes in the way they work, the people to whom they report, the information that they control, and the people who are their peers are important issues. Many people will resist change. Take cues from the style of the Collaborative Planner:

1. Emphasize from the very beginning of the enterprise that this time will come. There should be no surprise about the need to make these changes.
2. Create as much security before the changes as possible. For all the people who should remain with the enterprise, let them know there is a place for them: "We can stay connected."
3. Hold meetings to explain the issue. Let everyone know that changes are needed to make the work processes more rational and efficient. Doing this before the crisis period makes a big difference.
4. Hold meetings to inventory facts and feelings regarding what everyone does. Empower others to organize this process.
5. Analyze the elements of what people do and arrange them more logically and rationally. Don't tolerate errors and inefficiency. The simple process of writing steps down, taking out the company jargon, and asking a newcomer to organize it will take you pretty far down the path. Consider getting a consultant for this step.
6. Hold more meetings to explain and ask for comments and refinements.
7. Hold more meetings to announce and describe the new structures and processes.

Timing is everything. If you do these things too late, developing the new mode of operation will consume too much business momentum. Chapter 9 shows the signs of delay. Again, keep in mind that if you begin Foundation Building early you can do it more quickly.

A Fork in the Road

After the first Transitional phase, you should make a conscious choice as to which momentum-generating growth phase you will enter next. Your next move should accommodate the demands and opportunities your business environment presents. There are generally three broad types of business environments for an innovative venture after it has established its business infrastructure. Some are more beneficial and easier than others for certain types of firms. Subsequent chapters will present each in detail.

After the first Transitional phase, you should make a conscious choice as to which momentum-generating growth phase you will enter next.

Chapter 6: If you're lucky and have access to a rapidly expanding market for one of your products, take advantage of this opportunity. It's a land grab: use this opportunity to gain as much marketplace real estate as possible and accumulate financial strength for subsequent phases of growth. If this Rapid Market Expansion phase of growth is available to you, it's the one that gives you the greatest long-term advantage. Build a Producing organization, a mode of operating appropriate for firms that need to deliver a product quickly and efficiently.

Chapter 7: Not all firms are going to have a land-grab opportunity; instead, they may face a Crowded Marketplace, one in which competition on features and price is intense. If this describes your situation, the next most advantageous path is that of the Crowded Marketplace phase and a business environment that is complex and challenging, but stable. Deep efficiency in the key functional areas important to the product can allow you to compete effectively. The Planning mode is appropriate for firms operating in these environments.

Chapter 8: You may also have the option of serving a number of different market niches that, if positioned well, will pay a premium for a version of your product customized to serve their needs. This business environment is complex, much like the Crowded Marketplace phase, but it also changes relatively quickly, which makes extensive central planning futile. This is the Niche Development growth phase. The Adapting mode is most appropriate here, because of its focus on adapting the practices of your enterprise to the various segments of diverse markets. This may enable you to take advantage of higher profit margins for adapting to customers' unique demands.

Don't be tempted to select the target mode based only on which one is most comfortable. Consider comfort. But also consider the business potential of the opportunities available in the market. The selection process requires a strategic assessment of not only the market but also your firm's capabilities.

Subsequent Transitional Phases

The nature of each restructuring is similar; the focus is on replacing existing power structures and work processes with processes and practices that will support the new growth.

Your organization will move through other Transitional phases requiring Foundation Building as it goes from one momentum-building mode to another. The nature of each restructuring is similar; the focus is on replacing existing power structures and work processes with processes and practices that will support the new growth. Differences occur because practices that need to be developed are different. The new practices that should be in place for each growth mode noted in this book are the preconditions of that growth phase.

Vic Reconfigures His Organization

Vic felt that the company was working smoothly internally, although it was somewhat overbuilt with a hint of bureaucracy.

"I hate filling out these purchase orders and time sheets," Vic complains. He realizes the value of such records in determining the real cost of what his company does, but it still seems like just so much paperwork.

Vic's organization has the decision-making system that's typical after an initial restructuring—the heads of production, sales, and administration all report to Vic:

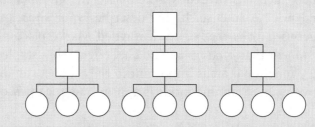

One of the key business decisions Vic and his team made during this phase was to create a product strategy, finding ways to eliminate some of the specialized features. They met with current and prospective customers, reviewed their immediate competition, and studied new market segments in order to evaluate the production implications of various versions of Model 3000. They decided to offer essentially two slimmed-down versions of Model 3000, named Model 3001 and Model 3002, and to target Finch Enterprises and others in that market segment.

The slimmed-down versions incorporate the fewest extra features that will give access to the widest number of prospects in this segment. These versions incorporate the fundamental breakthrough innovation in a specific, tangible, and obvious way. The models are simple to produce, even at high volumes, and relatively low in cost to the customer, considering the benefits of the breakthrough innovation. Sales should be fast—and exposure to other market segments through this segment should be broad.

Limitations and Vulnerabilities

The primary limitation of the Foundation Building mode is foreshadowed in the strength of its naturally effective management style—refining, research, developing consensus. The style is not bold and brash. And, since the Foundation Building phase consumes business momentum rather than building it, you can't use this mode indefinitely and stay in business. The classic undesirable legacy of restructuring is perpetual introspection. Decision making can become slow and ponderous. Every issue is reviewed from various perspectives to make sure that no point of view is excluded. Deliberation takes precedence over action and bold decisions rarely emerge.

Perpetually Introspective: Pelican Tools

Pelican Tools, an LA-based manufacturer of mining equipment, had brought in a new CEO to help get its house in order after a successful Concept Development phase. The leader was systematic and good with people, just the right combination for Foundation Building. This CEO solved many of the problems that were apparent when he arrived.

The firm got a formal decision structure and people were made accountable for certain areas of decision making, with the authority to make decisions and implement them. Personnel evaluation policies and the training program were widely seen as fair, systematic, and appropriate. Pelican began keeping records on the cost of everything to support informed decision making in the future.

However, it soon became apparent that the company was not moving aggressively enough to capture attractive segments of the market. Its products were available; the organization operated smoothly—perhaps too smoothly: selling was not a top priority for its leaders. Sales targets that were set were all well researched, comfortable, and realistic.

A far less methodical competitor appeared in the firm's key market. This new competitor set audacious goals and acted quickly—no questions asked. Pelican had not anticipated this bold new competitor; its presence was clearly a barrier to growth. After Pelican began to rapidly lose market share, a new leader was brought in to recast the firm's priorities.

A good sense of timing can help you bring the Foundation Building phase to a close before major commercial hazards appear. Ideally, you should begin to focus attention on internal issues shortly after your innovative business concept has been validated in the market. When restructuring is begun early enough, the momentum of the company's initial product success will carry it through the restructuring period. You can also set specific objectives for the Foundation Building mode so that once the company reaches them, everyone knows it's time to move on. For example, you might decide to develop all methods of control just to a workable level, with the idea that they will be refined in later phases.

Once this phase is complete, your attention should be on growth. Realize that this change, like all the other changes discussed here, requires subtle alterations that may be difficult to recognize and achieve. But as long as you are prepared for change, you will be able to respond in ways that ensure your business continued success.

The following chapter will take us one step back before we move on to an in-depth look at the Rapid Market Expansion mode of development in Chapter 6. The correct transition to and through Foundation Building is critical for growing companies, but leaders frequently miss the signals that it's time to get the process going. These are some clear red flags—what I call classic indicators. In the next chapter, I'll introduce you to five of them. These are potent signals that it's time to initiate a Foundation Building mode.

Phase of Growth—Summary Table

Phase of Growth	Foundation Building
Goals	• An efficient business infrastructure capable of supporting future growth
Mode of Operation	**Foundation Building (modeled by Collaborative Planner)**
Preconditions	• Sufficient business momentum to sustain a transitional period of restructuring • Valid product and business concepts that retain their effectiveness after being made more systematic • A suitable target for future growth

Mode of Operation	Foundation Building (modeled by Collaborative Planner)
Control Lever Settings	
Supervision	20
Business Vision	10
Cultural Priorities	10
Organizational Hierarchy	20
Formal Plans and Processes	20
Expertise of Team Members	10
Formal Feedback and Evaluation	10
Total Control	100%
Organizational Structure	▪ Functionally segmented team
Cultural Priorities	▪ Open discussion, simplification, systemized work processes
Business Processes	▪ Transparent, logical, and efficient
Product Strategy	▪ Simplified product that can be produced in high volume
Inherent Weaknesses	▪ Consumes business momentum
Beneficial Legacy	▪ Efficient initial business infrastructure ▪ Rationalized processes and procedures to execute initial innovation ▪ Identification of initial target market niches and related niches

■   ■   ■

The following three chapters detail each of the three other growth phases—Rapid Market Expansion, Crowded Marketplace, and Niche Development. Review these chapters to determine which is best for your business. Use the profile of control levers and other details of the target phase to guide your Foundation Building activities as you prepare for future growth.

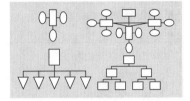

Chapter 6

Going for
Market Share

THIS PHASE IS ABOUT FOCUS.

Most growth enterprises encounter a point in time when they can decide to pursue growth by doing new things or by doing more of something they're already doing. Rapid Market Expansion represents the latter option. The extent to which you should focus depends on several variables; understanding these variables will help you gauge if this phase of growth and its appropriate operational mode are right for you.

In this and other chapters, I refer to "preconditions" that must be met before you can commence a growth phase. This term implies the sense of an absolute requirement, but that is not the precise intent here. My intent with the word "precondition" is to reinforce two ideas. First, it is better to enter a phase of growth only when you've met some requirements. Success is more likely when you attempt a growth phase after developing specific capabilities. Others you can develop during the growth phase. Second, you have choices to make. You can choose to avoid a phase of growth if meeting the preconditions is too costly.

These are the important preconditions for entering the Rapid Market Expansion phase of growth.

Precondition 1: *Commercially compelling product.* This is most important. It could be a pet rock, a breakthrough medical innovation, or an in-demand fashion, but your product must be in or create a product category with strong demand.

Precondition 2: *Efficient initial business infrastructure.* This is what you built using the Foundation Building mode in the Transitional phase. It's important because you will need effective and efficient processes in this and other phases as you turn your attention to dominating a market niche.

Precondition 3: *Protection from competitors.* Important forms of protection include technological, expertise, geographic, and legal barriers, along with any other barriers to potential competitors getting on your turf. Protection may also be simply because you have a head start: others are later to the game.

You have some control over these first three preconditions and they will help you prepare for the Rapid Market Expansion phase. However, you really cannot enter Rapid Market Expansion and operate using the Producing mode unless you really have a rapidly expanding market. Thus, the fourth precondition.

Precondition 4: *Strong and stable market demand for your product.* It is important for the market demand to be strong, and predictably so. Strong, unquestioning demand will allow you to safely focus only on production and sales as a way to drive business growth without jeopardizing long-term prospects.

There are gradations of these four preconditions. The extent to which one of your products experiences strong demand will determine the level of focus advisable. You act on the first three preconditions and hope the market recognizes the compelling nature of the product and produces strong demand, which gives you the fourth. There is no guarantee that if you meet the first three preconditions the fourth will happen. But if the fourth does happen, whether through your efforts or luck, the decisions you make about how you operate to take advantage of this fortunate situation will have a huge impact on your business.

There is no guarantee that if you meet the first three preconditions the fourth will happen.

The actions you can take to make the fourth precondition happen is an important topic and is covered by many other books on marketing and marketing strategy. Of course, meeting all four of these is the dream of every business leader in the world—or at least one would assume so.

Yet some enterprises that meet all four prerequisites do not take advantage of this phase to produce high volumes, to gain market share quickly, and to put money in the bank. Instead, they operate in a manner that fits what they did prior to getting to this fortunate place. They do not operate in a manner that takes advantage of the business opportunities available to them now.

Helping you take see this opportunity is the purpose of this chapter. Let's take a look at the defining characteristics of this phase of growth and its most effective operational mode. This will help you visualize what you might be building for in the Foundation Building phase and, if you enter this phase, how you should operate to make the most of this situation.

Rapid Market Expansion

Five, four, three, two, one, blast off! You developed a breakthrough product in the first phase. You constructed your launch pad and set your sights on the moon in the second phase. This is the point where you can ignite all rockets.

During this phase, you will not have time to think deep thoughts or experiment with new paths. The course has been set and you must make the most of the situation. Focus and speed will be distinct competitive advantages in this growth phase—and to your long-term success as well.

Vic Puts the Pedal to the Metal

"OK, everyone," says Vic in a loud voice to get the attention of all the people gathered in the warehouse. "Our objectives for the next six months are to increase sales of the standard 3000s by 100 percent and to reduce warrantee repairs by 90 percent."

Cody, a Decisive Commander and the newly appointed head of sales, is ecstatic. She has a product. She has a story. She has a list of prospects. She's on the road.

Vic and Cody are a great team. They both relish meeting prospects and making the sale, but they differ on two important strategic questions. The first is how much customization and servicing to do for customers. The second is how long to keep new sales the dominant business priority.

Customization comes naturally to Vic. His discussions with prospects often become blue-sky sessions during which he and the prospect leapfrog each other's ideas to create magnificent variations on the original. Everywhere Vic looks, he sees opportunities for valuable new features. More importantly, Vic can easily see the technical possibilities for solving customers' problems. He keeps mental notes of all the features that he and prospects talk about.

Vic also remembers with considerable angst, however, his earlier attempt to grow by marketing dozens of versions of Model 2000. Although it was readily accepted in the market, it was a nightmare to design, build, sell, and service all the different versions. Overall, the 2000 fell short of what they could have done in design, production, and sales because the company had spread itself too thin. It was and still is a small company. With the 2000, quality and reliability fell—as did customer satisfaction.

Cody sees the blue-sky discussions as a waste of time. To her, the faster they find that a prospect doesn't want one of their current two versions of the 3000, the faster they can move on to the next. It's a numbers game: the more prospects they meet, the more they sell. To their good fortune, they've done their homework well. The slimmed-down 3000 is a hit with many customers. Ultimately, Vic defers to Cody's judgment and they avoid adding bells and whistles. Cody sets sales targets and her staff meets them—or else.

The dominance of sales as the major management priority is something that Vic contemplates a great deal. Vic also knows they're a small company competing with large companies. As such they can't be competitive by giving top attention to everything. They have to be selective and they have to select the right priorities.

While the team did a good job of developing the current production system in the Foundation Building phase, it's reaching capacity limits. Pat, the Collaborative Planner and the head of production, now has about a dozen people in his production department. Adding people increased capacity, but capacity is becoming a greater issue as time goes on. To Pat, the systems issues are top priority.

"I believe we've had enough discussion here," interjects Cody during a discussion of production issues at the weekly operating committee meeting. "We have a great product. I acknowledge that it's theoretically possible to make improvements, but they are not needed to meet our sales targets. Product quality is much better than before, primarily because we are not trying to be all things to all people. Let's just get on with it."

Vic recognizes that the nature of the weekly meetings has changed from coordinating tasks and problem solving to simply assigning sales and production targets and pushing aside any barriers to meeting those targets. It seems to him that much is being swept under the rug, but he also knows they're operating in a privileged time, with a hot product, high margins, and little direct competition.

"The priorities must be driven by the situation," Vic reflects. Pat said they could produce 20 units a day, so Vic replies, "Give me 25." Cody smiles.

With Cody's encouragement, Vic instructs Pat to make quick fixes to the current production system and to sound the alarms only when he believes that production volumes or quality are likely to drop. Quick fixes are more expensive long term, but they're now gathering customers quickly at high profit margins. While Sparrow Inc. can afford the higher cost of quick fixes, it can't afford missing the chance to place product and expand market share while doing so is relatively easy.

Vic instructs Pat to keep detailed notes of what production changes are needed but to hold off on major restructuring because the company can't afford the down time. Vic visits the production area from time to time, which he thoroughly enjoys, to make a few improvements, just as he helps Cody's team refine its discussion of the 3000's features and close sales.

This is a heady time. However, although rapid sales are exciting, to Vic, if it isn't breaking new ground, it isn't interesting. He longs for the old days.

A Land Grab

During the Concept Development phase, you were extremely aware of your customers' lives and could identify what they needed. During the Transitional phase, you inventoried all your customers' interactions with your product and company to identify the simplest, most easily mass-produced package of essential elements of the product.

During the Rapid Market Expansion phase, your opportunity is take this simplified product and put it into the hands of a large number of customers. In this phase of growth, you are essentially producing a product that stands alone in the marketplace because of its features or its fashion. Your pioneering customers of earlier phases have given way to a wider market. Now you can target one of the most attractive classes of buyer: the pragmatists.

Pragmatists are interested in making big or fundamental changes if doing so will make their lives better.

They are a large class and are eager to buy a product or service that another class of buyers (pioneers) has found to be valuable. They adopt earlier than the conservatives, who tend to be more resistant to change in general.

Pragmatists do not crave new products based on some larger vision of the future. They may even prefer change that's evolutionary rather than revolutionary. But they are interested in making big or fundamental changes if doing so will make their lives better. They seek to adopt innovations only after a record of performance has been established. References from people they trust are important. When they decide to adopt a new idea, they do so quickly and completely in order to make a clean break and to build all future efforts on the new paradigm. They prefer to buy from the perceived industry leader, not because of superior technical qualifications but because they believe the rest of the world will build to this standard and therefore make their investment more durable.

The demands of this group are more narrowly focused than are those of the pioneers you targeted in the Concept Development phase. The larger size of this customer group and its lesser need for customization enable you to focus on a narrow range of products or services and still experience rapid growth. This is the time to gain market share before competitors become fully aware of the business potential of your product or service. It is a time to build a solid revenue stream to support future efforts.

Not all companies have access to a marketplace fitting this description. Service companies experience this least frequently and it is typically for shorter periods of time. The customers of service companies tend to demand more product variation and the barriers to entry for new competitors are relatively low.

Success in this phase depends on the speed at which the product or service is put into the marketplace and how quickly production can meet demand. The more extreme version of this phase is a hyper-expanding market; it corresponds to the "tornado" in Geoffrey Moore's sequence of marketing strategies.[1] Just as one never knows exactly when or where a tornado will touch down, you can't know if or when you'll experience a market expanding so rapidly that only sales and production matter. Nor can you determine when the tornado will stop. But all of us do know that tornados eventually dissipate and die—and we know that success will attract competitors. When your initial production capabilities are straining and competitors are becoming active, it's time for your firm to move on to the next phase.

The customers of service companies tend to demand more product variation and the barriers to entry for new competitors are relatively low.

The Naturally Effective Management Style for Rapid Market Expansion: Decisive Commander

The style of management most effective in the Rapid Market Expansion phase is that of a Decisive Commander. This leader's natural interest is in specific objectives and in getting the job done. He or she quickly assesses the situation and prefers to act immediately. This leader values specific task-oriented objectives and crossing those objectives off "to-do" lists when complete. The attributes that look successful to a Decisive Commander are getting things done quickly, doing something or seeing some action, making a quick decision, and accomplishing tasks.

The limitation of this management style is a tendency to place a low priority on detailed long-term planning. The focus is on the here and now. His or her orientation is to see things in black and white; understanding a complex and varied set of future possibilities does not receive high priority.

1. Geoffrey A. Moore, *Inside the Tornado* (HarperBusiness, 1995).

The Decisive Commander models effective leadership for this phase because of his or her interest in speed, the here and now, and specific task-oriented objectives.

The Producing Operational Mode

In the Producing mode, objectives are fairly clear and simple: expand in the market, set objectives for employees, and monitor results. You should continue to keep the product as simple as possible and avoid the temptation to enhance it. You were attentive to what customers wanted in the first two phases; you should now listen less. The priority is on getting new business and reducing errors in your company's basic production process. These themes are typical themes of Producing organizations:

▶ Keep it simple.

▶ Do it.

▶ Don't fix it if it isn't broken.

Even if there's no competition right now, if you're truly good, believe me—it's coming.

The offering of a Producing organization contains all the essential elements of the innovation but is not highly differentiated for various market segments or customers. Customization is minimal. When Henry Ford was in this operational mode, he said that people buying his cars could have any color they wanted as long as it was black. His focus was on getting the product out and selling to more people than anyone else. Even if there's no competition right now, if you're truly good, it will come.

By keeping the product simple, you can indeed increase volume and productivity as well as improve product quality. High volume and repetitive cycles of work are a shakedown for your enterprise. Right now, you're typically using the first-generation production systems developed during your Transitional phase. With high volumes, the inevitable weaknesses of your systems will be exposed.

Controlling a Producing Organization

The most important control levers in the Producing mode are "Direct Supervision by the Leader" and "Formal Feedback and Evaluation Disciplines." The control levers chart (Table 6-1) illustrates the relative importance (weight) of each in controlling the organization.

The direct supervision of the leader in endorsing objectives for success

Phase	Concept Development	First Transition	Rapid Market Expansion
Operational Mode	*Innovating*	*Foundation Building*	*Producing*
Control Lever Settings	**Relative Weight, %**		
Supervision	60%	20%	30%
Business Vision	25	10	5
Cultural Priorities	5	10	10
Organizational Hierarchy	0	20	15
Formal Plans and Processes	0	20	15
Expertise of Team Members	10	10	5
Formal Feedback and Evaluation	0	10	20
Total Control	100%	100%	100%

Table 6-1. Control levers

makes a comeback in the Producing mode. Explicit objectives are set and successful performance is expected. While this type of business practice seems so obvious that it is unremarkable, it does represent an important departure from what has been appropriate in the past. Objectives in the Innovating mode are broad and flexible (e.g., an entirely new way of doing things, initial validation of a product or business concept). In the Foundation Building mode they are qualitative (e.g., agreement among the informed about a course of action, determining the right processes).

In the Producing mode, specific objectives are needed.

In the Producing mode, specific objectives are needed. These might be "sales of 20,000 units by June" or "production of 45 machines by December." Many leaders and organizations find it difficult to make this change to specific and objective targets. Keep in mind that the objectives should be SMART (specific, measurable, actionable, realistic, and targeted). The feedback and evaluation system initiated during Foundation Building should promote these attributes of good objectives and they will be used extensively.

The image of control levers suggests that if control is to remain always at 100 percent and some levers have become more important, others must become less important to compensate. Indeed, the control levers of

"Organizational Hierarchy" and "Formal Plans and Processes" are less important than in the Foundation Building mode and are weighted more lightly.

In the Producing mode, "Organizational Hierarchy" has less impact on controlling the organization than it did in the Transitional phase. Please note that, in order to highlight the shifting control mechanisms from mode to mode, I have treated "Direct Supervision by the Leader" and "Organizational Hierarchy" as separate control levers. Clearly, they are connected. But I'd like to display clearly the control exerted by the organizational hierarchy outside of the personal interaction of the leader. In addition, "Supervision" and "Organizational Hierarchy" as control levers are developed separately and one can exist without the other.

In the Producing mode, other members of the leadership team tend to have less impact on how the enterprise operates than in the Foundation Building mode. This is due in large measure to the narrow focus on sales and production. The heads of other department act in support of these functions. The effective organizational structure of the Producing mode can be characterized as a "platoon of implementers." Based on the general structure developed in the Transitional phase, members are added incrementally as the enterprise grows.

Because objectives are fairly simple and stable over time, there is little need for an extensive middle management function. The organization is flat: there are few levels of hierarchy and the senior people have many people reporting to them. A typical organization chart for this mode is shown in the diagram below, with implementers indicated as triangles.

The leader formally supervises a relatively large number of staff, often over ten people, and has informal but direct influence over many others.

In the Producing mode, "Organizational Hierarchy" has less impact on controlling the organization than it did in the Transitional phase.

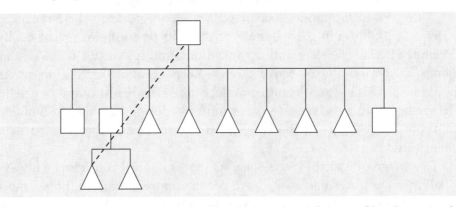

Figure 6-1. Producing mode: organizational hierarchy—"platoon of implementers"

Compared with prior modes of operation, there is more of a one-way flow of information from the leader to the staff. This information usually consists of basic instructions about the tasks that must be accomplished. Leaders operating in the Producing mode will go around any mid-level staff directly to the line staff to see the action firsthand. This informal linkage is illustrated by the dotted line in the diagram.

The Quick Fix

When production problems are exposed in a Producing mode, fix them quickly, even temporarily, and resume production as soon as you can. If it's possible to differentiate between an effective quick fix and a fundamental solution, favor the quick fix. The deeper, more fundamental fixes and improvements should be designed into your systems during the next Transitional phase. Growth covers up many mistakes. If you stop production for a long time to implement a fundamental solution, you will miss sales and the opportunity for a larger market share. In the more crowded marketplace that is sure to follow, you'll appreciate the larger market share you gained here.

When production problems are exposed in a Producing mode, fix them quickly, even temporarily, and resume production as soon as you can.

When you operate in a market that has a strong demand for your product, extensive long-term planning is not a high priority, because it will not pay off as in other situations. The resources devoted to developing formal alternative plans will, in many cases, distract from your priority of generating more sales in increasing production.

Interestingly, business vision and the team members' expertise have less impact during this operational mode. Any sense of a "noble cause" embodied in the business vision is dwarfed by an interest in short-term gains in market share and revenue. Staff members' autonomy is reduced as the multiple objectives and developmental projects associated with earlier periods are pushed aside: everyone must focus on a few very specific sales-oriented objectives. Those who thrive on major projects and initiatives or an all-for-one atmosphere find this phase unpleasant. The business has lost its soul, many will say—it has sold out its noble causes. But this too is a phase.

The atmosphere of the firm at this point brings to mind a classic cartoon, a personal favorite. The main character is driving an old jalopy with his partner at his side. A villain is chasing them and they need to go faster in order to escape. Our hero looks down at the speedometer and notices that the needle shows that the car has reached its top speed: 40 mph. In a stroke of brilliance that saves the day, he breaks the glass cover of the speedometer and writes 45, 50, and 55 on the speedometer. He then moves the needle to those higher numbers, making the car go faster, and they make their escape.

When Foundation Building Didn't Happen

There are several errors common to this phase of growth. The first occurs when a company attempts the Rapid Market Expansion phase without an initial business infrastructure. Basically, the enterprise skips the Transitional phase and has few systems and procedures to help it ramp up production. Work processes follow the patterns set in Concept Development and cannot support the higher production volume. The glass cover of the speedometer is removed to make the machine go faster, but the machine is already going faster than its safe operating speed.

This mistake is usually made by Decisive Visionaries with a very strong Decisive component in their management style. They want the speed and focus, but have, for the reasons described in Chapter 3, little or no affinity for the Foundation Building processes required in transitional phases. They start the enterprise effectively, but skip Foundation Building in their interest in getting on to the Producing mode. By skipping the important Transitional phase, they are unprepared for the Rapid Market Expansion phase, regardless of how well the Producing mode fits their personal preferences. Here's an example.

Leaving the Door Open—to the Competition

Red Hawk Bioscience, a Miami biotech firm, created an affordable and effective breakthrough approach to drug delivery. The treatment is novel in how it is delivered (through the nasal passages) and is protected by patents. The company's brand was enhanced by the academic research supporting this technology. It had done the scientific work and developed the innovation, but failed to accurately read the market. The CEO was a Decisive Commander and slipped quite naturally into the Producing mode.

Unfortunately, the transition to the Producing mode came so naturally that they essentially skipped the Foundation Building mode. The Decisive Commander's intense personal supervision of all activities—and an office manager who never slept—kept the processes moving.

But this left the company unprepared for Rapid Market Expansion. Because of Red Hawk's poor accounting systems, management was unable to understand the costs of selling and supporting their products. They were also unable to analyze current customers' buying patterns. They were late in doing objective market research that would have helped position the company better in key market segments.

Part of the problem was inadequate financing in the earlier stages. Those resources could have helped the company build a stronger infrastructure in areas like accounting and market research. But the clear lack of business processes and objective data about the marketplace limited their ability to interest investors.

New staff hired to help never worked out because few processes were rational and transparent. Instead of addressing these issues early on, when they could have been resolved more quickly and cheaply, management delayed.

Their innovative products sparked a Rapidly Expanding Market, even a hyper-expanding market. While watching this market grow at top speed, they were unable to determine how to position their product in that segment. They had no information to guide a decision about which of their current products and channels they should abandon to free up resources for the newer innovation that was obviously expanding.

Red Hawk was unable to take full advantage of the rapidly expanding market segments it helped launch. Competitors took advantage of the firm's research and product characteristics and copied the product and the message. Red Hawk didn't benefit from the expanded market as much as its competitors did.

Failing to Focus

A second common error is one of the great ironies of new ventures, one we've encountered repeatedly over the years: *enterprises that have the greatest opportunity to benefit from a focused effort on a single product are the least inclined to do so.* The more commercially compelling your innovative breakthrough from the Concept Development phase, the greater your opportunity will be in the Rapid Market Expansion phase. However, the more a company is able to create a breakthrough in Concept Development, the more it typically wants to do it again.

Stated in management style terms, the greater the Visionary component of the Decisive Visionary management style a leader has, the more potential there is for him or her to ignite a true breakthrough—and the *less* likely he or she will be focused on capitalizing on it. Simply, Creative Visionaries want to create.

Enterprises that have a truly breakthrough innovation and meet the four preconditions discussed earlier are often the ones least interested in the

Stated in management style terms, the greater the Visionary component of the Decisive Visionary management style a leader has, the more potential there is for him or her to ignite a true breakthrough.

113

Producing mode of operation. Rather than taking advantage of the opportunity to focus on expanding market presence in a controlled and forceful manner, they continue to place a high priority on adding bells and whistles to existing products, developing new products, and coming up with the next breakthrough.

An example of this idea is PARC—the Palo Alto Research Center. Many of the most notable technological innovations that made fortunes in the personal computer business were not developed by the firms commonly associated with them. The graphical computer interface now associated with Microsoft Windows was patterned after the Apple operating system, which offered it years earlier. But Apple did not create that concept. PARC, a subsidiary of Xerox Corporation, did the Concept Development phase of that technology. PARC also pioneered the mouse and other technologies that were then made famous by other firms. PARC is an Innovating organization; that is what it does.

PARC's mission is to innovate and license the innovations to others for development and sales. Thus, its avoidance of the Producing mode and foregoing Rapid Market Expansion for its great ideas is consistent with its goals. Yet there are many enterprises that attempt to cover all growth phases. So it is important to understand the opportunity that is forgone by skipping Rapid Market Expansion in order to make the decision that is right for your enterprise.

Irony begets tragedy when much of the business growth prompted by an innovation that accrues during this phase doesn't go to the enterprise that developed it, but goes instead to the enterprise that adopts or imitates it and operates effectively in a Producing mode. The race goes to the swift.

A Better Mousetrap—But Not a Better Game Plan

A Seattle-based manufacturing company developed a fuel pump for the aerospace industry that was recognized as the best designed and most rugged in its class. The company had built a better mousetrap, but the world was not beating a path to its door. The firm's leadership knew of this problem and considered it important, but most of management time was spent developing new products.

Despite the company's great reputation, sales of the fuel pump were not as high as those achieved by its competitors. A competing firm not noted for innovation had emulated the functions of the pump and aggressively marketed and supported its product in the marketplace. Soon the competing pump dominated the market.

The leaders of the Seattle firm felt the market had been taken from them. But, in fact, they had failed to take it when they had the chance. They chose to diversify to other innovative products rather than focus on growing a narrow product line. Their products in general were viewed as innovative but more costly. While no formal decision was made, personal interests and the desire to repeat past successes dominated this company's strategy. Despite its innovative success, it never achieved the business success justified by its innovations or management's expectations. Ultimately, growth leveled off.

While riding the success of early innovations, innovative leaders enjoy the exhilaration of monetary rewards for creative innovation and want to keep doing more of it. Any hint that efforts should begin to focus is met with scorn. The party line is "We are an entrepreneurial company; we are going to keep innovating. Don't mess with success." As a result, the enterprise devotes its energies to developing a broader and broader product line.

Not only do the leaders of the enterprise recoil, but also the younger members have a stake in maintaining "the entrepreneurial spirit" with respect to product development. They see the success and rewards going to the more senior members of the enterprise for their new product development efforts and want the same. "It's our culture and heritage," they say.

Assessing Where You Are

Given the volatile nature of the markets for new ventures, it's sometimes not possible to accurately select the narrow set of products or services on which to focus. While in the Foundation Building mode, you should assess your product objectively and identify the "bowling pin" cluster of market segments that will benefit most from your innovation. Identify more than one in order to diversify your risk, but make sure the selection of multiple products and market niches is driven by a business need rather than solely a cultural bias or personal preference for doing things right.

The greater the number of products needed to reduce business risk to a reasonable level, the less likely you are actually in a Rapid Market Expansion phase. If a number of products are needed to maintain a reasonable level of business risk, consider a Planning or Adapting mode. Begin to work them. If you find that one of these segments begins to grow very rapidly, give it more exclusive focus—possibly shifting to the Producing mode.

Also while assessing your situation in the Transitional phase, carefully inventory the barriers that protect you from competition. Is the opportunity

While in the Foundation Building mode, you should assess your product objectively and identify the "bowling pin" cluster of market segments that will benefit most from your innovation.

115

there just because you were there first? Are there technological, expertise, or other barriers that protect you? Get some objective advice on these. Monitor these barriers systematically—and be ready for a more complex and volatile world when they're breached.

But carefully consider the focus of the Producing operational mode. Even if experienced for a short period, this operational mode introduces a more focused and sales-oriented perspective into the culture and structure of the enterprise that will be a benefit downstream.

Limitations of the Producing Approach

The Decisive Commander management style is a good model for effective leadership during this phase, but the limitations of this style foreshadow the inherent weakness of the Producing mode—poorly developed long-term plans and poorly developed complex systems and processes. Those who excel in this phase tend to assume it will last forever, that the future will be like the present. Yet, success in this phase will attract competitors just as the blood of a fresh kill attracts sharks, which then swarm the prey. Your business environment will become much more unpredictable and complex when the barriers of technological innovation or intellectual capital are lowered or there are changes in what's considered "hot" and other companies start to crowd onto your turf.

In the world of investment management, we've worked with Decisive Commanders who were very successful investors. Just as I describe here, they look at the facts (preferably numerical facts) and make decisions quickly. These decision makers tend to look for tactical investment opportunities rather than long-term strategic ones. Their investment philosophies are more instinctive than formal and developed. They look for specific characteristics when evaluating an investment and move quickly through the evaluation process.

Again, some very strong individual investors have this style, but the drawback here is that these leaders' investment principles and processes tend to be instinctive rather than process-oriented. They find that it is difficult to incorporate other professionals meaningfully into their investment processes. Thus, investment approaches built on the views of a Decisive Commander tend to have difficulty scaling up to accommodate more decision makers and supporting more products. If these leaders begin to manage broader-based investment portfolios, more people, or several different products, their effectiveness and success drop rapidly. Care must be taken to maintain a sharp focus while the thrust of the investment activities is based on the views of a Decisive Commander.

This element of success in investment management has implications for other businesses as they attempt to ramp up production of an innovation. Success in the focused environment well suited to the Decisive Commander does not always foreshadow success in more complex situations.

Responding to Changes in Your Market

You should expect the Rapid Market Expansion phase to end and you should be prepared for it. Trees do not grow to the sky. The key indicator that it's time to move on to the next phase is when multiple competitors begin to grab market share despite your focus on sales. Your situation becomes much more complex and unpredictable, a new phase for which the Producing mode of operation is not suited.

You should expect the Rapid Market Expansion phase to end and you should be prepared for it.

Of course, to de-emphasize the expansion of your market too soon is to give up market share, perhaps permanently. To make the shift too late puts you at a disadvantage because competitors have already defined the basis on which they will compete with you. They will begin to define the variations and differentiated product lines that become important in the Crowded Marketplace phase.

The lack of an immediate need for formal planning can be deceptive. Commercial success without elaborate plans and procedures during this growth phase sometimes lulls an enterprise's leaders into thinking that it is solely their genius that got them there and not the whims of the market. They erroneously conclude that they don't need formal plans. They fail to realize that they were operating in a privileged situation and that when the situation changes, they too will need to plan.

The sequence of phases that follows the Rapid Market Expansion phase depends on the nature of the market opportunity. The work that must be done to assess those market opportunities systematically and objectively fits best with the Foundation Building operational mode. Returning to our Mario Andretti analogy, it's time to shift gears.

Since we have already experienced the first transition and have built the basic infrastructure, the subsequent transitional periods are targeted to retooling the enterprise for the next phase of growth. The next transitional phase need not take long, but it requires the Foundation Building mode to be most effective and expeditious. You should adopt this mode and assess your circumstances to make the best strategic decisions regarding your developmental path. Subsequent chapters will discuss these phases; what follows is just a quick preview.

The Shift to Niche Development

Many software and service companies shift directly from the Rapid Market Expansion phase to the Niche Development phase. They must move quickly from being the only producer in their field to being one of many competitors trying to retain market share. To continue growing, they must develop the ability for mass customization. They provide customers or groups of customers with unique solutions to their problems and they increase or maintain their profit margins. This business environment is complex, it differs from niche to niche, and it changes relatively quickly.

The Shift to Crowded Marketplace

Enterprises that have a strong manufacturing or production component often find the next battlefield is on price and functional efficiency. For these, the shift is from Rapid Market Expansion to Crowded Marketplace. Growth is achieved by turning out high volumes of standardized products that embody commercially attractive features and are sold at competitive prices. Efficiency and specialized expertise in marketing, manufacturing, and so forth are needed to achieve growth in this way. The business environment of this phase is complex—many different issues must be handled effectively and in a coordinated way—but stable. The environment is stable enough to justify developing elaborate plans for contending with these complexities.

Phase of Growth—Summary Table

Phase of Growth	Rapid Market Expansion
Goals	• Expand market presence faster than anyone else

Mode of Operation	Producing (modeled by Decisive Commander)
Preconditions	▪ Viable business concept ▪ Efficient initial business infrastructure ▪ Market demand that is stable enough that simple task instructions give members sufficient guidance ▪ Protection from competitors, such as technological, financial, legal, and other barriers to market access
Control Lever Settings	Relative Weight, %
Supervision	30%
Business Vision	5
Cultural Priorities	10
Organizational Hierarchy	15
Formal Plans and Processes	15
Expertise of Team Members	5
Formal Feedback and Evaluation	20
Total Control	100%
Organizational Structure	▪ Platoon of implementers
Cultural Priorities	▪ Narrow focus on production and following instructions
Product Strategy	▪ Commoditized version of innovation offered to customers willing to pay premium prices
Inherent Weaknesses	▪ Poor long-term planning; few contingencies in place for when protection from competitors ceases
Beneficial Legacies	▪ Focused production, sales and production power

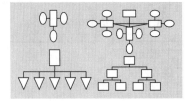

Chapter 7

Crowded
Marketplace

YOU HAVE AN INNOVATIVE PRODUCT AND AN EFFICIENT INITIAL BUSI-
ness infrastructure and you have focused to make the most of a
rapidly expanding market. Now it's time to step back a bit from
pushing these frontiers and fortify your position. The Crowded
Marketplace phase is about efficiency, reliability, and scale.
Your potential customers in this phase, the *conservatives*, know about the
product you're selling, even if they're not aware of you and your company.
They will compare your product with those of competing enterprises, looking for the best features and value.

The conservatives are a customer group that tends to be more pessimistic
about achieving significant benefit from a new product or service; they will
buy only after the trend toward its use is clear and well established. This is
a large group and competition for their spending can be intense. If they
become customers, they become lasting customers. They are price-sensitive,
skeptical, and demanding on issues of quality and reliability. They will consider competing products carefully. Although conservatives tend to have
complex needs, their interest in going with established practices means their
demands are more predictable than those of groups encountered before
them—the pioneers and the pragmatists.

The business opportunity is immense and long-lasting, but challenging.

Competition is strong and the conservatives' insistence that your innovation fit in seamlessly with their lives presents many challenges to overcome. However, because their demands are usually stable over time, your investment in meeting their needs can pay off over the long run.

Vic Adjusts

"Copycats! There's nothing original there."

"Parrot Products is nothing but a bunch of cloners."

Vic got the picture. It had taken special insight for him to create the idea, develop it, and begin to dominate the market. But any business with a healthy profit margin is bound to attract competition. Sure, he had blazed the trail, but that just made it easier for others to follow in his path. Vic still has some key advantages: nobody understands the concept the way his team does, they have the edge in quality, and they still own the brand.

The battleground is on price. The new competitors are selling a product essentially the same as the Model 3000 for 20 percent less. They got this advantage because they could take a fresh look at the product and how it was produced—and they didn't have to invest in development. Luckily, Vic has market share and money in the bank. He can afford to meet prices and build a new plant at the same time.

The new plant will have greater efficiency and capacity than the current production facilities. They'll finally be able to iron out some of the production problems that had bothered Pat for some time and to offer more variations of the 3000.

Cody is focusing her efforts on building market share. But selling has changed. It's tough for her team to shift their pitch from simply presenting the 3000 and taking orders to describing its features and benefits—and how these compare with competing products. The biggest hurdle is that the sales reps have never been in the habit of asking prospects about their needs and wants. This new dialogue is difficult.

Vic is placing a high priority on operational efficiency. He's developed a broad framework for how all the processes of various departments are coordinated and combined. He's finally been able to delegate complete authority to Cody, Pat, and others for their respective areas.

Formal planning is crucial. Sparrow's operations are going to be much more complex and the new plant will be very expensive to build; they must build it right. Planning includes defining future business objectives, assessing progress, and dividing work among the various internal manufacturing functions and external subcontractors. Everything has to be planned out in advance to make sure that manufacturing produces a product that meets customer demands.

The weekly operations meetings have changed yet again. Much less time is spent on sales and production targets and more on long-term planning. Many issues are handled within the various departments, outside the weekly meeting. Any problem that doesn't clearly affect other groups is discussed within that functional group, not at the higher level. Each group has a set of specific responsibilities for current production and sales and for increasing capacity. Vic has to be very careful to avoid giving direction without first confirming that the direction is consistent with the plans.

In some ways, Cody and Pat are at risk. Both have grown with the company, but they lack the specialized training and experience with other companies that would enable them to provide the depth needed in their functional areas. Ultimately, although the company's recent success has been due to Pat's and Cody's efforts, Vic realizes that they're not fully prepared to lead their groups in the future. Higher-level skills are needed. Vic decides to hire people with stronger experience in manufacturing, finance, and management. Fortunately, business is unfolding as planned and, as members of the founding team, Pat and Cody are rewarded for their contributions. Vic also realizes that this, too, is a phase and that their expertise will be highly valued later on.

The operating committee decides to offer three standard variations of their core product: Models 3001, 3002, and 3003. These will serve the bulk of the demand in major market segments. With their gains in production efficiency, they can compete with any firm.

Complex but Stable

The demand for your product is more stable than you experienced in the Concept Development phase. What you offer is acceptable to a large class of buyers. All of this sounds good, but the large market and stable demand usually mean that you have significant competition, unlike what you experienced in the Rapid Market Expansion phase. Your world is made much more complex by competitors, different distribution channels, and the need for well-developed business functions.

The upside of this situation is that there is some predictability in your business environment. Because of its stability, you can ultimately understand and accommodate its complexities in how you operate. You can determine what is required to excel. Successful growth will depend on how well you can plan and coordinate construction and how well all the pieces will fit together. You are now in the Crowded Marketplace phase of growth.

The automobile industry and other manufacturing-oriented industries are classic examples of this type of environment. But it's not limited to manufacturing companies. Many service companies exist entirely or partially in a similar "complex but stable" environment.

The Crowded Marketplace phase is the business environment where a multitude of enterprises find themselves—at least for while. It is often a natural consequence of business competition.

But you should verify that you are meeting or can meet the preconditions for success before investing in a Planning operational mode. There are four basic preconditions for this phase of growth.

Precondition 1: *A commercially viable product or products.* These products need not be wildly innovative, but just offer attractive features at competitive prices.

Precondition 2: *Presence in or access to a sufficiently stable and predictable business environment that will allow for extensive use of defined structures and processes.* This precondition is a key element in defining this phase. For the necessary investments in formal and systematic processes to pay off, stability is required. The more stable the environment, the longer the useful lives that the structures and processes will have. If stability is insufficient to justify your investments in structures and processes, then this growth phase is not right for you.

Of course, determining "sufficient stability" is difficult; it's a function of both the external environment and your enterprise's ability to efficiently create effective systems. The concept to keep in mind is that if you can develop cost-effective structures and processes that can effectively handle the dynamics of the environment, you probably have sufficient stability.

It's important to assess your circumstances accurately. Let me give you an illustration.

When I started interviewing management teams about 20 years ago, I always asked leaders about their decision-making environment. Everyone I asked—and even those I didn't—said something like "I operate in a rapidly changing environment and I'm doing a great job of managing my way through it." I stopped asking this question after about five years. Then, not so long ago, I met with the head of a management team who said, "Our situation is really quite stable." *He was the only person in two decades who had volunteered this answer.*

Yet as we have worked with many different management teams over the years, it's clear that some of them are dealing with situations that are more volatile than others. The question is, can they anticipate largely what they'll need to do to be successful in, say, 18 months? Many firms operate in cir-

The Crowded Marketplace phase is the business environment where a multitude of enterprises find themselves—at least for while. It is often a natural consequence of business competition.

cumstances where this is largely possible. In other words, some environments are inherently more complex than others.

Precondition 3: *Operational practices that can remain—or will become effective when they're institutionalized in formal rules.* Rules can refer to systems, plans, and processes—or any rule-based way for making decisions and guiding actions. Some enterprises have key practices that do not lend themselves to becoming formal processes. Recall that I made a similar point about the formalization of processes in the Transitional phase.

In some ways, this phase of growth is a continuation of the same practices and priorities that were appropriate when you originally rationalized your initial informal work processes. The key difference is that the Transitional phase focused on rationalizing the processes developed in an earlier trial-and-error Innovating mode and on building an initial internal infrastructure. That period did *not* produce growth or business momentum. The Crowded Marketplace phase does produce growth and increase business momentum because of its focus on designing and building new structures and processes for the main operational practices that will drive that growth. You do this to be more competitive in a competitive marketplace.

Precondition 4: *You have personnel with appropriate technical expertise in specialized areas.* You will need staff who can learn and ultimately master the various elements and sub-elements of your operational processes. For many enterprises, this precondition will not be a challenge; many have access to a large number of people who can readily become effective. For others, this will be a challenge because what they design as the elements and sub-elements of the process may not be suitable for the people available.

If you meet these preconditions, you can enter the Crowded Marketplace phase and hone your operations in a competitive environment.

Developmental Goals

If you meet these preconditions, you can enter the Crowded Marketplace phase and hone your operations in a competitive environment. Your enterprise will grow during this phase by mastering the major business functions of marketing, manufacturing, sales, and whatever else is required for your business—and by your ability to be very efficient and effective in bringing all the functions together. These are the developmental goals of this phase of growth:

▶ Integration of your business with the rest of the business world
▶ Functional efficiency at high volumes

▶ Leveraging high-expertise people across a larger base of people with less expertise

Naturally Effective Management Style for Crowded Marketplace: Analytic Planner

Improving the quality and lowering the average cost of each function require a planning orientation, which is why the Analytic Planner is most effective during this phase. Planning-oriented individuals like to gather information and analyze it carefully before making decisions. They make decisions based on the information analyzed and they value precision and reliability. This approach allows these leaders to consider a large number of variables in decision making. Analytic Planners like formal structures with clear accountabilities and responsibilities. They like to make the trains run on time.

The Analytic Planner is biased toward working with the tasks and the technical sides of issues, as opposed to considering the human side or looking at a situation holistically. Attributes that look and feel successful to Analytic Planners are long and detailed reports, consistent execution of plans and procedures, and following disciplines.

The downside of this style is "analysis paralysis," an endless cycle of collecting and analyzing information before making a decision. Analytic Planners also tend to see the world in terms of tasks and technical issues and underweight the human element and a holistic perspective when developing plans and making decisions.

The qualities of the Analytic Planner that serve as the model for the Planning mode are analytical depth and rigor, a focus on solving complex problems, and determining a course of action *after* the facts have been analyzed.

The qualities of the Analytic Planner that serve as the model for the Planning mode are analytical depth and rigor ....

The Planning Mode of Operation

Planning organizations excel at bringing together a wide range of functions and creating solid solutions. Your priorities in this phase are to specialize, refine production techniques, and train staff members. You should develop greater efficiency, reliability, and scale in your firm's main functional areas, such as manufacturing, sales, and accounting. Engineer these functions to ensure that quality is high and improving while costs are decreasing. The output of these functional groups must come together in a planned and organized manner.

Typical themes of Planning organizations are:

- Measure twice, cut once.
- Let the data drive decisions.
- Select the right ruts: you'll be in them for a long time.

Be careful when making plans and strategies. The decisions you make will influence your business for a long time to come. Double-check the information on which you base decisions to make sure it is correct and right for the situation. After you've gathered reliable information and analyzed it thoroughly, base your decisions on the outcome of the analysis. But be careful about the disciplines, procedures, and practices you select. Once selected, they will color your view of the world and how you operate in it. Any inappropriate biases will be built into your practices.

Controlling a Planning Organization

Organizational hierarchy and formal rules, which include plans and processes, are important control levers in a Planning organization.

Organizational hierarchy and formal rules, which include plans and processes, are important control levers in a Planning organization. These are "hard" controls: they explicitly guide how people work and are visible in process flow charts, reporting relationships, job descriptions, and accountabilities. Consider it in a cause-and-effect framework: the structures and rules are the *cause* and the behavior and actions of the members of the enterprise are the *effect*.

The Crowded Marketplace column in the profile of control methods chart (Table 7-1) shows the relative importance of the different control methods in a Planning organization.

"Formal Plans and Processes" shows the greatest increase in importance from the Rapid Market Expansion phase; "Supervision" as a form of control shows the greatest decrease in emphasis.

One of the hallmarks of this phase is that individuals and departments need to perform as expected; otherwise, the whole system will not. Deviation from expectations is not valued in the organization's culture.

Your task is to formally define the actions you expect and then to design the plans and processes to produce the desired actions. During the earlier phases, new activities were developed using a trial-and-error method. Now many of these activities have become routine. You must refine the methods and develop systems and processes to handle the complexities of the business that have become routine. The efforts of each individual must fit with

Phase	Concept Development	First Transition	Rapid Market Expansion	Crowded Marketplace
Operational Mode	*Innovating*	*Foundation Building*	*Producing*	*Planning*
Control Lever Settings	Relative Weight, %			
Supervision	60	20	30	5
Business Vision	25	10	5	5
Cultural Priorities	5	10	10	15
Organizational Hierarchy	0	20	15	25
Formal Plans and Processes	0	20	15	30
Expertise of Team Members	10	10	5	10
Formal Feedback and Evaluation	0	10	20	10
Total Control	100	100	100	100

Table 7-1. Control levers

those of others within his or her department; the same is true among different areas of the company. If this fit isn't achieved and maintained, your larger goals may be jeopardized. In this way you design reliability into your process. It is often worth the effort to do painstaking research to determine the right patterns and processes: *measure twice, cut once.*

A Hierarchy of Functional Groups—The Strength Is in the Structure

The structure of a Planning organization is, to no surprise, a "hierarchy of functional groups." In this formal hierarchy, reporting relationships and responsibilities are clear and stable. Departments are often formed along the lines of whichever functions require the greatest degree of leverage, such as marketing, manufacturing, or accounting. By organizing around functional areas, the expertise of a small number of staff can be leveraged and used to train other staff. This structure is indicated in the diagram on the next page.

Decision making is highly structured. Big decisions or projects are separated into smaller decisions, again usually along functional lines. The decisions about how to build a factory, for example, may be divided into components addressed by a group of specialists with expertise in related areas; their output would come together according to an integrated plan.

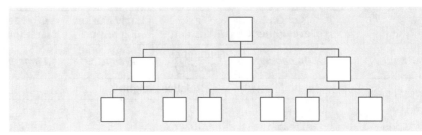

Committees and coordinating groups are important in bringing together the various views and talents of different departments when an integrated decision—one that cuts across departments—must be made. Expertise can be leveraged from a small group of individuals to many more. The enterprise typically has limited specialized expertise in certain areas; when market demands are stable, a hierarchy of functional groups can be effective in leveraging this expertise. This gives the enterprise's key functions new scale and efficiency.

Training becomes important. You may need skills that are unique to your firm and you may be unable to hire staff with extensive relevant experience. You may also need to hire people who have the needed expertise from bigger companies. By organizing your firm along functional lines that are common in your industry, you have a better chance of finding people with previous experience relevant to your needs who can be effective quickly.

In this phase of growth, the broad functional departments are usually not the place to create wildly innovative structures or work practices that are not important to your innovative edge. If you structure by functional definitions for your industry, this can give you access to new staff already trained in relevant functions and facilitate training the staff. All of these can efficiently accelerate growth. But don't entirely stifle that creative and innovative edge increase capacity. You will need it later on.

Taken together, these two control levers, "Formal Plans and Processes" and "Organizational Hierarchy," provide over half of the control of a planning organization. They form the blueprint for how all the pieces need to come together to create the whole. Any change in the dimensions of one piece directly affects the others. Indeed, the purpose of the enterprise is apparent in this blueprint. Manufacturing does manufacturing. Marketing does marketing. The interaction of these two functional groups can and should be defined as a specific set of inputs and outputs of specific dimensions and quality.

*B*y organizing your firm along functional lines that are common in your industry, you have a better chance of finding people with previous experience relevant to your needs who can be effective quickly.

128

Cultural Controls—Often Underdeveloped

The informal priorities embedded in the enterprise's culture have a greater impact in this operational mode than is required in earlier phases. The design of the structure and rules is important, but the culture of the organization must be relatively strong and support both. Individuals within the organization should sense not only the importance of performing their different roles effectively and reliably, but also how each role integrates with all the others. This cultural glue is important, but often overlooked. Developing this sense of integration is one of the key challenges in developing an effective Planning organization.

Typically, segmentation and specialization of duties during Planning are so pervasive that it's easy for people to develop a "box-ticker" mentality. Each individual has a list of tasks to accomplish and actions to perform. People have been told that that there's cleverness in how all the jobs and tasks have been designed and come together to create a great product. When this point is widely promoted to encourage people to do what they are supposed to do and it is finally accepted, individuals tend not to think about how it all comes together in the end. When they complete a task, they check off the box corresponding to the task. When all boxes are ticked, the job is complete. Everyone sleeps well at night knowing that all pieces will fit together.

But even in very stable situations, there will always be exceptions to rules, specific elements that can't be reduced to rules and formal processes, or subtle changes that make past rules less suitable. Unfortunately, since culture is a soft control and this operational mode is guided by hard controls, culture is not considered an important control lever. Because of these understandable tendencies, it is an important cultural bias to consciously develop a "concern about the whole."

Even in very stable situations, there will always be exceptions to rules, specific elements that can't be reduced to rules and formal processes, or subtle changes that make past rules less suitable.

Performance Monitoring and Feedback—Surprisingly Less Important

Interestingly, relatively little control is driven by "Formal Feedback and Evaluation." This control involves measuring performance and providing feedback on performance to relevant groups and individuals. It seems counterintuitive that a rules-based operational mode like the Planning mode would be light on performance monitoring and feedback as a control mechanism, since it sounds like a hard control. But over the years, we have seen this time and time again. The systems exist because these organizations like to build and operate systems, but they are not used to influence operations. Evaluations are minimal.

This inconsistency is reconciled when one considers some common assumptions about Planning organizations. The key assumption is that success is planned into the blueprint. Of course, evaluation and feedback exist and are important, but in the Planning mode, most of the control is built into the plans and structure of the organization. Everyone is expected to follow the plans.

The low importance of performance monitoring and feedback as a control lever is evident when the enterprise tries to become more adaptive and grant more autonomy in the next phase of growth, which I'll discuss in the next chapter. During the current phase, however, the wise leader will develop a stronger and more flexible performance evaluation system than is currently required. It will be needed in the next growth phase.

If you've made it this far into this book, I'm sure you've caught onto a core thesis: if you know what's coming, you can lay the right groundwork and speed the transition from one growth phase to the next.

Cleverness Built into the Plan

In considering what real-world company I should use as an example of a Planning organization, what first leapt to mind was a Rust-Belt manufacturer. But this unfairly pigeonholes Planning organizations as traditional command-and-control hierarchies that many say no longer have a place in today's knowledge-based economy. It would also imply that the Planning operational mode does not apply to service companies.

Instead, I'll use an example from the investment industry to show how a Planning organization can be effective in a service business. JP Morgan Investment Management became one of the most successful investment management businesses in the world because of its highly disciplined approach to investing in U.S. stocks. Morgan's clients for this service have historically been some of the world's largest pension funds, which have entrusted Morgan with billions of dollars of assets.

In the mid-1980s, after some major setbacks, Morgan management decided to take a fresh look at how the company was conducting its investment activities. Careful research led them to conclude that if they organized their research analysts effectively and had disciplined portfolio construction practices, they would make the most of their reliable strengths and would

If you've made it this far into this book, I'm sure you've caught onto a core thesis: if you know what's coming, you can lay the right groundwork and speed the transition from one growth phase to the next.

have a good chance of producing better investment performance than their competitors.

Morgan had determined that a strong investment process could be based on the insights of analysts if they built cleverness into the system. They carefully engineered how the analysts were organized, how they worked, and how the output of their efforts came together in portfolios of stocks for clients. The traditional role of portfolio manager, which usually dominates an investment process, would be reduced and replaced by a system of portfolio construction decision rules. If the insights of the analysts were assembled carefully and effectively, these could produce competitive returns.

Morgan's new Planning-oriented approach was different from the more common approach, in which a portfolio manager, perhaps assisted by analysts, executes an investment process that largely reflects his or her personal investment philosophies and biases. If this sounds to you like an Innovating operational mode like that associated with the Concept Development phase, you're right.

Instead of having portfolio managers attempt to select stocks from the entire stock market, Morgan divided the market into about 25 economic sectors and had one analyst or small group of analysts evaluate all companies in that sector. Using essentially the same methodology across all sectors, analysts would use their insights and analytical talents to understand and assess the future prospects of each company.

Thus, through a highly engineered and proprietary stock evaluation process, each analyst ranked all stocks in his or her sector from best to worst. The analysts followed their companies closely. When their views changed, they could change the inputs to the system and re-rank the companies within their coverage area. This highly systematic process and set of disciplines produced portfolios of many securities representing all sectors. There was no second-guessing the analysts' ratings, as the analysts were closest to the information about the companies. Cleverness was designed into the overall structure.

The Morgan approach was commercially successful because:

1. It worked: it produced good returns.
2. Its design was clever and thorough.
3. It used people and systems effectively and was realistic about what each could do.
4. The power and strength of what Morgan did was easy to communicate to prospects and clients.

Morgan's investment strategy was apparent in the blueprint of its structure. This gave clients confidence that the strategy would be rigorous, disciplined, and consistent over time. It was an institutionalized approach and less sensitive to the departure of any person—a chronic concern in the investment industry, as strong individual portfolio managers often leave larger bureaucratic firms to form entrepreneurial investment shops, essentially vaulting from a Planning to an Innovating mode.

Limitations of the Planning Approach

No formal process in investment management or elsewhere is without limitations. Morgan's is no exception. In its original form, it produced basically just one type of investment portfolio. The formal structure of the approach gave it a particular fingerprint. The fingerprint was attractive to many prospects and clients, but there were some who wanted something other than what this approach produced. Thus, there were some commercial limitations.

In addition, as analysts worked in their specialized roles for a period of time, they sought to move forward in their careers and advance to the role of portfolio manager, which is generally viewed in the industry as the more senior role. The relatively large number of analysts and small number of portfolio management roles created a career bottleneck for analysts.

This was an internal stress on the system, as some analysts found they did not want to play the narrow and specific role defined by Morgan's approach for their entire careers. Also, the highly skilled portfolio managers who enjoy operating in the Innovating mode found Morgan's mode unappealing and left. Despite these limitations, Morgan's approach to investment management was very successful—and has been emulated successfully by other firms.

Other versions of a Planning organization exist in the investment industry. In some, analysts are organized like at Morgan, but a portfolio manager or committee makes the final security selection decision instead of following a set of decision rules. Typically, larger committees make decisions too slowly and are too removed from those with the information advantage—the analysts—to make effective decisions in today's dynamic stock markets.

Some investment companies that have tried this approach have succeeded while others have not. The common thread weaving though those that have been unable to make it work has been that the markets are rarely completely stable. There are always small shifts in the nature of the market that require some adjustment to the grand plans. As Planning organizations rely on designing the cleverness into the system, they tend to not accommodate these small but frequent shifts. When all the pieces of the structure come together, they don't fit as planned because the world has changed slightly. It is like building the bridge across a river, starting from both banks and planning to meet in the middle. Everything goes according to plan, but because of small seismic shifts over the construction period, the two sides of the bridge do not meet exactly in the middle as planned.

Structure and Rationality: A Must for the Toolbox

The Planning mode of operation should be in every leader's toolbox, right alongside the other operational modes. Many entrepreneurial ventures can benefit from having a large portion of the entire enterprise adopt this operational mode. Others may benefit from having just a small portion of their organization adopt this mode. This organizational type is often maligned, however—it is the bureaucratic structure. But if your business success requires it, as leader, you should be able to see that requirement and initiate developing it. And you should be proud of using it, even if it doesn't fit in with the management hype about entrepreneurial ventures.

Many entrepreneurial ventures can benefit from having a large portion of the entire enterprise adopt this operational mode.

Many successful entrepreneurial companies have this dimension. Despite this fact, I have worked with many entrepreneurial companies that avoid this mode of operation altogether. Within some of these enterprises, staff members working in areas that require structure and formal processes yearn for it desperately. For real business purposes, they need a clearer definition of their roles and responsibilities and they seek clarity and rationality in how the entire organization is structured. Yet, for a variety of reasons, some of which relate to their historical legacy, culture, and leaders' personal preferences, this clarity of structure and rules does not develop and the enterprise misses the opportunity to be more effective and targeted—and operate with greater scale.

Strengths and Weaknesses

Just as every tool in the toolbox has a specialized use, so each mode has particular strengths and weaknesses. You should have realistic expectations for each operational mode. There are some things that the Planning mode tends not to do well; one of these is creating breakthrough innovations. Recall the

Chasing Rabbits

An investment firm headquartered in South Africa had a highly successful domestic investment product. It was led by a man recognized in the South African domestic market as a "money maker." Philippe worked with a small team of research analysts and was the key decision maker. He was a highly experienced investor accustomed to analyzing a variety of industries personally; further, he was comfortable buying companies in highly cyclical sectors of the economy. His comfort with his own assessments of stocks showed in the firm's highly concentrated portfolios.

Philippe worked closely with the analysts, who would all focus their analytical efforts on a few companies he identified. When they were finished with that set, they all dropped that work in order to focus on another set of companies. While performance was sometimes extreme, it usually worked in favor of investors. Philippe's firm was comfortable marketing his track record and approach to a broad swath of investors.

The firm decided that in order to grow, it needed to go beyond domestic investing. It created and marketed an investment product that invested in international equities. Because its domestic product had been so successful, the firm tried to replicate that approach. As the original product was based on labor-intensive fundamental research, the firm hired a large number of research analysts to cover stocks outside of South Africa. They developed a very progressive research template that reflected Philippe's strong thinking—and some of the best thinking globally. The firm also promoted some of its people internally to manage the international portfolios. They reported directly to Philippe.

The firm ran into several problems in building its new international investment team. First, it was difficult to hire experienced research analysts in its home market. Many young, promising individuals left South Africa to seek their fortunes in London or New York, which were perceived as offering much greater personal opportunity. Thus, the remaining talent pool was, on average, younger and fairly inexperienced.

Second, the portfolio managers promoted internally were not of the same caliber as Philippe in terms of investment judgment and original, intuitive thinking. They were also faced with managing a much larger pool of information across more markets in an international product, and with information filtered for them by less experienced analysts.

Third, Philippe replicated the domestic investment approach and tried to work closely with the larger team of analysts, but the number of analysts needed to cover the global equity markets was simply too large to be guided in the same fashion as before. It was slow and unresponsive. Successful habits die hard and Philippe tried to light fires under the analysts to get them to move faster.

Philippe would command the analyst team to research one of his new investment ideas or themes. The team would then drop what it was doing and scamper off in a new direction. After doing this several times and producing little of value, the analysts came to refer to these new ideas as "rabbits." Philippe would release a rabbit and they'd all chase it this way and that until it finally dropped down a rabbit hole. While they chased rabbits, their training in using the new research template and building their new country-specific disciplines was put on hold. For Philippe, chasing rabbits had the look and feel of the successful actions early on, but it produced none of the successful results.

Ultimately, Philippe found himself no longer working at the "coal face" of the firm's work. In the early successful days, he was definitely the senior professional, but he was working in the coal mine right alongside the others. He saw what they saw. He could see the subtle dynamics in what was being discussed—dynamics that are not apparent in more formal and structured communications. He was part of developing the information advantage. Conversely, in the international product, he was insulated from the information of the market. He was getting everything secondhand.

Following a stretch of particularly bad investment performance, Philippe left the firm, leaving no one to pass on the judgment and experience that created its original investment success. The remaining team had critical mass in terms of research coverage, but little in the way of direction to go with it in creating top-quartile portfolios.

map of the four growth phases and five operational modes. (The Transitional phase is the fifth mode.) The Planning and Innovating modes are at opposite corners. This positioning is intended to convey that their appropriate uses are very different. Enterprises that excel at planning tend to be weak at developing breakthrough innovations. When innovative companies progress to the Crowded Marketplace phase and find success using the Planning operational mode, they sometimes—frequently unsuccessfully—attempt to develop a second breakthrough. Here's what to watch for.

The Sequel Is Not as Good as the Original

The scenario goes like this. A company's initial breakthrough product is introduced into the marketplace and proves extremely successful. The company gains significant momentum from the first burst of sales. As the product begins to mature, management decides to initiate the next major innovation as a way to rejuvenate the business.

They decide to introduce a sequel to the initial groundbreaking innovation with the hopes that their new product will rewrite the rules of the industry, just as their first one did. They believe that success is ensured: after all, the firm can now provide all the support, depth, and guidance that were lacking when the first innovation was developed on a shoestring budget.

The enterprise creates a second innovation using its current Planning operational mode. People representing the relevant disciplines form a task force or design team to develop breakthrough innovation #2. The best design work, best technology, and best of everything else the firm has to offer are brought to bear on the design process.

Inevitable design tradeoffs are made as the design team tries to get the best mix of attributes for the innovation. Yet team members, by virtue of their own experiences with innovation #1, focus only on the areas they know and they try to avoid all the mistakes they made with it.

Market research and understanding external market dynamics sometimes were not an important part of their past successes with innovation #1. (Remember: earlier on the enterprise knows more about what the market wants than the market itself.) But in attempting breakthrough #2, they want to rewrite the rules of the industry again. While all the best departmental expertise is represented, these efforts typically must contend with several barriers to success.

First, the design team is basically a committee. Committees tend to make defendable decisions that can stand up to the scrutiny of group discussions and objective analysis. These decisions often represent consensus, however, which, while perhaps not the lowest common denominator, quite often does not represent the boldest of the ideas expressed. Individuals, on the other hand, can make decisions based primarily on insight and intuition.

Second, to achieve breakthrough innovation, an individual or team must be able to deviate from the expected and accepted and to cut across (and indeed at times offend) the company's functional divisions while immersed in information relating to the innovation. Unfortunately, such far-reaching individual autonomy is not consistent with the formalized structures and practices associated with the interests of a design team or a successful Planning operational mode. The sequel, sadly, misses the target: it is notably mediocre and does not rewrite the rules of the industry. The marketplace is influenced little by its arrival.

Although many years ago, the classic example of this was Apple's introduction of the Lisa computer after its very successful Apple II computer.

Apple's Lisa

Apple hoped to repeat the staggering success of its first computer. By now, the creation of Apple is the stuff of legend. The first Apple computer was developed in a garage and serendipity played a big part in its successes.

For their second computer, Apple management decided to research target market segments and systematically profile the various needs and benefits sought by those buyers. They would then determine how to market the product effectively to each buyer segment. They planned to use an external manufacturer to develop the prototype; all final design decisions would have the full support of the organization. A skilled project manager was brought in to oversee the process and ensure that it went smoothly and efficiently. Apple allocated millions of dollars to the project to make sure that it was funded adequately. Eventually about 300 people were dedicated to the new effort.

The Lisa project was launched in 1979. Apple developed a design that met the needs of the target market segments and was approved by the firm's leaders. They developed a prototype and subjected it to the review of key staff in charge of various functions, such as production, marketing, support, and research and development. Each person reviewed the prototype against a checklist of issues that were raised by members of his or her groups. The prototype was approved with just a few changes, although some staff members expressed concerns about production costs. Some of the required manufacturing techniques were new to Apple—but the conclusion was that these details could be worked out later, during production.

More than three years later, Lisa was introduced to the market with great fanfare as the rightful successor to the original Apple computer. Market expectations were high and potential customers reviewed Lisa carefully. But after some initial excitement about the product, interest faded. What Apple believed to be revolutionary turned out to be not clearly superior to other computers in established segments. And because of the risk inherent in new technology, few programs were written for Lisa by outside developers that supported its radically new user interface. Lisa never grabbed the market; the plug was pulled after about 18 months.

In retrospect, Apple realized that Lisa embodied some very creative ideas but that the overall execution lacked the bold purity of thought characteristic of its initial computer design. The process was too complicated, too many design changes had been made to satisfy the large numbers of participants in the development process, and production issues were not addressed appropriately.

Avoiding the Weak Sequel

One key reason why the Lisa strategy fell short is because the process of developing breakthrough innovations is individualistic and influenced by intuition. Innovation cannot be put on a daily "to do" list. It cannot be reliably delegated to others, especially to a committee. Instead of creating an Innovating group within the company to push forward the new product, Apple, essentially at this point a Planning organization, recreated itself in the new group and expected it to behave like an Innovating unit.

In addition, Apple had continued to develop enhancements for its existing product lines, including the Macintosh, that incorporated many of Lisa's innovations. It was essentially competing with itself as well as outside competitors.

To avoid the weak sequel problem, recognize that the Concept Development phase requires a specialized organization: an Innovating organization. Set aside a small team and allow the members to focus on a limited number of issues. Immerse them in information, put them at the coal face, and give them freedom to create. This means creating an Innovating organization within or alongside the larger organization, making it possible for a team to work outside of the structural and cultural impediments of the rest of the company. This skunk works team consists of mavericks and creative thinkers and may have relatively little interaction with the Planning side of the firm. But make sure what you're inventing is truly new—get good market intelligence to see if you are re-creating the wheel.

Innovation cannot be put on a daily "to do" list. It cannot be reliably delegated to others, especially to a committee.

Signs of Success

You'll know that you're succeeding in creating a Planning mode if you're able to compete successfully on price, deliver high volumes to large markets, and still maintain your edge in quality. This is no easy feat. Your success in this mode will show up in these ways:

- ▶ Your systems, such as accounting and production, are refined enough to accommodate the stable complexities of doing business.
- ▶ Product consistency is high.
- ▶ Your larger staff is trained to a higher level.
- ▶ You are able to compete in price.

In addition to the signs of success listed above, when you use the Planning operational mode, you may also notice that higher margins may be available in niche markets that are not well served by your standardized products. These are specialized niche markets with their own sets of demands and potential rewards, which I'll discuss in the next chapter.

Stuck in an Obsolete Rut

You may also realize that, because of fundamental changes in your business environment, the preconditions of success that prompted you to apply the Planning mode are no longer valid. The state to which you should be especially alert is the precondition of *a sufficiently stable and predictable business environment*. Business environments can be stable for a period of time and then experience significant change or instability that can continue for some time. You should be careful not to blindly dedicate your enterprise to the Planning mode in perpetuity. If you are in a rut that becomes obsolete, it will be apparent in one or some of these ways:

▶ The company appears slow and unresponsive to the dynamics of the marketplace.

▶ Junior members of the organization lack advancement opportunities and, internally, staff members feel frustrated because of the rigid power structure.

▶ Hierarchy, plans, and processes inhibit the breadth of thinking and other creative processes that would allow the firm to be more responsive and flexible.

Business environments can be stable for a period of time and then experience significant change or instability that can continue for some time.

Because changes to the power structure that would address these problems can be threatening to those in power and what they've built, the status quo is frequently protected. It's also likely that the enterprise's leaders do not recognize the signs that they are stuck.

The expertise of experienced staff is often leveraged by having them lead functional groups. Once the staff has been trained, however, the senior staff are often reluctant to allow newer staff members to use their individual initiative. In this way, the Planning organization's hierarchy can serve to limit staff advancement and initiative. Long cycles of analysis and planning slow down action and threaten growth. The following sidebar provides an example of how a Planning organization can become entrenched and inflexible.

The first step to getting out of an obsolete rut is to recognize that you're in one. What kinds of communication avenues are in place in your organization for line staff to report snafus? What means does management have for staying current with the needs of their markets? If, as in the example above, you must forgo a market opportunity, make sure it's a well-reasoned

Unhitched in Kalamazoo

A Michigan-based manufacturer of trailer hitches depended on operational efficiencies for its success. Virtually all of its business was with the major car manufacturers; without exception, these customers placed orders well ahead of required delivery. The company had engineered its production techniques and clearly identified all the steps required of each worker. Decision making was formal and production procedures were highly developed. Each person played a well-defined role in the process and the contributions of all workers came together according to an established plan and schedule. The firm was successful in reducing costs and meeting needs it had anticipated in advance.

The company launched a new business initiative: selling its hitches through the national chains of muffler shops. These chains were anxious to add sales and installations of hitches to their list of services. Sales were brisk and profitable. But muffler shops don't stock large numbers of hitches and they can't accurately predict how many they'll sell well in advance of delivery. In addition, the range of hitch models mushroomed; each muffler chain wanted the hitch assemblies to be modified to fit its own shop practices.

Back in Kalamazoo, management did not quickly understand the full impact of these diverse requirements. Of course they'd try to accommodate the new requests, but they viewed these special requirements as exceptions to their practices rather than normal circumstances of this market segment that would be simply part of how business must be done.

The sales team serving the muffler shops complained that the production department was being unresponsive. They were concerned because one of the top muffler chains was seriously considering another supplier.

The production department countered that they were doing all they could: the production runs did not allow any more variation. Revamping current practices would require the attention of the most senior production people—who already had their hands full with their other responsibilities. There was not much that could be done; change would have to be put off until the current quotas were met.

Ultimately, sales to the muffler chains began to decline and this was management's first clue that there was a problem. The production group saw this as evidence that the muffler shop business was unreliable and didn't justify any fundamental changes. But the sales team believed they gave away the business: other hitch manufacturers had been more responsive—and developed highly profitable businesses serving these chains.

choice. Regardless of your organizational structure, team members need to experience their roles as valued parts of the greater whole and have an opportunity to contribute, corroborate—and advance.

If you're in a Planning mode, you should take pains to define which aspects of your business need to be more adaptable. Certain core portions will remain stable, but others can be segmented away from the regular production cycle to accommodate the various demands of different market segments. Internal processes should be realigned away from functional distinctions and toward the different market segments. This new alignment is characteristic of the Adapting mode, which I'll treat in depth in the next chapter.

Transitions

After a successful stint in the Crowded Marketplace phase, you will be ready for a transition. Two types of transition are common.

Niche Development. The tough price competition typical of the Crowded Marketplace phase may cause business leaders to seek out the higher profit margins available in a niche market. Further, when there's a fundamental change in the nature of your current markets that requires you to be more adaptable and flexible, your business could well be entering a Niche Development phase. The transition to Niche Development is difficult because it requires shifting from hard controls, like plans, processes, and procedures, to softer controls, like vision, culture, and the informed judgment of individuals. It also involves structural changes. The organization will be organized more by customer or client segment and less by internal functions.

This transition requires a complete realignment of the power structure of the firm. In the Planning mode, the leaders of functional groups tended to dominate and sales and customer service were support functions. In the Adapting mode, individuals responsible for client or customer service and satisfaction gain relatively more power. This shift is not easy because people do not give up power easily. Ironically, though, the best preparation for the Adapting mode is the depth and experience gained during the Planning mode. So the challenges you encounter doing this are an expected part of the development process.

A new and different stable market. In this second type of transition, you will still need to operate in a Planning mode, but the difference is that your stable practices require change. This transition is less difficult, because the structure does not require dramatic reconstruction, just realignment.

As with the transition to the Niche Development phase, the transition to a new, rejuvenated Planning mode first requires a Transitional phase and the

Foundation Building mode. Planning organizations are notorious for becoming rigid and completely inflexible. They often fail to update themselves to accommodate the inevitable small changes that occur constantly.

Change occurs in all business situations. For most Planning organizations, small changes require little fine-tuning. Over time, however, as the small changes in the firm accumulate, it goes out of sync with the requirements of its environment. Ultimately, a change is needed and the old system must be reviewed, purged of useless practices, and replaced with new ones. A new Planning organization may be built, but it will be one with different stable practices. The Foundation Building mode, with its careful inventory of facts, feelings, and future paths, is suited to this realignment process.

Neither of these two alternatives is inherently better than the other. The right path depends on what is actually available to you and whether you can properly execute any changes. A mistake that some leaders make is to assume that an Adapting mode is always the target mode.

Vic Realizes the Need for Change

"We're running neck and neck with those hotshot competitors on price and our margins have dropped," Vic thought. "We're at a crossroads again."

Although Vic's company had achieved dominance in the industry and everything was working well, he sensed that they could be doing more business. He began to make the rounds of his industry, touching base with contacts and talking with customers and prospects.

Phase of Growth—Summary Table

Phase of Growth	Crowded Marketplace
Goals	• Efficiency • Scale • Reliability • Integration with the business world

Mode of Operation	Planning
Preconditions	▪ A commercially viable product or products ▪ Reside in or can move to a sufficiently stable and predictable business environment to allow for extensive use of defined structures and processes ▪ Operational practices that can remain or become effective when institutionalized in formal rules ▪ Access to personnel with appropriate technical expertise in specialized areas
Control Lever Settings	Relative Weight, %
Supervision	5%
Business Vision	5
Cultural Priorities	15
Organizational Hierarchy	25
Formal Plans and Processes	30
Expertise of Team Members	10
Formal Feedback and Evaluation	10
Total Control	100%
Organizational Structure	▪ Hierarchy of functional groups
Expertise Profile of Team	▪ Some high, some low
Cultural Priorities	▪ Data-driven decisions, defined strategies, refinement, cost reduction, consistency
Business Processes	▪ Clear, robust, and logical
Product Strategy	▪ Standard product line to a large number of price-conscious customers in stable market segments
Inherent Strengths	▪ Efficiency, reliability, scale
Inherent Weaknesses	▪ Lack of responsiveness ▪ Bottlenecks for career progression and innovative ideas
Beneficial Legacies	▪ Deep functional expertise ▪ Operational efficiency

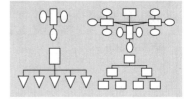

Chapter 8

Niche Development Phase

YOU DEVELOPED YOUR PRODUCT CONCEPT IN THE FIRST PHASE, grabbed market share and got the world's attention in the second, and then systematically fortified and expanded your market presence in the third. After each of these growth phases you carefully prepared for the next phase by initiating the right operational mode. With these successes and retaining the capabilities that produced them, you move forward.

Your market opportunities in this growth phase center on the diverse and evolving needs of the sophisticates[1]—the customer group that will pay a premium for products and services that are targeted to their individual needs and demands. These customers present numerous niche situations for which standardized products are a poor fit or they have changing needs that make them leery of long-term commitments to a brand or product. In both cases, they require personal attention and advice that will coax them into buying. They believe they have unique demands and are willing to pay a premium for products or services that meet them. This makes them sophisticates in terms of what they look for in a product or service. The business

---

1. This group is similar to Moore's group called Conservatives, but sophisticates are more willing to pay a premium for customized products and services. It is perhaps a subgroup of Moore's Conservatives.

opportunity presented by sophisticates is typically large, but it is also more varied from segment and changeable over time than the stable conservatives who defined the Crowded Marketplace phase.

Sophisticates can be grouped into market niches and present you with a wider range of opportunities than were available or were recognized in the Crowded Marketplace. However, adapting your enterprise to simultaneously meet the needs of a wide range of niches is challenging. Each niche has slightly different needs and demands and each may evolve over time in its own way. Meeting these needs efficiently is important to making the sometimes slim premium worth your while. This is a new growth phase, the Niche Development phase.

A dapting your enterprise to simultaneously meet the needs of a wide range of niches is challenging.

Now is the time to bring out the innovative spirit and insight of many members of your enterprise. Fresh ideas and perspectives are needed. Responding effectively to this changing situation defies being reduced to formal plans and procedures. Instead, you must depend on the flexibility and initiative of your people, who will adapt your systems and processes and products to customer needs.

This is not the time to dictate the way individuals work. You need to establish quality standards for their work, guide them with a broad vision, set goals for them to meet, bathe them in relevant information, and then let them determine the strategy right for their market niche. You will need to trust your people to implement that vision effectively for their market niches. This is a tricky phase of growth because the enterprise must be very sophisticated in its underlying infrastructure and in management's use of different control levers. Yet it must operate with a deceptively informal and flexible structure.

Niche Development: Mission Possible?

It's important to keep in mind that not all enterprises will have the opportunity to pursue Niche Development. As I've discussed in previous chapters, much depends on the opportunities on offer in your marketplace. Clearly, if the seeds are there for you to develop a customized, high-margin product, you should consider cultivating these seeds. When considering the potential of entering this phase of growth, you must be honest about the opportunities that exist. It may be that this growth phase is not open to you. Perhaps current and potential customers for your product are not willing to pay enough of a premium to justify the costs of customization. Perhaps the way you would customize will be too costly.

In addition, for some products or services, there are no practical ways to customize or improve them enough to encourage customers to pay a premium. Some business firms must continue to grow by Crowded Marketplace maneuvers, by competing on price, reliability, and other strategies within reach—rather than through the developmental innovation of Niche Development. These issues should be considered in the Transitional phase as you contemplate whether this growth phase and its Adapting operational mode are right for you.

Vic's New Opportunities

"Our Model 3000 is everywhere, but each customer has different needs," Vic, the visionary leader of the company, announces at a company meeting. "We have 250 employees and many of them have developed into experts in their fields. Our business infrastructure is solid and our core production disciplines are second to none. But before our competitors mimic everything we do, let's be the first to take the next step and pepper the market with dozens of versions of the Model 3000. We can charge higher prices because we're meeting more of our customers' needs. That will make it more difficult for competitors to challenge us head to head."

Vic is stepping back into his element. Visualizing possibilities is what he likes best, but he has to hold himself back a bit. Rather than promoting fundamental revolutions in the industry, his mission is to listen to his customers and give them what they want—down to the smallest detail.

The company designates people from the sales, production, and design departments to form teams, with representatives from each function on each team. The teams are asked to find out everything there is to know about a particular niche of customers, particularly how customers are presently using the Model 3000. The teams are seeking to understand the entire context of activity in which the model is used or can be used. Their goal is to make its use more efficient and effective for different customers.

A big challenge for the company is to create the new teams. People must be taken from the functional departments and put together to form working teams in a matter of weeks. A bigger challenge, however, is determining how these new teams should be integrated with the internal functional departments that were put in place in earlier phases.

Peter, the recently hired head of the manufacturing department (an Analytical Planner), is concerned because manufacturing is no longer experiencing the rapid growth it once was—or garnering the management attention to which he had already become accustomed. Peter resents what he sees as the rise of marketing to a higher stature than manufacturing.

"These teams have some of the best people from my department," Peter complains to Vic. "They know their stuff and their suggestions are rational and doable, but we're no longer in control of our own destiny."

For Vic, the creation of the market-niche teams is reminiscent of the early days. Staff members who can engage in blue-sky discussions are the most helpful. In fact, Vincent (a Visionary), an energetic designer selected to be on one of the teams, is making an immense contribution. He understands intuitively what's happening inside his customers' shops. Together with other team members, Vincent specifies customized products that are enthusiastically accepted by customers who once thought their needs were too unique to benefit from the Model 3000.

Vincent's team is able to design the customizations and work with manufacturing to make it happen efficiently. Effective product design and team collaboration come about with the help of computer systems and communication techniques. Everyone can stay current with each team's progress and input.

Vic realizes that he has to promote a new sensitivity to client demands. He wants the company to build on the operational efficiency developed in the last phase—but to emphasize listening to the customer. He even encourages parts of the company that didn't change structurally to think more about the customers' situations and look for opportunities to provide solutions.

The nature of the regular meetings shifts again. They are now monthly strategy sessions. Less time is spent on the long-term planning of specific, measurable objectives. Those tasks are well taken care of by the business units and the functional departments that are now given much more discretion in how they develop and execute their plans.

The strategy sessions are more about targeting new business opportunities and trying to understand the subtleties of markets. In addition, personnel issues have become important topics of discussion. This is not so much to solve individual issues, which is done within the teams, but to address how to hire, train, and motivate employees, as well as how to channel their energies and interests. More and more, staffing is becoming the constraint that limits growth and the ability to implement the business strategy.

Vic realizes the risk of fragmentation inherent in having a number of semi-autonomous teams. "What is the glue that keeps them from being wholly autonomous?" he wonders. "What keeps them performing in a manner consistent with their past reputation?"

He can't develop all their strategies. He can't personally supervise them. Nor should he. He knows that the teams are held together by a number of forces. First, the basic business disciplines are similar across the teams, as most of the staff members worked together in the past, with the financial group, they were "educated in the same classroom and speak the same language." Second, the staff has, on average, a high level of expertise in relevant business and operational matters—they had hired well and trained well. Third, internal communication is excellent—their culture of trust and open communication (not to mention their strong internal communication systems) keep people informed. But Vic wonders if these measures are enough to keep the company from fragmenting.

Vic and the heads of the business units, each of whom oversee a number of teams, set the broad direction for business growth and monitor results. The strategies used by the units to support the business direction are left up to the units as long as they don't violate the company's broad guidelines and standards. To ensure consistency with the intangible aspects of policy and culture, Vic and others make it a habit to walk around the company every week.

They talk to people, listen, exchange views, and coach. Vic knows that every person in the company is making several decisions a day that have an impact on the business. In addition, most of the people in the company are closer to the customers than are Vic and the management team. The ideas, thoughts, and concerns of the front-line people are vitally important.

Naturally Effective Management Style for Niche Development: Collaborative Visionary

Collaborative Visionaries listen to others, seek consensus, and place a high value on interpersonal communications.

The naturally most effective style of management for the leader during the Niche Development phase is the Collaborative Visionary. They are visionaries and can see opportunities on the horizon. These leaders create a vivid, broad image of the industry, the company, and its opportunities. They infuse the organization with a strong culture that helps guide the actions of its members. Collaborative Visionaries listen to others, seek consensus, and place a high value on interpersonal communications. They act as a clearinghouse for strategic information concerning the various units of the organization. They provide people with ample information for making their own decisions. They place high value on corporate culture as an important guide for the independent decision-making efforts of the staff. They accommodate a variety of solutions to a problem.

The weakness of this management style is a lack of specific focus and a reluctance to rigorously scrutinize members of the enterprise. They have the big-picture and opportunistic side of the creative Visionary and the nurturing side of the collaborative Facilitator.

What looks and feels successful to Collaborative Visionaries is broad, integrated visions expressed in the actions of people; when people demonstrate a clear understanding of the mission and goals of the enterprise. These are the attitudes that model the practices and priorities of the Adapting operational mode.

The Adapting Mode of Operation

These preconditions must exist before you attempt an Adapting operational mode.

Precondition 1. *Customers willing to pay a premium for a product customized to their needs and demands.* The presence of such customers is a key economic rationale for this mode of operation. If this type of customer does not exist, then a more systematized and programmed way of operating (i.e. the Planning mode) is more appropriate.

Precondition 2. *An efficient and effective business infrastructure.* The very flexible customer interface required by this phase of growth must be grounded in a robust business infrastructure. There must be systems for inventory, sales, manufacturing, accounting, and internal communication. They will need some modification for this phase of growth, but a strong foundation in the important business areas is essential. This is why the Planning mode is good preparation for Adapting mode.

Precondition 3. *Individuals with sufficient expertise and information to handle the higher level of discretion in making decisions for their market segments.* You must be able to depend on team members to develop and execute the strategies that will drive your economic growth. This expertise can be developed by formal education, experience with other firms, experience in your firm, and their own personal efforts. The Niche Development growth phase of growth is riskier when attempted with people who are not suited to the higher levels of discretion associated with the Adapting operational mode.

Precondition 4. *Strong performance monitoring and feedback systems and practices.* You'll need these to help you oversee the wide variety of market segments, strategies, and patterns of results that will emanate from the market-driven teams. While these systems could be considered part of the infrastructure mentioned above, they deserve special mention. The breadth and complexity of your efforts during this phase will require a systematic monitoring and evaluation processes.

If these elements are in place, you can build on this foundation and create an Adapting organization. The typical themes of an Adapting organization are:

- Collaborative synergies
- Listening to the customer
- Cross-functional teamwork

The most pressing issues during the Niche Development phase vary from market niche to market niche. The tastes of your customers, the capabilities of your suppliers, and the activities of your competitors are varied and may change quickly and thus make it difficult to accurately predict in a centralized manner how all your efforts should be coordinated. You may not be able to develop detailed plans. Adaptability is essential. Therefore, your critical business objectives at the broad enterprise level are to listen well and adapt effectively.

To meet these objectives, dismantle some of the rigid functional departments and re-form them around the opportunities presented by different market niches. These market-driven teams, which are usually used for just a portion of your firm, will each be able to produce goods that are more attractive to a specific market segment. Each will use its creativity, energy, and agility to adapt your basic products or services to the particular needs of its market segment.

Controlling an Adapting Organization

Within the market-driven teams, people don't have the benefits—or the restrictions—of direct supervision by the central leader. They also don't have rigid plans, procedures, or processes that prescribe the right decisions. Instead, the enterprise depends on its members to use their own initiative, judgment, and interpretation of the organization's broad visions and objectives to set their own course. Because the hard control levers of "Organizational Hierarchy" and enterprise-wide "Formal Plans and Processes" cannot possibly be specific enough for every situation encountered, the enterprise relies more heavily on soft controls (see Table 8-1). Four of the seven control levers are important in the Adapting organization.

- **A compelling and loyalty-inspiring business vision.** The enterprise may have had a compelling business vision early in its development, but it is often forgotten, watered down, or heavily influenced by the market-

Phase	Concept Development	First Transition	Rapid Market Expansion	Crowded Marketplace	Niche Development
Operational Mode	Innovating	Foundation Building	Producing	Planning	Adapting
Control Lever Settings	Relative Weight, %				
Supervision	60	20	30	5	5
Business Vision	25	10	5	5	20
Cultural Priorities	5	10	10	15	20
Organizational Hierarchy	0	20		25	5
Formal Plans and Processes	0	20	15	30	10
Expertise of Team Members	10	10	5	10	20
Formal Feedback and Evaluation	0	10	20	10	20
Total Control	100%	100%	100%	100%	100%

Table 8-1. Control levers

ing messages of the day. The importance of other, harder controls in the operational modes for two earlier phases, Rapid Market Expansion (and its Producing mode) and Crowded Marketplace (and its Planning mode), typically leave this control underdeveloped. If possible, embed a "noble cause" in the vision—one that influences the hearts and minds of the enterprise's members and truly conveys what you are about.

▶ **The organization's culture.** A unified, success-oriented, fair, positive, and supportive culture improves adaptability. The culture must reinforce the broad vision and goals of the enterprise and the actions that serve the enterprise.

▶ **The expertise of its members.** Personal discretion is important to the success of the Adapting mode. The level that's appropriate is a function of the expertise of the people involved. Generally speaking, the higher their expertise, the more autonomy they can be given. The training benefits of the Planning mode make it good preparation for the Adapting mode.

▶ **Formal evaluation and feedback practices.** These practices should be on the forefront for two purposes:

   – Highlighting performance so the teams can self-correct.

   – Initiating processes at high organizational levels for deeper corrective action, as required.

The Soft Touch

Soft controls are important in creating an effective Adapting organization. You will be delegating a great deal of decision-making responsibility and authority. You cannot and should not try to second-guess or over-manage those closest to the markets they are responsible for. But you do want to channel your team members' actions in effective but flexible ways. The soft controls can do this.

You cannot and should not try to second-guess or over-manage those closest to the markets they are responsible for.

Investment shops highlight the importance of these soft controls. Among those who evaluate investment management teams, a key indicator of a successful large team is a strong and well-articulated investment philosophy. There is not the same requirement for small investment teams in which all team members are in constant contact. A small investment team can operate very effectively using an informal Innovating organization; it can operate without formal statements of philosophy and process descriptions. But a larger investment team, an investment group of more than six or seven people, requires philosophies and distinguishing beliefs about what it considers to be an attractive investment and what risks are worth taking. These must be articulate and clear and known by each member of the investment team.

The reason for this is that most investment processes work best when those who are closest to the information make the decisions—they can make decisions faster. This means the front-line investment people, those doing the research and those working at the coal face of the market. Investing is a competitive activity; slow decision-making processes are disadvantaged. Thus, delegation of decision-making responsibility is in many firms a requirement for long-term decision-making success. Large organizations need a clearly articulated investment philosophy and guiding principles to enable each investment professional to correctly interpret those ideas for his or her work and to make decisions in a manner consistent with the views of the firm.

Weak Soft Controls Are Commonplace

It's common for organizations moving into the Niche Development phase to have weaker soft controls than they need. For enterprises following the default developmental path presented here, "culture," "vision," and "individual expertise" have not been important control levers in the past. Leaders who know the requirements of an Adapting organization consider the development of these control levers a crucial effort during the transitional phase leading to this phase. They develop them early because these controls take time to develop and doing so help the enterprise traverse business momentum-consuming transition to an effective Adapting mode more quickly and effectively.

A particularly common weakness of organizations moving from a Planning mode to an Adapting mode is an inadequate performance evaluation and feedback system. Although such a system is typically developed in the Crowded Marketplace phase, it is not an important control lever during that phase. It often must be strengthened to be an effective method of control during the Niche Development phase.

Aside from the very important benefit of providing feedback so the teams can correct their actions, the system is important because of the protection Adapting organizations give their teams. If you refer back to the map of the operational modes, you'll see that the Adapting mode resides in the upper right. It requires insight and innovation to be successful. To its left is the Innovating mode, which excels in the development of breakthrough innovations. One might be tempted to think of an Adapting organization as a collection of many Innovating organizations. They do have similarities: the teams are informally organized and there is a certain amount of trial-and-error development in each.

But when you look at businesses that successfully progress beyond the Concept Development phase, you're looking at only a small sample of those that have attempted it. Most fail—they have worked at the coal face of the marketplace and have not survived: they didn't come out of the mineshaft. In an Adapting enterprise, the larger business is essentially saying to the smaller teams, "We will not let you fail." The larger business has its brand and franchise at stake and it protects the smaller units from the harsh realities of the mine shaft. While Darwinian market forces clear out the weak among independent Innovating organizations, the weak can easily find refuge inside a larger organization in the Niche Development phase. The weak are protected. In some of the larger investment shops around the world, one can find investment teams operating as Innovating organizations that clearly could not survive on their own.

Perhaps because formal feedback and evaluation systems appear rigid and seem to go against the flexible nature of an Adapting organization, they are often not given adequate attention by otherwise effective leaders of Adapting organizations. They seem bureaucratic and Big Brotherish. Yet, true Adapting enterprises have strong internal evaluation practices.

Aside from the very important benefit of providing feedback so the teams can correct their actions, the system is important because of the protection Adapting organizations give their teams.

Your teams may complain that the scrutiny is intrusive, but you can remind them of the implied contract of an Adapting organization. Compared with a fully independent Innovating enterprise, internal teams are protected from the harsh market, team members have almost as much autonomy, they benefit when another team does well, and their efforts probably have a bigger footprint in the market. In exchange, they must meet operational standards and be held accountable for meeting team goals.

An Information Bath

A final element of an Adapting organization that is important, but not one of the seven control levers, is an *information bath*. I am not speaking of a particular database or library, which many firms have, but instead the ideal practice of keeping everyone informed as possible. An information bath could be as simple as regularly e-mailing information about industry trends to 20 percent more people than you would otherwise. It is not an effort to figure out what every person and role should have, but what they might find useful. Some firms send around news alerts and with a clear note that the information is saved in a particular place and the e-mail can be deleted. People can skim or read carefully depending on their needs.

Together, the strong and fully aligned soft controls, the performance monitoring and feedback systems, and the information bath, which are all supported by robust core business process (a beneficial legacy of the Planning mode), make a very sophisticated organizational context for your market-driven teams. This rich context is crucial to supporting them. It will guide them in directions that make sense for the teams and make sense for the entire enterprise. The purpose of this sophisticated context is to make you organization as "holographic" as possible.

A Holographic Organization

Let's take a look at what being holographic represents. A holographic image, let's say of a ship, exists in a plate of glass. When the plate is broken into smaller pieces, each piece shows the complete picture of the ship. Instead of one large ship, there are hundreds of smaller ships as recognizable as the larger one. This is the intent in an Adapting organization: to have the image of the large represented in the small.

Every person on the cross-functional market-driven teams should convey the sense of the vision of the enterprise, how it works, and how his or her work is consistent with those frameworks. This holographic nature helps the semi-autonomous teams chart their courses and proceed forward in a manner consistent with the enterprise's overall goals.

The holographic nature of Adapting organizations contrasts sharply with Planning organizations, in which knowledge of the overall plan of how all the pieces fit together is not required for a person to do his or her specialized job. So long as the person works in a way that meets the specifications of the job, he or she can contribute to achieving the overall goals of the enterprise.

Most Effective Structure

An Adapting organization is a "federation of market-driven teams." A market-driven team is established to serve each segment of the market in a manner tailored to the needs and demands of that market. The teams typically cut across the functional areas, including marketing, production, sales, product design, and so forth, to bring all functions together to serve that market segment. While organizational diagrams tend not to show the strengths of an Adapting organization, the following diagram is fairly typical.

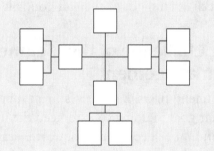

Indeed, there are many organizational structures that could be consistent with an Adapting structure.

One of the challenges in building this type of organization is that it lacks a specific formal structure. In contrast, the structure of a Planning organization is very important and the organization's purpose is more readily apparent in its blueprint. The manner in which you build a Planning structure is just like that of building a physical structure—a bridge, for example. You survey both sides of the river and riverbed. You engineer the bridge and develop specifications for each piece. The pieces are assembled end to end until the structure is complete. The strength and power are in the structure.

In contrast, an Adapting organization is like a nuclear reactor. The structure of the reactor is critical, of course, but the work—the point of building the structure in the first place—is done by the nuclear reaction taking place inside it. You need to understand the nature of the reaction and you need to channel and direct the reaction in order to make it productive. Importantly, you need to monitor it carefully to ensure it's operating the way it should. From the outside, the reactor's structure doesn't convey much about the strength of the reaction, and the structure without the reaction inside is useless.

Very often, those who excel at building a Planning organization and its systems of hard controls cannot see or trust the strength and abilities of an Adapting organization.

Very often, those who excel at building a Planning organization and its systems of hard controls cannot see or trust the strength and abilities of an Adapting organization. They look for strength in the structure of the reaction and simply see nothing; if they do see something, they see chaos. It is like the visual perception test done with cats. Kittens born and raised in boxes painted with only vertical black and white lines did not develop the physiological capabilities to perceive horizontal lines. When freed from their boxes, they could not perceive horizontal lines in their environment. We use and overuse the Planning operational mode—the hierarchy of functional group is easily designed and people at the top like the concentration of power—but we get accustomed to the apparent strength of the hard controls and can no longer see the strength of the soft controls.

The Marketing Challenge of the "Segment Approach" to Investment Management

A number of investment firms have investment operations that use the Adapting mode. Their goal in doing so is to keep the innovative spark of an Innovating organization, but deploy it with greater scale than possible in an Innovating mode. To address this need, they use what some in the investment industry call a *segment approach*. This approach calls for one investment portfolio to be divided into three to five segments.

Under this framework, one portfolio manager (or a portfolio manager and a few analysts) is assigned to manage each segment. The segments are combined to create the single portfolio for the client. Each segment manager can pursue whatever approach he or she believes will perform the best. The segment managers exchange views among themselves and review the aggregate portfolio to make sure that they're all comfortable with the overall portfolio delivered to clients, but the firm makes no attempt to micromanage each segment manager's activities.

156

Segment managers can develop and implement insights quickly. They like the ability to develop their own investment strategies. While many firms use this approach with great success, the best-known and largest practitioner is Capital Research, manager of the American Funds. This firm has performed exceedingly well for its clients and is widely respected in the industry for its investment and business success. It is also viewed as a very attractive place to work.

But on the flip side, Capital Research has experienced significant marketing challenges. Many potential clients want to hear about robust investment processes and clear accountability and decision rules, much like they hear from JP Morgan about its approach—which I've already described as an example of a Planning organization. Without those easily described features, Capital Research is able to tout only the expertise of its professionals, its in-house training, low staff turnover, and strong culture. But while these are impressive qualities, they tend not to carry the weight that specific, ironclad processes and structures do. In other words, JP Morgan probably has an easier time painting a compelling picture of its process. Yet Capital Research's investment results (in terms of investment performance and business growth) are strong and speak to the strength of what the firm has accomplished.

The Capital Research example is useful for another point. This firm does just one thing. The segment approach is what it focuses on—their people have mastered its fine points. Other larger investment shops that have several products may have some investment teams using a Planning structure and others using an Adapting one. While this diversity can work, it's more challenging to make it work well. A control lever that Capital Research relies heavily on is its culture. It is very strong, but it is designed to fit the segment approach—the only thing it does. Other investment shops with a greater diversity of operational modes cannot use the soft control of culture to the same extent: culture tends to be a powerful control, but one not adaptable to fine-tuning for widely different circumstances. They must rely on other controls, such as monitoring systems, to ensure that each team operates effectively.

Correcting Undesirable Legacies of Prior Growth Phases

Two undesirable legacies from earlier phases typically surface in this phase; both can be addressed by successfully developing the Adapting mode. These legacies emerge from historically successful structures, practices, and priorities that have outlived their usefulness.

Defiant Innovation Becomes Defiant Isolation

When a new young company makes a big splash in the marketplace with a bold innovation, it may make the headlines and be the talk of the town for a time. This taste of fame can be heady stuff, enough to convince the leaders that their defiance of the norm has contributed to their success. Defiance of conventional wisdom is often a crucial ingredient in the creation of a breakthrough innovation. This belief that you can create a new product or business where none has existed before can become a part of the company's self-concept.

During the period of breakthrough innovation, an insightful and effective entrepreneur often defies prevailing practices and techniques and the articulated demands of the market.

During the period of breakthrough innovation, an insightful and effective entrepreneur often defies prevailing practices and techniques and the articulated demands of the market. In the early days, he or she and the team were working at the coal face—directly in touch with the market. They probably knew more about what the market needed than the market could articulate, so listening to what was said wasn't important at the time.

Unfortunately, defiant innovation in the early days can easily atrophy into defiant isolation later on. As time passes, the decision makers become removed and insulated from the coal face of the market by organizational layers and the distractions of running a business. Yet the attitudes of defiance have become part of the organization's culture. Listening and responding to the market are simply not part of what they believe is important. These innovators continue to believe that they know more about what the customer wants than the customer does.

If this behavior continues, the company can become out of touch with the market and its own customers. It can fail to keep up with the development of the very market it helped to create or fail to take advantage of the market's demand for variations of its initial product. Defiant innovation can easily become defiant isolation.

Defiant isolation surfaces as a problem most ironically when the company's early breakthrough innovations become part of the conventional wisdom. Once the groundbreaking innovation has been accepted and integrated into the marketplace, the market will give ample feedback about the product and how it can be improved and customized to meet more specialized needs. Companies suffering from defiant isolation often don't listen. If they do, they do not take it seriously. As a result, they can miss significant opportunities for future growth.

Left Behind in Boston

A Boston-based company specializing in medical devices was first to introduce an innovative blood-sampling device that changed the market. The device sold well and several other firms introduced copycat products. The firm took pride in creating a new market segment and held itself out as the industry leader. The company was confident that the fundamental merits of the device would serve it well in terms of business growth. It devoted attention to producing a large volume of the devices and then going on to the next great breakthrough. However, the buyers of the device were diverse and found many different ways to use it. Demand for customized applications was so great that several competing companies introduced products to be used in conjunction with the device that made it better suited to various medical situations.

To the market, the initial version of the product was out-of-date and not versatile enough. Competing firms bent over backwards to work with customers to modify the device to make it better suited to their needs. In sum, although the market was taking off, the Boston company's business was not keeping up.

The cell phone maker Nokia displayed a dollop of defiant isolation regarding flip or clamshell phones. Nokia had earlier developed ergonomically simple and stylish "brick" phones, which were so successful that Nokia took significant market share away from Motorola, the market leader. Nokia believed that people didn't need the ergonomics of a flip phone and therefore didn't offer them. But consumers had a different idea. Nokia didn't hear them until it had lost significant market share.

In the Innovating mode, you can lecture to the market. Later on, you must listen to the market.

In the Innovating mode, you can lecture to the market. Later on, you must listen to the market. You must make a conscious cultural shift from the attitude of defiant innovation typical of a successful Concept Development phase to the more market-driven innovation of the Niche Development phase. This is a cultural change that is essential in making the enterprise truly responsive to the commercial marketplace.

A Flotilla of 100 Rafts

In this undesirable legacy, a company that is especially good at adding more staff and introducing new products and business units experiences poor coordination and cooperation among the various business units. The organization and its business become fragmented and none of the lines of business are developed to their fullest potential. The only coordination is done by informal agreements between or among the heads of the individual businesses.

159

Instead of being a coordinated venture seeking to maximize its activities as a whole, the firm is a collection of boutique efforts, with few becoming well developed and with little synergy among the entities. Rather than being a well-coordinated fleet of a dozen ships able to move in a coordinated fashion to meet objectives, the organization is a flotilla of 100 rafts moving with the currents and unable to focus its efforts.

The skipper of each raft competes with the skippers of other rafts for favorable winds and guides his or her raft to wherever the winds seem strongest. When there are alliances between or among skippers, the lines are not tied tight. It's clear to each skipper that all the rafts are just barely staying afloat; one can never tell which raft will go under. Independence from the other groups is a survival strategy. Observant employees may suspect that two separate business lines within the company serve the same segment of the market with redundant and overlapping functions.

The flotilla-of-100-rafts legacy has its roots in the bias toward innovation and trial-and-error opportunism characteristic of Innovating organizations. Starting new enterprises is what they do—and this thrust becomes ingrained as part of the culture. Developing plans and cultivating focus and reliability are not. When faced with the choice of marketing more of what one is already doing or doing something new, doing something new invariably wins.

Cut Adrift

A software company in the Northwest had so many different businesses that the firm was unable to create a single chart that reflected them all. Even long-time employees found it difficult to keep up with what the company did. Some business units were sizable and easily identified; others were small start-ups that were starved for corporate attention and resources. Because the firm consisted of many smaller enterprises, it had been able to benefit from many small changes in the industry.

The leadership of the firm, however, concluded that a major threat lay on the horizon. Competitors affiliated with larger companies had decided to be major players in the company's main marketplace and these competitors had the financial muscle to dominate the market. Unless the firm responded quickly and directly, it would lose its dominance. The leaders concluded that to protect their traditional businesses they needed to develop deeper capabilities and be able to respond more quickly to large-scale challenges.

Despite their accurate recognition of the competitive threat and the selection of a suitable strategy, the leaders were unable to coordinate their flotilla of 100 rafts. In total, they had the resources, but the fragmented structure of these resources made them practically useless for this challenge. Each business unit was so busy simply staying afloat that it could not carve enough time to coordinate with other units. In addition, the heads of each unit were competitive for resources and owning a market segment.

The leaders team could not marshal their resources because they were unfamiliar with the important details of each business and because of territorial squabbling among the business heads.

Under the strain of this competitive pressure, the firm's major lines of business no longer had the resources for rapid growth. While some in the firm were happy they had alternative businesses to fall back on, none of these side businesses was able to support the size of the total organization. The reduced growth of the major business lines forced the firm to cut loose some of the business-unit rafts and let them fend for themselves. The firm was no longer a high-growth enterprise and most of the business units that were cut adrift failed.

One of the most interesting aspects of this story is this: prior to the single large threat, the leaders of the firm were quite happy with their flotilla of rafts. There were many people doing many things. Each raft looked like an entrepreneurial venture. While profitability was low, hope sprang eternal and there was anticipation that one of these rafts would become a boat—or even a ship—some day. There was a laissez-faire attitude about the teams and placing few controls on them seemed truly entrepreneurial. Each raft-like enterprise developed just to the point of requiring the formalization of a Foundation Building period, but it stopped there because of the costs entailed. The enterprise liked neither the cost nor the more bureaucratic feel of the Foundation Building mode. In the end, all of its raft-like enterprises needed the momentum-consuming Foundation Building at the same time. None had achieved any business significance; to build foundations for all of them would have drained company resources.

The overall enterprise was beginning to strain under the weight of all the undeveloped rafts tethered together. For some, the appearance of a single large threat forced them to make changes that were long overdue. Unfortunately, by not addressing these issues earlier, management had far fewer options for the course going forward. They also experienced large opportunity costs by not having any of their smaller enterprises proceed down a developmental path best for its individual business activity.

To address this legacy, you should identify the business units that have strong opportunities for growth. If they have business momentum and can sustain a period of restructuring, consider doing so when it is right for that business. They can be restructured and developed from makeshift rafts into more developed boats. Unfortunately, this recommendation goes against the grain of the kinds of cultures that typically develop in successful Innovating organizations.

Common Errors in Creating an Adapting Organization

These are some of the common mistakes and erroneous assumptions made when developing an Adapting operational mode:

1. Assuming that Adapting organizations evolve without specific intent. This is not the case. *The good ones are built carefully.*
2. Assuming that establishing the flexible and loose structure establishes the Adapting mode of operation. It doesn't. Without the sophisticated context of soft controls, high-expertise members, performance monitoring and feedback, and information bath, this is a recipe for a major performance failure.
3. Allowing the soft controls of business vision, culture, and performance monitoring and feedback to remain underdeveloped. As discussed earlier, the importance of these controls is often underestimated.
4. Failing to understand at a leadership level why some individual teams perform poorly while others do well. Without suitable performance evaluation systems, the enterprise typically cannot identify accurately the contributions made by team members pursuing their team-specific strategies. Unproductive biases appear in the compensation system.
5. Assuming that reliance on soft controls means lack of accountability. Teams need to be held accountable for meeting operational standards and for attaining their goals.
6. Failing to manage the teams strategically. The loose "feel" of adapting ambiguities sometimes allows leaders to be careless about product development and the introduction of new teams. Both product development and introduction must be well conceived.

Signs That the Niche Development Phase Is Coming to an End

The Niche Development phase comes to an end when differences between or among products cease to be economically meaningful to the customer, when they're unwilling to pay the premium. This can happen for various reasons.

One reason is simply because all customers no longer value the special service. When customers are no longer willing to pay a premium for more customized goods, the higher costs of fielding market segment teams force some firms to reconsolidate along functional lines in order to lower production costs. As practices become standardized, the less costly Planning operational mode is more effective.

The Niche Development phase comes to an end when differences between or among products cease to be economically meaningful to the customer, when they're unwilling to pay the premium.

Distinctions Without Making a Difference

A Madison Avenue advertising firm tried hard to listen to its clients. It established three separate teams to work with large, medium, and small clients. The culture and philosophy of service for the company was strong and enabled each team to deliver service that could be identified with the organization as a whole. The reputation of the firm was strong.

As time progressed, clients' businesses grew and changed. The classifications of large, medium, and small no longer related to differences in what each client required. The needs of the market segments were converging and stabilizing. This gave the firm an opportunity to consolidate some activities performed by each team.

Unfortunately, the different teams responsible for the segments wanted to retain their relative autonomy and did not want to be consolidated. They pointed out differences in how each segment was being served and how each team had developed its own reports evaluating account investment performance. Each report was different in appearance, run by different people, and based on different software packages.

Because of this duplication of efforts, costs were higher than needed, but more importantly, the organization's segmentation prevented any one person from seeing trends developing across the segments.

The teams were so focused on satisfying current market needs that they had little time to think about their business as a whole. The staff did not have the vision to anticipate broad trends and they were late to spot the really important trends affecting the whole industry. Because of this market myopia, a new firm consisting of just a few people successfully identified the emerging trend. Although the market served by both firms continued to grow, most of the growth went to the new firm.

Another reason is the commoditization of customization. It is still required, but you cannot get paid extra for it so you better be able to do it efficiently. When competitors are offering the same customizations, it's become a standard practice. It is now standard practice, for example, to be able to get a car in many colors other than black; auto manufacturers don't need an Adapting mode to produce a blue sedan.

An Adapting organization is able to be successful in a complex and volatile marketplace because it is responsive.

An Adapting organization is able to be successful in a complex and volatile marketplace because it is responsive. But this responsiveness comes at a cost in duplication of functions and resources. An enterprise establishes its products within these new niche areas and can command higher margins. As this happens, competing enterprises will be attracted to those margins and follow suit. The series of niche marketplaces may become saturated with a variety of products; this abundance of competitions can lead to reduced margins, making this higher-cost operational mode less attractive. Over time, the once-changeable nature of the market segments can become more predictable and the enterprise can benefit economically by identifying ways of systematizing the handling of what was once highly uncertain and complex and is now only complex. This is the interplay between the Adapting and the Planning parts of an enterprise. The Adapting side starts the customization and develops it and then passes it to the Planning side once it stabilizes. Once it is completely stable and no longer requires your enterprise's input, it is then outsourced from the Planning side. This is one of the great forces in a competitive market—the commoditization of special features in a grinding and relentless manner. What was once new and innovative and requires a flexible operational mode later becomes commonplace and most efficiently handled by systems and procedures that require little judgmental intervention.

Ready for a New Breakthrough

As Vic surveyed the facility his company had built, he realized that he had a state-of-the-art manufacturing facility and marketing and client service teams with deep knowledge of customer needs and the ability to respond to business opportunities. He also recognized that the Model 3000 technology had run its course. In addition, they had derived all the benefit possible from developing versions for niche markets. Peter grouped the 12 different customized versions that had been developed over the recent phase and identified how they were starting to stabilize and converge. It would be possible, he believed, to simplify the product line and still meet a wide range of client demands.

Recently, demand had indeed converged and there was less need for the market-segment groups to identify and serve the unique market niches. Vic decided to reduce the product line to four standard versions and cut prices to draw in customers who would not otherwise buy.

He also realized that it was time to develop the Model 4000, the next breakthrough innovation. Vincent's team had identified a significant problem for a customer and proposed a novel solution. Vic had assisted them on the effort and saw immediately the broader application for the technology. Quietly, Vic, Vincent, and a few others retreated to a small warehouse to develop the concept. Vic and Vincent were in their element.

Phase of Growth—Summary Tables

Phase of Growth	Niche Development
Goals	▪ Respond effectively to the complex and changing needs of different market niches and segments (mass customization) ▪ Innovation driven by the needs and demands of the market niche
Mode of Operation	**Adapting**
Preconditions	▪ Customers willing to pay a premium for products better suited to their needs. ▪ Employees with a high level of expertise. ▪ Stable and efficient business, information, and communication infrastructures. ▪ Strong and effective formal feedback and evaluation systems.
Control Lever Settings	Relative Weight, %
Supervision	5%
Business Vision	20
Cultural Priorities	20
Organizational Hierarchy	5
Formal Plans and Processes	10
Expertise of Team Members	20
Formal Feedback and Evaluation	20
Total Control	100%

Mode of Operation	Adapting
Organizational Structure	• Federation of market-driven teams
Expertise Profile of Team	• High across the organization
Cultural Priorities	• Informal communication, knowledge of market niche, flexible strategies, cross-functional teamwork
Business Processes	• Flexible
Product Strategy	• Customized versions of the products to a small number of customers in various market niches
Inherent Strengths	• Market-driven innovation
Inherent Weaknesses	• Internal scrutiny of teams
Beneficial Legacies	• Mass customization

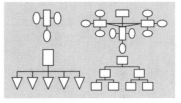

Chapter 9

Four Growth Phases, One Transitional Phase, and Five Operational Modes

I HAVE DESCRIBED THE GROWTH PHASES AND OPERATIONAL MODES IN A sequence that tracks the technology adoption cycle and that systematically prepares the enterprise for future needs. Consider this the ideal default sequence. This sequence—Innovation, Foundation Building, Producing, Planning, and Adapting—is a mantra that reminds you what mode should probably come next.

Table 9-1 summarizes key characteristics of each. At the top are listed the phases of growth, the primary customer groups each phase typically addresses, and the names of the operational modes. You adopt the operational mode indicated to make the most of the opportunity presented by the growth phase.

Below the name of each operational mode are the variables that define that operational mode. To develop a particular mode, develop or adopt the structures and practices described. These are variables over which you have some control. Keeping these aligned and well suited to the right phase of growth will help you operate optimally for your particular growth phase. But adopting these structures, practices, and priorities is difficult.

Growth Phase	Concept Development	(Transitional)	Rapid Market Expansion	Crowded Marketplace	Niche Development
Operational Mode	Innovating	Foundation Building	Producing	Planning	Adapting
Cultural Values *(People Factors)*	▪ Insight ▪ New ideas ▪ Action/Doing ▪ Agility	▪ Seeking opinions and listening ▪ Open discussion ▪ Consensus	§ Narrow focus § Being goal-oriented § Giving and following orders	▪ Stability ▪ Research ▪ Data-driven decisions ▪ Refinement and depth	▪ Pervasive communication ▪ Intimacy with market segment ▪ Responsive to customers ▪ Flexible strategies
Expertise Profile of Staff	Some high expertise, some low	—	Many relatively low expertise	Some specialized high expertise, some relatively low	High across organization
Naturally Effective Leadership Style	Decisive Visionary	Collaborative Planner	Decisive Commander	Analytical Planner	Collaborative Visionary
Total Members	Maximum of 10	Approximately 10 to 25	Approximately 20 to 60	Approximately 20 and up	Approximately 20 and up
Organizational Structure *(Business Processes and Structure)*	Team of focused generalists	Functionally segmented team	Platoon of implementers	Hierarchy of functional groups	Federation of market-driven teams
Business Processes	Informal	In transition	Focused and clear	Specialized and robust	Systematic but variable
Important Control Levers	Vision and Supervision	All controls initiated	Supervision/ assignments	▪ Organizational hierarchy plans, processes, and procedures	Vision, culture, performance feedback and evaluation, member expertise
Product Strategy *(Product Strategy)*	▪ Custom products ▪ Partner-like relationships with customers	Same as in prior growth phase	Commoditized product	▪ Standard product line, ▪ Price-competitive products	Products customized for market segments
Class of Buyers	Pioneers	Same as prior	Pragmatists	Conservatives	Sophisticates
Typical Strengths	▪ High performance ▪ Preferred by skilled staff ▪ Low cost ▪ Easy to manage	Important developmental phase	Market penetration	▪ Does not require high expertise of Adapting mode ▪ Consistent performance across products	▪ High business capacity and customer satisfaction ▪ Preferred by innovators
Typical Weaknesses	▪ One-generation activity ▪ Sensitive to personal chemistry and team dynamics ▪ Limited business capacity	Consumes business momentum	§ Promotes little insight or innovation § Lacks depth of expertise and diversity of strategy	▪ Produces optimal pieces, but a suboptimal whole ▪ Not responsive to varying customer demands	▪ Costly-requires scale and marketing muscle ▪ Requires sophisticated management and infrastructure

Table 9-1. Growth phases and operational modes

Review how the cultural biases of the organization shift across the modes. These represent dramatic changes favoring at different times innovation, consensus, thorough research, and responsiveness to customers. The changes in team structure are also significant. Moving from a focus team of generalists (in which everyone has direct contact with the leader) to several other structures to one in which team members operate with a high level of autonomy.

Note the different controls that are most dominant in that mode of operation. The concept of control levers helps us focus on the key organizational elements for a particular mode of operation. In the Planning mode, for example, the important control levers are the "hard" controls of structure, plans, processes, and procedures in place within the enterprise. However, during the Adapting mode, the important control levers are the "soft" controls of vision, culture, performance monitoring and feedback, and expertise of the team members. These changes represent significant shifts in the way the organization operates and will affect its members deeply.

While looking at Table 9-1, identify the current phase of growth for your current enterprise and how well aligned your current organization to its current goals. Consider changes you have observed and see if they can be placed on the table. Appendix B poses questions that will help you identify where you are.

Considering the changes implied by moving from phase to phase, you may decide that you do not want your enterprise to fully and effectively adopt the operational mode indicated. For some Visionary leaders, the costs of adopting the Producing mode are too great. You must then recognize that you may not be taking full advantage of this growth phase. If you own the enterprise, only you can determine that trade-off is right for you. If others own the enterprise, their views become relevant. Many investors hold companies primarily for their economic potential and this objective should weigh in the selection of the right developmental course. By making these assessments, you can begin to make trade-offs. The sequence makes a difference.

But, as mentioned earlier, not all phases and their modes will be right for all enterprises. You must review the opportunities before you and make some choices.

Considering the changes implied by moving from phase to phase, you may decide that you do not want your enterprise to fully and effectively adopt the operational mode indicated.

What's Behind Door #1, Door #2, and Door #3

After a successful Concept Development phase using the Innovating operational mode, you stand in the transitional phase for the first time and consider the type of foundation you must build. Consider the three alternative growth phases: Rapid Market Expansion, Crowded Marketplace, and Niche Development.

When you evaluate what is behind the three doors, consider:

1. The customer groups being targeted and the respective business potential
2. Whether or not you are willing to pay the costs to make that change
3. Whether it will help your business achieve its objectives

These are the important questions. Focus on these rather than only questions like "Is it familiar?" and "Will I like it?" and "Will it be interesting?" Review the extent to which each of these phases fits the opportunities available to you and your ability to execute effectively.

If your enterprise has started or can participate in a rapidly expanding market of pragmatist customers who are anxious to buy your product—if this is the opportunity the market presents to you—this is usually the most attractive business opportunity and you should consider the Producing operational mode.

If a rapidly expanding market is not available, you may find that you are serving primarily conservative customers.

If a rapidly expanding market is not available, you may find that you are serving primarily conservative customers. This group of customers has high demands for product reliability and competitive prices. But this group is typically large and these customers do not require continual innovations or a high level of customization to be satisfied. If you can leverage your capabilities very broadly, this Crowded Marketplace phase of growth can be appropriate. Consider the Planning operational mode and its "measure twice, cut once" orientation.

You may find that the most attractive business opportunity is the serving sophisticated customers willing to pay a premium for customized solutions. If so, this represents a Niche Development growth phase. Consider the Adapting operational mode and develop a sophisticated context for a federation of market-driven teams that can know intimately and execute the drivers of success in each niche.

As you consider what is behind these doors, carefully consider the costs associated with adopting each operational mode. The costs can be counted in terms of any direct expenditure and, often more critically, the changes to your organization's power structure and culture and the changes in promoting the different set of business priorities. These costs can be significant.

Reducing the Costs of Making the Transitions

The cost of the changes can be reduced by advance preparation for the targeted operational mode. If you can determine what mode of operation will be needed next, you do early groundwork. This involves developing the important control levers and testing them before they are needed. If you are going to need formal plans and processes, start developing them before they are needed in order to improve your skills in making them. If you are going to need robust performance monitoring and feedback, develop them earlier than needed. The control levers can exist without your relying on them heavily. Obviously, if every lever were free, you would build them all at once and use them as needed. But there are costs associated with them, so build them strategically.

If you are going to need robust performance monitoring and feedback, develop them earlier than needed.

Giving everyone advance notice of the types of changes that are likely to occur can reduce the cost of the changes. This notice will allow them to make the needed changes in their activities. In countries in which a change in work patterns means that some people will be displaced, there is anxiety about these changes. In countries with traditions of lifetime employment, these changes are viewed as more normal. In the U.S., we are unlikely to adopt lifetime employment and in Japan this tradition is changing. But if you initiate change early and openly, there is time to retool the enterprise and for your team members to retool themselves for the coming operational mode. Also, if the change is initiated early rather than late, the degree of change can be less dramatic. The enterprise will be less misaligned and there will be fewer new staff brought in to get a little bit more out of an engine that is already revving at 9,000 rpm. If all who are involved know changes are coming and if they realize that the structures and practices put in place may be only for a particular growth phase, your enterprise can be more flexible and more fully aligned to meeting its most pressing issues.

The cost of change can also be reduced by carefully developing the culture of the organization. If you seek to move through the different growth phases, avoid embedding in the culture any particular operational mode. Avoid embedding the belief that decisions will always be made in a certain way and that certain functions will dominate (e.g., sales dominates engineering or vice versa).

Organizational cultures are influenced by a variety of forces. The forces might include the priorities of the leader, what has been successful in the past, what the members of the organization like to do, and the general societal cultures. To promote flexibility and anticipating change, reduce the impact of some of these other forces and actively embed other values in the culture. Actively embed fundamental core values and elements that are distinctive but not tied to any particular operational mode.

Develop a culture that values success. If growth is your objective, the culture should value adopting the right operational mode for the right situation. If staying with one mode of operation is your objective, then the culture should value that mode and also value finding business opportunities that respond well to that mode.

Change can be made more easily if the leader openly and visibly endorses the changes.

Change can be made more easily if the leader openly and visibly endorses the changes. Some of the modes of operation will not be pleasant but are important. If the leader is seen embracing the needed changes, others will be more inclined to make similar changes.

Vic Unmasked

In the prior chapters, Vic was skillful in navigating the changes required to be effective in the different growth phases. Vic had been through this sequence before so it was easier for him to understand some of the trade-off required. He used a combination of emulating the management style that models effective leadership for each phase and collaborating with others within his enterprise to lead his enterprise through the various phases of growth. His enterprise produced physical products and there was an opportunity for Sparrow, Inc. to experience all growth phases. Vic was accustomed to all the phases and how to adjust structures, practices, and priorities to fit the circumstances of the enterprise. Vic decided to pursue these opportunities and to change the way his business operated to achieve the goals of his enterprise.

But, as mentioned at the outset of the Vic story, Vic as a specific person is fictitious, a composite of several leaders, some of whom navigate just one or two transitions. In my experience over the last 20 years, I have encountered just a few people who had the need to pass through all growth phases and made all the changes as deliberately as Vic.

But I have met many leaders of successful enterprises who say, "You must have been a fly on our wall. This is exactly what happened to us." However, they also say that their development through the phases was more or less accidental. They made the needed changes because they just happened to stumble onto the correct operation mode without advance thought or planning. They took on someone new, for example, and that new person brought the needed operational mode. To be sure, there are many who stumble onto the wrong mode. Nonetheless, the changes promoted by Vic are experienced by these ventures and by leaders who model the appropriate operational modes. While there are cases where firms, by design or luck, navigated the appropriate shifts from one operational mode to another, I have met with many more enterprises that struggle with growth and development.

Common Errors

Broadly speaking, there are several ways in which growing enterprises go off track. These are errors that tend to be related to fundamental human behavior and judgment.

Founding Entrepreneurs Do Not Give Up Control

Entrepreneurs invest a huge amount of energy, resources, and time in starting and developing their ventures. The ventures are their kids. Much of their self-esteem is based on their success as founders of such organizations. But at some point the founders must assess whether they have the appropriate vision, skill, inclination, and talent to guide the firm into the next phase. The marketplace isn't static and neither are organizations. A founder who holds tightly to the reins and doesn't allow those with needed talents and insights to participate in guiding the firm forward will weaken his or her kid's growth and development. This is a classic tale. The person who starts the business cannot give up control. In our consulting practice we have seen three situations.

First, there are leaders who haven't given up control, but should do so if the enterprise is to move forward. Much of the pain and uncertainty about ultimate success related to moving can be mitigated by an early focus on building the right operational mode for the future before the need for that mode is critical. If you shift gears when you still have some business momentum, you will have many more options. Preparing and then shifting gears in

At some point the founders must assess whether they have the appropriate vision, skill, inclination, and talent to guide the firm into the next phase.

173

a deliberate and disciplined manner can help these businesses achieve broader-based success. It may seem to the leaders that they are indispensable, because of their history with the enterprise and the unique contributions they provide. But many leaders are more dispensable than they believe.

Consider the realization of Matt Goldman, one of the founders of the Blue Man Group.[1]

> Their first real breakthrough didn't come until several years later, when they belatedly saw the wisdom of advice they received from noted business philosopher Penn Jilette, half of the irreverent Penn & Teller comedy-magic duo. "He saw the show in, like, the first month," says Goldman. … "He said, 'Oh, my God! You guys can do what Teller and I can never do! You can clone yourselves!' And we said, 'No, you don't get it, we're more like a band.' I actually thought he was, like … a wackhead."
>
> So they continued on, three friends, doing their show. Six days a week, three years without a break, more than 1,200 consecutive performances. There was one understudy, to satisfy the group's financial backers, but while he'd studied the show, he never so much as rehearsed it. The three began to feel like prisoners of their success. They weren't creating new material, just performing Tubes over and over. Finally Stanton cut his hand one day while fooling around with a router. The understudy stepped in—and it worked.
>
> "It was a catalytic event," Goldman says. Blue Man Group wasn't a cult of personality. The founders could oversee the show without necessarily being in the show.

There are founders who don't give up control and shouldn't—their day-to-day involvement is a key driver of the enterprises success.

The Blue Man Group now has hundreds of performers and dozens of shows.

Second, there are founders who don't give up control and shouldn't—their day-to-day involvement is a key driver of the enterprises success. The nature of what they do requires their highly personal contribution. About half of the investment management teams are in this situation. The weakness in this scenario is that the enterprise isn't highly scalable. One person can stretch himself or herself only so far, and business growth may far exceed one individual's capacity. If you want to overcome this limitation, develop a revised business model that does not require the innovative insights of the particular person and allows for scale. Clearly, sometimes getting out of the picture is not an option. But there are not as many leaders who actually are indispensable as believe that they are.

---

1. Fortune.com, Rob Walker, "Brand Blue," March 2003.

Finally, there are founders who haven't given up control; they should give it up, but they can't or won't. They not only refuse to build intermediate controls, but they actively work against their firm by releasing rabbits (coming up with ideas that distract from the focus) and withholding information. It's not that they want to bring their firm down; it's just that they simply cannot see the real situation around them and recognize that changes are needed. They are wearing blinders and see no reason to take them off. Positive change may simply not occur.

Gravitating to a Comfortable Operational Mode

Gravitating to a comfortable spot is understandable. The enterprise has a strong bias toward a particular operational mode. This is understandable because it is human nature to want to continue to do things we like and avoid those we don't know or don't like. Enterprises in this situation do the operational mode they like but do not obtain the benefits of earlier phases of growth. Prior growth phases or transitional phases are underdeveloped. In addition, these enterprises resist developing past their comfortable mode.

On the map of organizational modes (Figure 9-1), some operational modes are likely to be more favored than others.

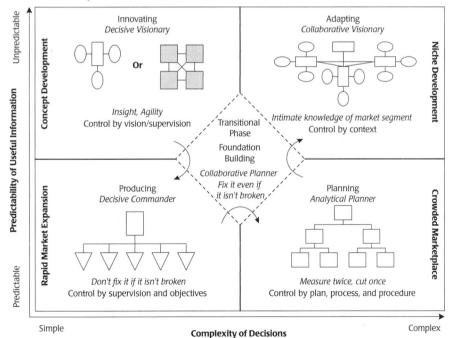

Figure 9-1. Organizational modes

Your enterprise may gravitate to that operational mode. This is not a problem of poorly aligned internal organizational elements, but rather a problem of aligning the enterprise with the external market opportunity. You may be missing business opportunities. The result is that organization skips growth phases; this may represent a significant opportunity cost.

For example, if the top managers like the Producing mode, this is what they do. They operate in the Producing mode and their enterprise probably lacks a breakthrough innovation that would position it well to initiate a rapidly expanding market. This type of enterprise will probably need to be opportunistic and move to whatever market is expanding rapidly and offer a product. The company is not likely to be growth-driven through owning a breakthrough innovation. This may work as long as the leaders are realistic and honest about what they are doing and why.

The chapter on Rapid Market Expansion discussed a phase that is commonly skipped: Visionary leaders who are successful in the Innovating operational mode tend to skip the Producing mode of operation and therefore do not take advantage of the Rapid Market Expansion phase that may be associated with their innovations. Instead, these leaders may be attracted to the Adapting mode of operation—it is more similar to the Innovating mode that they favor.

The Innovating mode and the Adapting mode both place a high priority on creativity and flexibility and involve a high level of sensitivity to customers. Formal planning and decision structures are not strong elements of either. Serving the various segments in the Niche Development phase requires customization similar to that demanded by customers during the Concept Development phase. The Adapting mode will seem familiar and the transition to this phase of growth is more practical than the transition to the Rapid Market Expansion phase and the Producing mode or to the Crowded Marketplace phase and the Planning mode. The change from Innovating to Adapting appears to be comfortable and easily done.

By doing this, they essentially skip the Rapid Market Expansion and Crowded Marketplace phases, both of which offer attractive opportunities. This path may be the right course for some enterprises. The effort required to change operational modes is significant and change does not occur immediately. But leaders should have some idea of the opportunity costs associated this strategy. To get an idea of the opportunity cost of pursuing a mode of operation based on life style as opposed to economic opportunities, let's go back and review the work of Geoffrey Moore (*Inside the Tornado*). If the

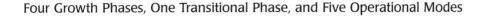

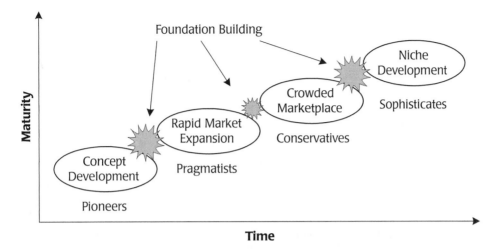

Figure 9-2. Growth phases with associated customer groups

enterprise does indeed have a breakthrough innovation, moving directly to an Adapting mode may not allow the focus and singular sales purpose that take fullest advantage of the opportunity available through the Producing mode.

Figure 9-2 shows the earlier stair-step image of enterprise growth. The customer groups are shown in relation to the phases of growth.

If leaders skip the Rapid Market Expansion and Crowded Marketplace phases, as is the tendency for Decisive Visionaries with an especially strong Visionary component, their company will not be taking advantage of a customer group with significant business potential. This is shown in the diagram below (Figure 9-3), which shows the customer groups and their relative business potential. A company that does not take advantage of the pragmatist customers will leave significant business on the table.

Also, by avoiding specialized Producing and Planning modes (associated with the Rapid Market Expansion and Crowded Marketplace phases, respectively), the company may underserve a significant portion of its potential markets. By moving directly to the Adapting mode, it will not serve the pragmatists and conservatives as quickly or effectively as it could have. Clearly, a company should consider whether or not to go after these very large customer groups only after considering the costs and benefits. If you are in a highly competitive market, someone else will serve them more directly and your company will be in a weaker competitive position.

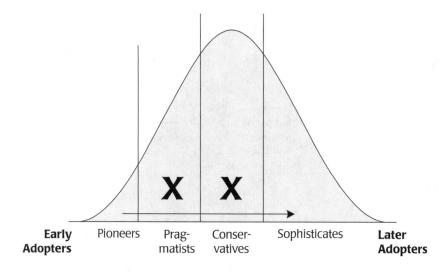

Figure 9-3. Life cycle and customer groups

Organizational Elements Follow Paths of Least Resistance

Many innovative firms start out in the Innovating mode of operation quite naturally: aligning structure, culture, and practices to the situation occurs easily. But these are small organizations, usually of fewer than ten people.

In virtually all the best larger firms, alignment happens intentionally—someone has designed the enterprise to align its various elements. This is quite a feat considering the extent of the changes required to obtain alignment and the discipline required to maintain it over time. Unfortunately, unless managed to maintain alignment, these elements follow paths of least resistance.

Let's first review the ideal progression for an enterprise that possesses a breakthrough innovation, from the Innovating mode through to the Adapting mode. It starts in the upper left corner of the map (Figure 9-1) and proceeds counter-clockwise around the map to take advantage of each successive market opportunity. Its organizational structure, cultural priorities, controls, and work processes would change to remain aligned with the changing circumstances.

When organizational elements follow paths of least resistance, they follow these paths as shown in Figure 9-4:

1. The cultural priorities typically shift directly toward the Adapting mode

of operation.

2. The organizational structure shifts toward the Planning mode.
3. The internal business processes remain in the Innovating mode (or perhaps the Transitional mode).
4. All the while, the business opportunity moves toward Rapid Market Expansion (which would be best served by the Producing mode).

The path of least resistance for the cultural priorities of the enterprise is a shift toward the Adapting mode. The historical success the enterprise has had with innovation cements cultural priorities of customizing products for small market segments, ad hoc processes and strategies, and expecting everyone to be involved in decision making. The enterprise continues to place high priority on flexibility and adaptability, similar to an Adapting organization. It values new innovation rather than fully exploiting opportunities presented by the first innovation.

The path of least resistance for the cultural priorities of the enterprise is a shift toward the Adapting mode.

The path of least resistance for the organizational structure is to make a beeline for the structures of the Planning mode—hierarchical and inflexible. When a small organization begins to grow, the new hires (second-generation staff) report to one of the first-generation staff. Several months or a few years later, the second-generation members say that they could be much more effective if they each had two assistants. Thus, the third generation is hired. Later, the third-generation members say they could be more effective if they had two assistants. And so on and on it goes. This is a path of least resistance because growth appears to be organic and there is no painful restructuring of reporting roles. Without periodic restructuring, informal organizations can quickly become rigid hierarchies.

The path of least resistance for work processes is to fix them only when they break. Rationalization of work processes requires painful restructuring and disruption of how people work and their responsibilities. Yet, particularly after the development of a successful breakthrough innovation (inherently a trial-and-error process), rationalization of work processes can produce tremendous benefits.

Again, if there is a breakthrough innovation, the business opportunity may well be in a Rapid Market Expansion phase.

The enterprise that avoids any realigning to develop new operational modes becomes neither strong nor compelling. It has

▶ A loose, consensus-oriented culture
▶ An inflexible, functionally oriented organizational structure

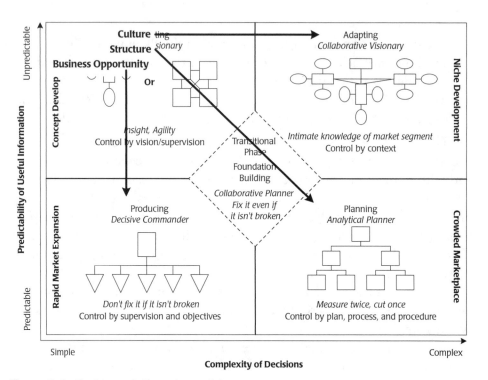

Figure 9-4. Choice and Change model

▶ Work practices that have not changed since they were originally pieced together in a trial-and-error fashion

The business opportunity available to the enterprise is to focus narrowly on selling a standardized product through a Rapid Market Expansion phase. Yet it is poorly suited to the focus, production orientation, and speed required to take full advantage of the rapidly expanding marketplace for the product. Its rigid structures make change difficult because of the strong departmental divisions, or silos. The consensus-oriented culture slows decision making. This situation represents a major missed opportunity.

Many of these problems relate to elements of human nature. People do what they like to do. They follow their interests and avoid things they do not like. These are some of the strongest forces guiding the shape of our organizations.

As individuals, this makes perfect sense as we want to gravitate to situations that we like and where we feel successful. People extrapolate successes from the past into the future. Rewarded behaviors are repeated. It is only natural to do so. A cougar returns to the sites of its kills. This is in many situations a success-oriented behavior.

180

But our enterprises are different. There are other stakeholders involved and the market may not provide support strong economic support for certain operational modes. The external environments of an enterprise change and leaders must be able to let go of practices that served well in a prior situation and find what will work in the present and future. This is what was described in *Who Moved My Cheese?* by Spencer Johnson.

People get hooked on their control and power. Part of the reluctance to change comes from a real need to maintain control. The lack of other workable control levers is a logical rationale. But some simply cannot let go.

To promote the growth of an economically healthy enterprise, you will have to manage these human forces. If you see the big picture and the trade-offs, you strike a better balance—one that makes sense for your situation. Even after reading this book, you may not be able to go through all the different phases and modes described. But you will know which operational modes are best for you and how to develop a business development plan that will allow you to optimize the success of your enterprise and the satisfaction of its members and various stakeholders. You will be better able to face the realities of your situation and make choices that help you achieve your goals and objectives.

Stepping Back

As the leader, you should continually be aware of which operational mode is right for your enterprise. One way is to track the customer group being targeted, as I have described in this book. Another is to look at your situation in terms of the complexity and unpredictability of the most important issues facing your enterprise. As shown in the map (Figure 9-1), each of the four modes of operation is associated with a specific type of business situation, management stylea and organizational structure.

In the diagram, the horizontal axis represents *Complexity of Decisions*, which refers to the number of issues or perspectives that must be considered when making an important decision in the future. It also reflects the number of decisions that must be made. Usually, the issues or perspectives relate to the business environment, your product and product development, your organization, and anything you need to make it operate. The more complex the decisions are, the more these decisions must be divided into smaller units and delegated to others. The less complex this decision-making environment is, the more decision making can rest with a single individual.

The more unpredictable the useful information, the more human judgment will be required to determine what is and will be useful and relevant.

181

The vertical axis represents *Predictability of Useful Information* that will be relevant to current and future decisions. The more unpredictable the useful information, the more human judgment will be required to determine what is and will be useful and relevant. The less unpredictable, the more the management of that information can depend on systematic processes for efficiency and effectiveness.

The Concept Development and Niche Development phases generally represent situations in which useful information is unpredictable: one cannot be sure what will be relevant and useful for decisions now and in the future. Rapid Market Expansion and Crowded Marketplace phases are more predictable: one can determine what constitutes useful and relevant information.

The Concept Development and Rapid Market Expansion phases generally involve situations with relatively few major issues that command the attention of leadership. In contrast, the Crowded Marketplace (market stabilization) and Niche Development phases are often more complex in terms of the variety of issues leadership must deal with.

As you can see in Figure 9-1, the complexity and unpredictability of your management situation changes for each phase of your organization's growth. To lead the organization effectively during each phase, you must understand the decision-making requirement of each type of situation.

Unpredictable, Simple Situations

Unpredictable situations that are relatively simple, those of the upper left quadrant, call for quick and intuitive decision making by individuals immersed in the situation, individuals working at the coal face. This situation is similar to a crisis when a major issue rapidly emerges to the forefront and other issues fade into the background. An individual has to assess information that is not easily identified in advance and must respond quickly to the situation. One person or a small team usually handles these situations most effectively. Focus, agility, and breakthrough innovations are key to success. These are characteristics of the Innovating mode.

Simple, Stable Situations

In situations that are simple and stable, those in the lower left quadrant of the chart, decisions can be made in a straightforward manner. It is obvious what should be done because the information required for the decision is simple and stable over time. Information can be evaluated and scrutinized by a number of people to identify the appropriate decision and predict the appropriate outcome. The standard, readily acknowledged decision or answer is probably most effective. Focus and the speed of decision making create the business advantage. These are characteristics of the Producing mode.

Complex, Stable Situations

In situations that are complex and stable, those in the lower right quadrant of the chart, decisions are typically made by devoting effort to researching and analyzing the situation to identify the best way to proceed. Because the relevant information is relatively stable over time, once the analysis is done and done well, there is no need to rethink the analysis and decision. Any systems or plans developed as a result of this analysis are useful for managing the situation in the future, thus making such an investment worthwhile. The situation can be determined and the response programmed in advance. Building any cleverness into the systems and processes and robust execution are key to success. These are characteristics of the Planning mode.

Unpredictable, Complex Situations

In unpredictable situations that are more complex, those of the upper right quadrant of the chart, more than one decision maker should be involved. It is not possible for a single individual to adapt quickly enough in all the situations that must be addressed. To be most effective, a team should make decisions holistically about one portion of the overall situation. For the leader to work through other people requires a more flexible and collaborative decision-making process. Teamwork and developmental innovation are important to success. These are characteristics of the Adapting mode.

Indirect vs. Direct, Knowledge vs. Efficiency

Based on the complexity and unpredictability axes, the right half of the map diagram indicates phases of growth that depend more on the leader working through the organization to achieve success. The left half indicates phases that depend relatively more on the leader's personal handling of an issue. The top half of the diagram indicates growth phases that depend most on individuals being knowledgeable about the volatile issues. In contrast, the bottom half indicates phases that depend on operational efficiency for success.

Recognizing the Inherent Weaknesses of Each Mode

Regardless of the mode in which your organization is operating, it will always face challenges in the areas in which it is inherently weak. To identify the inherent weaknesses for an organization in one mode, look at the strengths of the mode that is in the opposite corner of the map.

For example, if your organization is most like an Innovating organization, its key inherent weakness is the inability to act like a Planning organization, which is the mode opposite the Innovating mode in the map. If yours is a Planning organization, its inherent weakness is likely to be lack of innovation and agility. A Producing organization's weakness would be the inability to adapt or take on a problem-solving orientation with customers. If yours is an Adapting organization, the key weaknesses will likely be the inability to focus on one particular product or market segment and exploit it fully to gain large market share, which are the traits of a Producing organization.

Regardless of the mode in which your organization is operating, it will always face challenges in the areas in which it is inherently weak.

Past the Initial Five Phases—Leaders on the Leading Edge

The phases that I describe represent periods of time in which certain issues or opportunities command leadership attention. The sequence begins at the inception of the idea or product and progresses because of the growing scale of the enterprise and the evolving external market opportunities as the new idea becomes more widely accepted in the marketplace.

As an enterprise goes through these phases and adopts the appropriate operational mode, it does so on a progressively smaller portion of the enterprise. During each phase, the leaders develop and perfect an operational mode in order to address a specific need or serve a specific purpose. In some cases, these needs or purposes will continue to exist regardless of how the enterprise develops going forward. Thus, a portion of the operational mode developed for a particular phase will continue and remain dedicated to a particular purpose. For example, when you develop a strong internal business infrastructure using the Foundation Building mode in a transitional phase, part of the enterprise continues to operate in that mode while the leaders move on to the next operational frontier.

When you develop a strong sales focus using the Producing mode in the Rapid Market Expansion phase, this sales focus can remain within the enterprise, managed by someone other than the leader of the enterprise. Building on the beneficial legacies of prior growth phases and operational modes, the enterprise develops successive layers of organizational structures, control levers, and other practices needed to continue to succeed. After each phase, the leadership team moves on to identify the most pressing needs of the enterprise and initiate the development of the appropriate operational mode to meet those needs.

At inception, 100 percent of the enterprise uses the Innovating operational mode. Virtually all of the enterprise moves on to the Foundation Building mode to consolidate and make more rational the practices needed to produce the innovation on an ongoing basis. This is yet another reason why that first transition is so difficult. When all control levers have been initiated and the Foundation Building of that transition is complete, some portion, let's say 80 percent of the enterprise, moves on to the Producing mode during Rapid Market Expansion. A sales orientation is developed at this point. From there, a smaller portion, say 70 percent, moves on to the Planning mode for the Crowded Marketplace phase. From there, say 50 percent moves on to the Adapting mode for the Niche Development phase.

It is important for the leaders to be able to read the subtle clues that a change in operational mode will soon be needed and begin to make preparations for the change.

Thus, the transitions become progressively easier for the leader and the enterprise. They become more expensive, however, simply because of the greater scale of the later transitions. Yet, it is important for the leaders to be able to read the subtle clues that a change in operational mode will soon be needed and begin to make preparations for the change.

Vic in our case study navigates this path. He focuses his attention on the new areas that need to be developed to address the enterprise's most important developmental needs. He does each well and appropriately so that once it is established, he can safely turn his attention to the set of needs and objectives that represent the future. He queues up the enterprise and the next appropriate leader and gets them started. He then leaves each area in good hands and operating as it should. He will not have to turn his attention back later and fight rear-guard battles.

Past the initial use of the four growth phases and their operational modes, the enterprise becomes a portfolio of enterprises, each proceeding down its own developmental path. The role of the leadership team then becomes to make sure that each enterprise is operating the way it should and preparing as it should for its own next growth phase and initiating the development of new enterprises and winding down those that no longer contribute to the strength of the whole.

This is when your enterprise is firing on all cylinders. You have a business using multiple operational modes to achieve a diversified set of needs and objectives:

- The product innovation group is using something like the Innovating mode.
- The sales group is using something like the Producing mode.
- The manufacturing and operational infrastructure groups are using the Planning mode.
- The customer service and product enhancement groups are using something like the Adapting mode.

The leaders' role is to determine where the enterprise should place its focus and how that focus should be supported in terms of the organizational structures and operational practices that can take it where they want it to go.

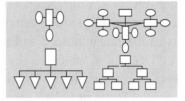

Chapter 10

Survival Tips

Lucky leaders come into a situation that happens to require their preferred way of managing, their preferred operational mode. To be effective over long periods of time and in different situations, however, a leader must know when to champion different practices and priorities, even when they are not those that are personally most comfortable. You must be able to determine the right moment to shift gears. You must have the wisdom to know that some discomfort associated with change will produce greater future benefits. The ten survival tips in this chapter will help you survive the challenges of leading a growing and changing company and provide your enterprise with the leadership it needs.

1. Know Yourself

To effectively manage your growing organization through the challenges that confront it, you must first understand your own biases. Think about what work situations you find most interesting. Consider the types of situations in which you have been most successful. Is there a relationship between the situations you prefer and those in which you are most successful? Think about what situations you find boring and what situations have been less than successful for you. Is there a relationship between these? An understanding of your preferences will help you identify the effective practices that are likely to develop as a natural result of doing what you like to do, as well as those that will need to be the result of a conscious decision.

Determine which of the four momentum-generating operational modes you are naturally most comfortable with. Then identify the mode that appears at the opposite corner of the map. This is your probable weak point, so you'll have to learn special skills to be effective in that mode. You can take cues from others. Confer with people who work well in that mode, especially those who prefer the mode that you prefer, people from whom you can learn. Observe how they set priorities and operate in different modes.

While a leader's preferences for managing are important, other factors such as wisdom and flexibility can ultimately be more important.

While a leader's preferences for managing are important, other factors, such as wisdom and flexibility, can ultimately be more important. You need the wisdom to see your situation realistically and to see the trade-offs that may be required. Flexibility allows you to change organizational priorities at different times.

2. See Your Situation Objectively

When you look at your business situation, see it for what it really is, as opposed to what you would like it to be. What people see is often heavily influenced by their expectations. Avoid the trap of looking for situations that will respond well to your favorite type of solution—"When all you have is a hammer, everything looks like a nail." Look objectively at the problems that confront you, try to understand them, and then determine what types of solutions would be appropriate.

Look closely at the developmental sequences shown in the road map in Chapter 9 (Figure 9-1) to assess your current location or position, keeping in mind as your destination your product's full market potential. Just as an automobile's optimum speed depends on road conditions, your speed through these phases will be affected by various challenges you encounter in your management situation. Consider predictable problems as roadblocks or detours and adjust your trip accordingly. The suggested growth phases are like recommended routes on freeways and highways. They are meant to be useful as a basic itinerary. Remember: your trip is unique.

3. Allow Personal and Organizational Objectives to Diverge

Over time, your enterprise's objectives will begin to evolve independently from your own. Be ready for those times, both personally and as the leader of the organization. Periodically review the original concepts of the business to see what your company's inception was based upon and how its current objectives may differ.

Originally, the objectives may have been to take advantage of a specific and narrowly defined market opportunity, to be creative and aggressive, to validate your vision, or to change the world in some meaningful way. As time goes by and your organization grows and matures, its objectives change. Issues that increase in importance are such essentials as financial soundness, customer and community relations, and supplier connections. These issues begin to overwhelm some of the earlier, perhaps more noble and exciting broad objectives. You may have to settle for high profitability rather than changing the world. The divergence of your enterprise's objectives from your personal objectives may be painful and difficult for you and the company.

When your enterprise involves people and business growth, change is inevitable. Even if you decide not to grow, change will occur. If people were hired as extensions of you while in the Innovating mode, they may ultimately want greater responsibility. The first people you hire are more likely to be motivated by the challenge and excitement of being in a new venture. As you hire more people, your organization begins to reflect the general population from which you're drawing. While the fifth person you hire may be motivated by your vision, the 50th person will be motivated more by a desire to pay the mortgage. The demographic forces of an organization will not allow your enterprise to stand still.

The first people you hire are more likely to be motivated by the challenge and excitement of being in a new venture.

4. Look for Subtle Clues of the Need for Deeper Change

Look for the subtle seismic movements in daily operations that represent deeper and fundamental changes to which you will need to adapt. When you continue to have a certain type of problem, it may indicate that you are using the wrong operational mode. Certain types of problems, especially personnel problems, are sometimes an early indication of the need for fundamental change. Recurring problems concerning uncertainty about responsibility and authority could indicate that a Foundation Building mode is needed.

Recurring issues about the lack of opportunity for advancement indicate that your firm is structured too rigidly. Recurring problems about a lack of responsiveness to customers may mean that defiant isolation is a general weakness. Unmotivated staff may mean that the leadership allelopathy is not ebbing properly.

There are people who are highly sensitive to certain deficiencies or problems in an organization and who can provide warning signals indicating the issues you must deal with.

Some people in your organization might serve a function similar to canaries in a mine shaft. These are people who are highly sensitive to certain deficiencies or problems in an organization and who can provide warning signals indicating the issues you must deal with. Carefully consider any comments that are delivered intensely, especially if they are part of a developing trend. If you assume that all problems are unrelated, you could miss early warning signs that bigger ones are looming on the horizon.

Do you remember the person in Thailand who saved a dozen people from the tidal wave in December 2004? He knew that before a tidal wave water levels drop quickly. He saw this sign and ran for higher ground. Understanding the meaning of that little clue made him a hero.

There is no naturally occurring force that will move you and your organization automatically from one mode of operation to the next. You need to make choices and initiate change. These take time. They are also less expensive if you do them earlier than later. Being sensitive to the subtle clues gives you advance warning.

5. Use Business Momentum Wisely

Success builds business momentum, which you can use to carry your company through transitional periods of Foundation Building. The Concept Development, Rapid Market Expansion, Crowded Marketplace, and Niche Development phases produce business growth and generate business momentum. In contrast, the transitional phase requiring the Foundation Building mode usually consumes business momentum. Use the momentum generated during a growth phase to carry you through the next period of Foundation Building. As you progress through the phases, the transitions can become shorter as you become better at anticipating the changes and building the needed control levers earlier.

6. Anticipate and Prepare for the Changes That Lie Ahead

A key role of the leader of a growing organization is to instigate appropriate changes before the need for the changes becomes imperative. Anticipate changes in both your organization and its marketplace. Be attentive to fundamental changes in the customer group and the nature of competition. Any changes in these may require you to change along with them. Identify the right time to shake up the existing structure and culture of the organization and to introduce more appropriate attitudes, priorities, and capabilities. Initiate timely revolutions, but don't purge every aspect of the practices developed in the prior phases. Carry the benefits forward and put down a new layer of capabilities when you move from phase to phase.

When you hire people, have an idea of how each job and role will change over time.

When you hire people, have an idea of how each job and role will change over time. Don't make promises about long-term roles and responsibilities that you won't be able to keep. This will help them and you to prepare for the requirements of those jobs. It also makes it less likely that some of these individuals will become redundant as the organization evolves. Regulate the power of individuals to prevent a particular structure from becoming too embedded in the organization.

7. Work with and Through Others to Achieve Objectives

You will discover that some operational modes come more naturally than others. Working with and through others can help you meet your objectives more quickly and effectively. Discuss with your staff why a change is needed, what will be accomplished if the change is made, and what will be required to make the change. Without this information, your shifts in priorities and modes of operation may confuse others. Assure them that practices of the past are not wrong, but they simply no longer fit the current or anticipated needs and it is time for a different mode of operating. If you initiate change early and allow your staff to participate in the process, you will be surprised at how forward-looking your staff can be. They will know that you are not held captive by the limits of your management style and that they should not be either.

When you create management teams, either formally or informally, you should try to both extend yourself and complement yourself. Identify people

191

who share your energy, but also select people different from you who can supplement your strengths. A team of diverse individuals will have a better chance of seeing what lies ahead and making the needed changes.

Depend more on different people in different phases. You will need to develop specialized modes of operation during appropriate phases, so look for complementary skills and management style biases and consider similar levels of energy and passions for success to give you more flexibility. Do not try to give all points of view equal weight at all times. To do so will not give you the competitive strength you will need in each phase. It will help greatly, however, to have everyone reading the same road map.

8. Sculpt the Culture of the Organization

An organization's culture is sometimes the most powerful force in determining how its members act. Seek not to limit the culture but to enlarge it to support the different practices needed in different situations. An organization's culture both reflects and affects attitudes about how things should be done and to which issues to give priority. When the members of your team are deciding how to prioritize their work, make compromises, and interact with others, your organization's culture is often what tips the balance toward a certain direction.

Realize that, as a leader, you have a tremendous impact on the culture of the organization.

Realize that, as a leader, you have a tremendous impact on the culture of the organization. Be very aware of the messages you send to others through your words and actions. Take an active interest in shaping the culture and mold it to be supportive of long-term success. Understand that it is appropriate for you to be highly decisive at certain times and slow and methodical at others. Ultimately, no single style of management should be so tightly woven into the culture of the organization that it cannot change. All must be represented.

Create an atmosphere of success. Reward people for responding to the true nature of problems. If the staff know that success and effectiveness are most important, they will be better able to handle challenges.

9. Broaden Your Own Range of Leadership Skills

Learn skills and techniques from others who are naturally well suited to situations you find difficult. Follow their lead and emulate their practices and priorities. Throughout the development of your business, you may need to use every operational mode discussed. You'll need to be able to set a variety of priorities, some contrary to what you're personally most comfortable with or interested in. Consequently, you may need to broaden your range of leadership skills to make the various situations more comfortable.

Then, when the situation requires a management style or operational mode different from your usual one, you can call on the new skills you have developed in these experiences to decide what direction is appropriate and help provide the kinds of leadership needed.

10. Find Ways to Make Natural Tendencies Pay

Given a free-flowing labor market, people will gravitate to situations where they find comfort and success. The successive phases of business growth may require leaders to focus on issues that they don't find interesting or handle particularly well. Many entrepreneurs resist a new phase because they don't know whether the change is going to be permanent or not. The fact that there are phases, however, presents the possibility that later phases may again be more personally gratifying. The key is to attend to the needs of the enterprise; then it can come back to a situation that's more comfortable and rewarding for the leader.

Just as you strive to create a situation that benefits from your personal preferences, also consider the interests of your staff. Find ways to make people's natural tendencies pay.

Just as you strive to create a situation that benefits from your personal preferences, also consider the interests of your staff. Find ways to make people's natural tendencies pay. While we all can behave differently from our preferences when it is clearly to our advantage to do so, if you have your people do what they enjoy, they will be more enthusiastic and productive. Use the tools in this book to understand your human resources and build on what you have or can access.

These disciplines will enable you to break free from the barriers to growth created by preserving once-successful practices in situations that require other approaches.

Vic Survived the Journey

As Vic looks back now at all his company has gone through, all the different phases of growth, he is amazed. He never imagined when he began a few short years ago that he would have to go through so much to turn his flash of inspiration into another stable business. All he had wanted to do was to bring his idea into reality.

Now he sits in his office and looks out onto a hive of activity in a state-of-the-art machine shop and busy assembly plant. Established products are being produced efficiently, new products are innovative, and the company is involved in relevant, rapidly expanding markets.

"All of this started from just a single inspiration," he thinks, but he also realizes that the initial business has been transformed several times to get to where it is today. Those were challenging times. But with the help of his dedicated team, they were able to grow through these changes. "Whew," he thinks. "I have survived."

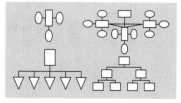

Appendix A

Management Style Should Be Different in Different Growth Phases

O THER WRITERS AND RESEARCHERS HAVE IDENTIFIED PHASES AND stages of growth and development for small businesses and that different management styles are appropriate at each phase. A few are described below.[1]

Eric G. Flamholtz identified six items that are critical in organizational development, as shown in Figure A-1.

Katherine Catlin and Jana Matthews explain what it takes to manage growth and achieve true entrepreneurial success. According to these authors, the way one leads a company should depend on its goals. But as the company changes, so does the role of the leader, shown in Figure A-2.

---

1. I am grateful to the Monterey Institute of International Studies for their work in identifying alternative frameworks.

Category	Stage I. New Venture	Stage II. Expansion	Stage II. Professionalization			Stage IV. Consolidation
			A	B	C	
Critical Development Areas	Markets and products	Resources and operating systems	Management systems			Corporate culture
Appr. Org. Size (Sales in Mil. $)	Less than $1	$1 to $10	$10 to $100			$100 to $500
Org. Structure	Prefunctional	Functional	Functional	Division-alizing	Divisional	COO, Complex
Management Development	On-the-job training	Fundamentals of management	Basic	Advanced	Leader-ship	Leadership
Control Systems	Personal observation	Personal responsibility, accountability	Basic	C&P Center	Compre-hensive	For decentralized management
Corporate Culture	Informal but understood	Attenuating	Tenuous			Explicitly defined
Management Systems	Informal	Informal	Formalizing			Formal
Operational Systems	Basic	Developing	Well-developed			Well-developed
Resources	Thin	Stretched thin	Increasing surplus			Strong
Leadership Styles	Benevolent autocratic/autocratic	Benevolent autocratic/autocratic	Consultative or participative			Consultative or participative

Figure A-1. Eric G. Flamholtz and Yvonne Randle, *Growing Pains: How to Make the Transition from an Entrepreneurship to a Professionally Managed Firm* (San Francisco, Oxford: Jossey-Bass Publishers, 1990).

Phase	Goals	Role of Leader
Continuous Growth	Dominate the industry	▪ Change Catalyst ▪ Organization Builder ▪ Strategy Innovator ▪ Chief of Culture
Rapid Growth	Lead the Market	▪ Team Builder ▪ Coach ▪ Planner ▪ Communicator
Initial Growth	Drive Sales	▪ Delegator ▪ Direction Setter
Start-up	Develop Product	▪ Doer/Decision Maker

Figure A-2. Katherine Catlin and Jana Matthews, *Leading at the Speed of Growth: Journey from Entrepreneur to CEO* (New York: Hungry Minds Inc., 2001), p. 125.

Larry E. Greiner considers five phases of organizational development. Each phase begins with a period of evolution, with growth and stability, and ends with a revolution, substantial organizational turmoil. The resolution of each revolutionary period determines whether the company will move to its next phase of evolutionary development (Figure A-3).

Category	Phase I Creativity	Phase II Direction	Phase III Delegation	Phase IV Coordination	Phase V Collaboration
Management Focus	Make and Sell	Efficiency of Operations	Expansion of Market	Consolidation of Market	Problem Solving and Innovation
Organizational Structure	Informal	Contralized and Functional	Decentralized and Geographical	Line Staff and Product Groups	Matrix of Teams
Top Management Style	Individualistic and Entrepreneurial	Directive	Delegative	Watchdog	Participative
Control System	Market Results	Standards and Cost Centers	Standards and Cost Centers	Plans and Investment Centers	Mutual Goal Setting
Management Reward Emphasis	Ownership	Salary and Merit Increases	Standards and Cost Centers	Profit Sharing and Stock Options	Team Bonus

Figure A-3. Larry E. Greiner, "Evolution and Revolution as Organizations Grow," *Harvard Business Review*, May-June 1998.

Neil Churchill and Virginia Lewis describe five stages of organizational development for a small business. Their model addresses corresponding types of the following categories in each stage: managerial style, organizational structure, extent of formal systems, major strategic goals, and the owner's involvement in the business (Figure A-4).

Category	Stage I Existence	Stage II Survival	Stage III-D Success-Disengagement	Stage III-G Success-Growth	Stage IV Take-off	Stage V Resource Maturity
Management Style	Direct Supervision	Supervised Supervision	Functional	Functional	Divisional	Line and Staff
Extent of Formal Systems	Minimal to Nonexistent	Minimal	Basic	Developing	Maturing	Extensive
Major Strategy	Existence	Survival	Maintaining Profitable Status Quo	Get Resources for Growth	Growth	Return on Investment
Key Problems	Obtaining customers and delivering the product	Relationship between revenues and expenses	To use the company as a platform for growth or as a means of support for owners as they completely or partially disengage from the company		How to grow rapidly and how to finance the growth	How to control financial gains and retain the entrepreneurial spirit

Figure A-4. Neil C. Churchill and Virginia L. Lewis, "The Five Stages of Small Business Growth," *The Entrepreneurial Venture: Readings Selected by William A. Sahlman* (Boston: Harvard Business School, 1999).

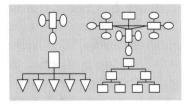

Appendix B

Evaluating Your Own Situation

S ELECTING THE RIGHT MODE OF OPERATION AND THEN CREATING IT requires that you know where you are now and what you have to work with. To help you review your situation, this appendix will prompt your thinking about four factors:

- ▶ Your organization's developmental path thus far
- ▶ Types of people in your organization
- ▶ The management and cultural priorities important in your organization
- ▶ Your organization's structure

You will gain a better sense of where you are on the road to entrepreneurial growth and which direction is best for you.

The Path Thus Far

To develop clarity and see your organization objectively, review the history of your organization's development and identify the legacies of the path that you have taken to get where you are now.

If your organization is large or diverse, consider your most recently developed or most important business unit, as opposed to trying to assess your entire organization, which may be a mix of business initiatives at different developmental phases.

Here is a summary of the phases to help you with your answer.

1. **Concept Development Phase.** Using the Innovating mode to serve pioneering customers with custom products, your priority is to develop and validate in the marketplace a breakthrough innovation that addresses a significant unmet need.

2. **Transitional Phase.** Using the Foundation Building mode, you continue to serve pioneering customers but you begin to rationalize your business infrastructure, product offering, and sales processes. Your goals are to simplify your product, develop an efficient business infrastructure, and select a pivotal market segment to target in the next phase.

3. **Rapid Market Expansion Phase.** Using the Producing mode, you serve pragmatist customers with a single version of your innovation. Your priority is to gain market exposure faster than anyone else.

4. **Crowded Marketplace Phase.** Using the Planning mode, you serve conservative customers with products that fit seamlessly into their lives. Your priorities are to refine production, lower costs, ensure consistency, and train staff.

5. **Niche Development Phase.** Using the Adapting mode, you serve customers with diverse needs, the sophisticates. Priority is on developing customized solutions for profitable niches driven by market demand.

Questions:

1. How far in the progression of phases has your main line of business come?
2. Is there a phase of business development that is clearly indicative of where your business is?
3. What type of dramatic changes have you recently seen in your organization's structure and culture?
4. How have you responded to new situations?
5. Was there a strong Concept Development phase of your organization when it was starting up and establishing a toehold in the market?
6. Does your organization have well-developed innovative capabilities?
7. Did you go through a transitional phase when you focused on internal issues?
8. During that transition, did you make sure that a robust business infrastructure was set in place and that it was efficient?

9. When did that restructuring happen?

10. How many people were employed in your organization during its first restructuring?

11. Did you cut one or two phases short because they were uncomfortable or unfamiliar?

12. Did you skip any developmental phases?

13. Is your organization an efficient producer of physical products?

14. Does your organization provide excellent customer service?

15. Has your organization successfully met the developmental objectives of each phase?

16. Are there any latent structural deficiencies in your organization that prevent it from taking advantage of future business opportunities?

What Type of People Do You Have?

Remember that the business environment is dynamic and your organization changes simply because of the passage of time. People gain higher levels of expertise and their career plans and aspirations change. These changes cause your firm to evolve because what you have to work with has changed. Consider the people you have in your organization and answer these questions.

1. Have you gathered a large number of people who simply do your bidding or are they truly independent decision makers?

2. Does your organization favor the highly articulate individuals who can give well-researched and thoughtful answers?

3. Does your organization tolerate the idiosyncratic and seemingly scattered innovative types?

4. Are your employees creative and always looking for a new solution?

5. Do your employees tend to do thorough research before making decisions or do they make decisions and then gather research to support their decisions?

6. Do you have only certain types of people working in certain areas of the company?

7. Do you have people of a similar age, decision style, or level of expertise?

8. Do you find that the people you hired in certain stages have now progressed and moved on to other kinds of functions for which they are not particularly qualified?

9. What are the levers that your organization uses to guide and control the activities of its members?

10. Do you place a high value on training and staff development?

What Are Your Personal Objectives?

Review your own objectives and determine where you would like to go as a leader and in your own personal development. Consider these questions.

1. Are your personal objectives and your business's objectives similar?
2. Are your objectives and your company's objectives compatible?
3. If there is close alignment between your personal objectives and the company's objectives, how much are others able to benefit by your meeting its business objectives?
4. Do you make it possible for others to expand their own horizons, take part in leadership, and feel a greater sense of fulfillment and commitment, or are you setting up the organization primarily to meet your own objectives?
5. What kind of people should you be hiring in order to meet those differing objectives?
6. Are you building an organization that will live beyond your current needs and objectives?

What Are Your Enterprise's Management Priorities?

To assess the management priorities within your organization, start with the three most recent major problems that your organization has addressed and think about how your organization went about solving them. Consider typical priorities of each decision-style component and choose which of the following approaches best describes how each of your three most recent problems was handled.

Were they handled by:

▶ Acting quickly? This is a Decisive Commander management style component.

▶ Performing careful analysis to understand the key components of the problem and to identify in a logical way what should be done? This is a methodical engineer management style and an analytical decision style.

▶ Taking an innovative approach, seeking to come up with a new answer? This would indicate a creative visionary management style and a conceptual decision style.

► Reviewing the opinions of internal or external experts? This is a collaborative facilitator management style and a behavioral decision style.

1. Looking back at these three situations, did they actually require the kind of solution or attention that they received?
2. If they didn't, how was the solution driven? By a personal preference? By an organizational habit?
3. If all three problems received the same kind of solution, was it because your organization has mastered only one way of doing things?
4. What other problem-solving approaches have been more effective?

Now, consider your organization's three biggest successes and answer the same four questions as above. Then answer the following questions.

1. Are there similarities in how the successes and failures were handled?
2. Does your organization manage a new product and an old product in the same manner, with the same decision structure and cultural emphasis?
3. Did you let each situation drive its solution or did your organization impose a solution on them?
4. How much decision-making flexibility does your organization have?
5. Does your organization value different approaches to management in different situations, different departments, and for different tasks?
6. How much emphasis does your organization place on displaying a certain kid of management style?

What Are Your Firm's Cultural Priorities?

Your organization's cultural priorities reflect the memory of what has been successful and what has not. They are forces that influence how people act and indicate what is or is not acceptable behavior.

1. What are the key priorities embedded in the culture?
2. Is it a priority to be defiantly innovative, ignoring current practices and market wisdom, or to be highly sensitive to market conditions, opportunities, and other external forces?
3. Is it a priority simply to gain market share and press your product into the market place, or is it to be deliberate, organized, and thorough in making decisions?

4. How does the culture of the organization compare with your own style of management?
5. Can the culture of your organization adapt to the changes of the environment, regardless of your personal priorities?
6. Does your organization have biases similar to your own?
7. Does it place high priority on the same issues as you do?

Another way to assess the firm's organizational culture is to have everyone complete the decision-style questionnaire included in this book. Review the average scores of the people who have been there the longest or who are the cultural leaders of the firm. This will give you an idea of the priorities that are being set and reinforced from day to day.

What Is Your Organization's Structure?

To review your decision-making structures, think about how you organize your work and your people.

1. Are people organized by functions or are they organized in customer-oriented teams?
2. After you've introduced multiple products, have you developed a functional organization where a particular functional group serves a variety of products?
3. What control levers are most important in your organization?
4. Is the structure of your organization the same as the structure with which you are personally most comfortable?
5. If you thrive on rigid structure, is your organization too rigid to meet the demands of the current situation?
6. If you have a large, diverse organization, are there blind spots built into your organization?
7. If you tend to avoid highly structured situations, is your firm avoiding needed structure?

Is the Time Right for Shifting Gears?

Use periods of high momentum to prepare for future needs. Don't wait for your business momentum to run out before making the needed changes.

1. Have you developed goodwill among your clients and customers?
2. Do you have a strong position in the market that will allow you to sustain a Transitional phase when you can shift some of your management attention to internal issues?

Index